T&P BOOKS

DICTIONARY

THEME-BASED

British English Collection

ENGLISH ARABIC

The most useful words
To expand your lexicon and sharpen
your language skills

7000 words

Theme-based dictionary British English-Egyptian Arabic - 7000 words
By Andrey Taranov

T&P Books vocabularies are intended for helping you learn, memorize and review foreign words. The dictionary is divided into themes, covering all major spheres of everyday activities, business, science, culture, etc.

The process of learning words using T&P Books' theme-based dictionaries gives you the following advantages:

- Correctly grouped source information predetermines success at subsequent stages of word memorization
- Availability of words derived from the same root allowing memorization of word units (rather than separate words)
- Small units of words facilitate the process of establishing associative links needed for consolidation of vocabulary
- Level of language knowledge can be estimated by the number of learned words

T&P Books Publishing
www.tpbooks.com

This book is also available in E-book formats.
Please visit www.tpbooks.com or the major online bookstores.

EGYPTIAN ARABIC THEME-BASED DICTIONARY
British English collection

T&P Books vocabularies are intended to help you learn, memorize, and review foreign words. The vocabulary contains over 7000 commonly used words arranged thematically.

- Vocabulary contains the most commonly used words
- Recommended as an addition to any language course
- Meets the needs of beginners and advanced learners of foreign languages
- Convenient for daily use, revision sessions, and self-testing activities
- Allows you to assess your vocabulary

Special features of the vocabulary

- Words are organized according to their meaning, not alphabetically
- Words are presented in three columns to facilitate the reviewing and self-testing processes
- Words in groups are divided into small blocks to facilitate the learning process
- The vocabulary offers a convenient and simple transcription of each foreign word

The vocabulary has 198 topics including:

Basic Concepts, Numbers, Colors, Months, Seasons, Units of Measurement, Clothing & Accessories, Food & Nutrition, Restaurant, Family Members, Relatives, Character, Feelings, Emotions, Diseases, City, Town, Sightseeing, Shopping, Money, House, Home, Office, Working in the Office, Import & Export, Marketing, Job Search, Sports, Education, Computer, Internet, Tools, Nature, Countries, Nationalities and more ...

TABLE OF CONTENTS

PRONUNCIATION GUIDE

T&P phonetic alphabet	Egyptian Arabic example	English example
[a]	[ṭaffa] طفّى	shorter than in 'ask'
[ā]	[eχtār] إختار	calf, palm
[e]	[setta] ستّة	elm, medal
[i]	[minā'] ميناء	shorter than in 'feet'
[ī]	[ebrīl] إبريل	feet, meter
[o]	[oɣosṭos] أغسطس	pod, John
[ō]	[ḥalazōn] حلزون	fall, bomb
[u]	[kalkutta] كلكتا	book
[ū]	[gamūs] جاموس	fuel, tuna
[b]	[bedāya] بداية	baby, book
[d]	[sa'āda] سعادة	day, doctor
[ḍ]	[waḍ'] وضع	[d] pharyngeal
[ʒ]	[arʒantīn] الأرجنتين	forge, pleasure
[ẓ]	[ẓahar] ظهر	[z] pharyngeal
[f]	[χafīf] خفيف	face, food
[g]	[bahga] بهجة	game, gold
[h]	[ettegāh] إتّجاه	home, have
[ḥ]	[ḥabb] حبّ	[h] pharyngeal
[y]	[dahaby] ذهبي	yes, New York
[k]	[korsy] كرسي	clock, kiss
[l]	[lammaḥ] لمّح	lace, people
[m]	[marṣad] مرصد	magic, milk
[n]	[ganūb] جنوب	sang, thing
[p]	[kaputʃino] كابتشينو	pencil, private
[q]	[wasaq] وثق	king, club
[r]	[roḥe] روح	rice, radio
[s]	[soχreya] سخرية	city, boss
[ṣ]	[me'ṣam] معصم	[s] pharyngeal
[ʃ]	['aʃā'] عشاء	machine, shark
[t]	[tanūb] تنوب	tourist, trip
[ṭ]	[χarīṭa] خريطة	[t] pharyngeal
[θ]	[mamūθ] ماموث	month, tooth
[v]	[vietnām] فيتنام	very, river
[w]	[wadda'] ودّع	vase, winter
[χ]	[baχīl] بخيل	as in Scots 'loch'

T&P phonetic alphabet	Egyptian Arabic example	English example
[ɣ]	**[etɣadda] إتغدّى**	between [g] and [h]
[z]	**[me'za] معزة**	zebra, please
['] (ayn)	**[sab'a] سبعة**	voiced pharyngeal fricative
['] (hamza)	**[sa'al] سأل**	glottal stop

ABBREVIATIONS used in the dictionary

Egyptian Arabic abbreviations

du	-	plural noun (double)
f	-	feminine noun
m	-	masculine noun
pl	-	plural

English abbreviations

ab.	-	about
adj	-	adjective
adv	-	adverb
anim.	-	animate
as adj	-	attributive noun used as adjective
e.g.	-	for example
etc.	-	et cetera
fam.	-	familiar
fem.	-	feminine
form.	-	formal
inanim.	-	inanimate
masc.	-	masculine
math	-	mathematics
mil.	-	military
n	-	noun
pl	-	plural
pron.	-	pronoun
sb	-	somebody
sing.	-	singular
sth	-	something
v aux	-	auxiliary verb
vi	-	intransitive verb
vi, vt	-	intransitive, transitive verb
vt	-	transitive verb

BASIC CONCEPTS

Basic concepts. Part 1

1. Pronouns

I, me	ana	أنا
you (masc.)	enta	أنت
you (fem.)	enty	أنت
he	howwa	هوّ
she	hiya	هي
we	eḥna	إحنا
you (to a group)	antom	أنتم
they	hamm	همّ

2. Greetings. Salutations. Farewells

Hello! (form.)	assalamu ʿalaykum!	السلام عليكم!
Good morning!	ṣabāḥ el χeyr!	صباح الخير!
Good afternoon!	neharak saʿīd!	نهارك سعيد!
Good evening!	masāʾ el χeyr!	مساء الخير!
to say hello	sallem	سلّم
Hi! (hello)	ahlan!	أهلاً!
greeting (n)	salām (m)	سلام
to greet (vt)	sallem ʿala	سلّم على
How are you?	ezzayek?	ازّيك؟
What's new?	aχbārak eyh?	أخبارك ايه؟
Bye-Bye! Goodbye!	maʿ el salāma!	مع السلامة!
See you soon!	aʃūfak orayeb!	أشوفك قريب!
Farewell!	maʿ el salāma!	مع السلامة!
to say goodbye	waddaʿ	ودّع
Cheers!	bay bay!	باي باي!
Thank you! Cheers!	ʃokran!	شكراً!
Thank you very much!	ʃokran geddan!	شكراً جداً!
My pleasure!	el ʿafw	العفو
Don't mention it!	la ʃokr ʿala wāgeb	لا شكر على واجب
It was nothing	el ʿafw	العفو
Excuse me! (fam.)	ʿan eznak!	عن إذنك!
Excuse me! (form.)	baʿd ezn ḥadretak!	بعد إذن حضرتك!
to excuse (forgive)	ʿazar	عذر
to apologize (vi)	eʿtazar	أعتذر

My apologies	ana ʾāsef	أنا آسف
I'm sorry!	ana ʾāsef!	أنا آسف!
to forgive (vt)	ʿafa	عفا
please (adv)	men faḍlak	من فضلك
Don't forget!	ma tensāʃ!	ما تنساش!
Certainly!	ṭabʿan!	طبعاً!
Of course not!	laʾ ṭabʿan!	لأ طبعاً!
Okay! (I agree)	ettafaʾna!	إتّفقنا!
That's enough!	kefāya!	كفاية!

3. Cardinal numbers. Part 1

0 zero	ṣefr	صفر
1 one	wāḥed	واحد
1 one (fem.)	waḥda	واحدة
2 two	etneyn	إتنين
3 three	talāta	ثلاثة
4 four	arbaʿa	أربعة
5 five	χamsa	خمسة
6 six	setta	ستّة
7 seven	sabʿa	سبعة
8 eight	tamanya	ثمانية
9 nine	tesʿa	تسعة
10 ten	ʿaʃara	عشرة
11 eleven	ḥedāʃar	حداشر
12 twelve	etnāʃar	إتناشر
13 thirteen	talattāʃar	تلاتّاشر
14 fourteen	arbaʿtāʃer	أربعتاشر
15 fifteen	χamastāʃer	خمستاشر
16 sixteen	settāʃar	ستّاشر
17 seventeen	sabaʿtāʃar	سبعتاشر
18 eighteen	tamantāʃar	تمنتاشر
19 nineteen	tesʿatāʃar	تسعتاشر
20 twenty	ʿeʃrīn	عشرين
21 twenty-one	wāḥed we ʿeʃrīn	واحد وعشرين
22 twenty-two	etneyn we ʿeʃrīn	إتنين وعشرين
23 twenty-three	talāta we ʿeʃrīn	ثلاثة وعشرين
30 thirty	talatīn	ثلاثين
31 thirty-one	wāḥed we talatīn	واحد وتلاتين
32 thirty-two	etneyn we talatīn	إتنين وتلاتين
33 thirty-three	talāta we talatīn	ثلاثة وثلاثين
40 forty	arbeʿīn	أربعين
41 forty-one	wāḥed we arbeʿīn	واحد وأربعين
42 forty-two	etneyn we arbeʿīn	إتنين وأربعين
43 forty-three	talāta we arbeʿīn	ثلاثة وأربعين
50 fifty	χamsīn	خمسين
51 fifty-one	wāḥed we χamsīn	واحد وخمسين

52 fifty-two	etneyn we χamsīn	إتنين وخمسين
53 fifty-three	talāta we χamsīn	ثلاثة وخمسين
60 sixty	settīn	ستّين
61 sixty-one	wāḥed we settīn	واحد وستّين
62 sixty-two	etneyn we settīn	إتنين وستّين
63 sixty-three	talāta we settīn	ثلاثة وستّين
70 seventy	sabʕīn	سبعين
71 seventy-one	wāḥed we sabʕīn	واحد وسبعين
72 seventy-two	etneyn we sabʕīn	إتنين وسبعين
73 seventy-three	talāta we sabʕīn	ثلاثة وسبعين
80 eighty	tamanīn	ثمانين
81 eighty-one	wāḥed we tamanīn	واحد وتمانين
82 eighty-two	etneyn we tamanīn	إتنين وتمانين
83 eighty-three	talāta we tamanīn	ثلاثة وثمانين
90 ninety	tesʕīn	تسعين
91 ninety-one	wāḥed we tesʕīn	واحد وتسعين
92 ninety-two	etneyn we tesʕīn	إتنين وتسعين
93 ninety-three	talāta we tesʕīn	ثلاثة وتسعين

4. Cardinal numbers. Part 2

100 one hundred	miya	ميّة
200 two hundred	meteyn	ميتين
300 three hundred	toltomiya	تلتميّة
400 four hundred	robʿomiya	ربعميّة
500 five hundred	χomsomiya	خمسميّة
600 six hundred	sotomiya	ستميّة
700 seven hundred	sobʿomiya	سبعميّة
800 eight hundred	tomnomeʾa	ثمنمئة
900 nine hundred	tosʿomiya	تسعميّة
1000 one thousand	alf	ألف
2000 two thousand	alfeyn	ألفين
3000 three thousand	talat ʾālāf	ثلاث آلاف
10000 ten thousand	ʿaʃaret ʾālāf	عشرة آلاف
one hundred thousand	mīt alf	ميت ألف
million	millyon (m)	مليون
billion	millyār (m)	مليار

5. Numbers. Fractions

fraction	kasr (m)	كسر
one half	noṣṣ	نصّ
one third	telt	ثلث
one quarter	robʿ	ربع
one eighth	tomn	تمن
one tenth	ʿoʃr	عشر

two thirds	teleyn	تلتين
three quarters	talātet arbāʿ	ثلاثة أرباع

6. Numbers. Basic operations

subtraction	ṭarḥ (m)	طرح
to subtract (vi, vt)	ṭaraḥ	طرح
division	ʾesma (f)	قسمة
to divide (vt)	ʾasam	قسم
addition	gamʿ (m)	جمع
to add up (vt)	gamaʿ	جمع
to add (vi)	gamaʿ	جمع
multiplication	ḍarb (m)	ضرب
to multiply (vt)	ḍarab	ضرب

7. Numbers. Miscellaneous

digit, figure	raqam (m)	رقم
number	ʿadad (m)	عدد
numeral	ʿadady (m)	عددي
minus sign	nāʾeṣ (m)	ناقص
plus sign	zāʾed (m)	زائد
formula	moʿadla (f)	معادلة
calculation	ḥesāb (m)	حساب
to count (vi, vt)	ʿadd	عدّ
to count up	ḥasab	حسب
to compare (vt)	qāran	قارن
How much?	kām?	كام؟
sum, total	magmūʿ (m)	مجموع
result	natīga (f)	نتيجة
remainder	bāʾy (m)	باقي
a few (e.g., ~ years ago)	kām	كام
little (I had ~ time)	ʃewaya	شوية
the rest	el bāʾy (m)	الباقي
one and a half	wāḥed w noṣṣ (m)	واحد ونصّ
dozen	desta (f)	دستة
in half (adv)	le noṣṣeyn	لنصّين
equally (evenly)	bel tasāwy	بالتساوى
half	noṣṣ (m)	نصّ
time (three ~s)	marra (f)	مرّة

8. The most important verbs. Part 1

to advise (vt)	naṣaḥ	نصح
to agree (say yes)	ettafaʾ	إتّفق

to answer (vi, vt)	gāwab	جاوب
to apologize (vi)	e'tazar	إعتذر
to arrive (vi)	weṣel	وصل
to ask (~ oneself)	sa'al	سأل
to ask (~ sb to do sth)	ṭalab	طلب
to be (vi)	kān	كان
to be afraid	χāf	خاف
to be hungry	'āyez 'ākol	عايز آكل
to be interested in ...	ehtamm be	إهتمّ بـ
to be needed	maṭlūb	مطلوب
to be surprised	etfāge'	إتفاجئ
to be thirsty	'āyez aʃrab	عايز أشرب
to begin (vt)	bada'	بدأ
to belong to ...	χaṣṣ	خصّ
to boast (vi)	tabāha	تباهى
to break (split into pieces)	kasar	كسر
to call (~ for help)	estaɣās	إستغاث
can (v aux)	'eder	قدر
to catch (vt)	mesek	مسك
to change (vt)	ɣayar	غيّر
to choose (select)	eχtār	إختار
to come down (the stairs)	nezel	نزل
to compare (vt)	qāran	قارن
to complain (vi, vt)	ʃaka	شكا
to confuse (mix up)	etlaχbaṭ	إتلخبط
to continue (vt)	wāṣel	واصل
to control (vt)	et-ḥakkem	إتحكّم
to cook (dinner)	ḥaḍḍar	حضّر
to cost (vt)	kallef	كلّف
to count (add up)	'add	عدّ
to count on ...	e'tamad 'ala ...	إعتمد على...
to create (vt)	'amal	عمل
to cry (weep)	baka	بكى

9. The most important verbs. Part 2

to deceive (vi, vt)	χada'	خدع
to decorate (tree, street)	zayen	زيّن
to defend (a country, etc.)	dāfa'	دافع
to demand (request firmly)	ṭāleb	طالب
to dig (vt)	ḥafar	حفر
to discuss (vt)	nā'eʃ	ناقش
to do (vt)	'amal	عمل
to doubt (have doubts)	ʃakk fe	شكّ في
to drop (let fall)	wa''a'	وقّع
to enter (room, house, etc.)	daχal	دخل
to exist (vi)	kān mawgūd	كان موّجود

to expect (foresee)	tanabba'	تنبأ
to explain (vt)	ʃarah̩	شرح
to fall (vi)	we'eʿ	وقع
to fancy (vt)	ʿagab	عجب
to find (vt)	la'a	لقي
to finish (vt)	χallas̩	خلّص
to fly (vi)	t̩ār	طار
to follow ... (come after)	tatabbaʿ	تتبّع
to forget (vi, vt)	nesy	نسي
to forgive (vt)	ʿafa	عفا
to give (vt)	edda	إدّى
to give a hint	edda lamh̩a	إدّى لمحة
to go (on foot)	meʃy	مشى
to go for a swim	sebeh̩	سبح
to go out (for dinner, etc.)	χarag	خرج
to guess (the answer)	χammen	خمّن
to have (vt)	malak	ملك
to have breakfast	fet̩er	فطر
to have dinner	etʿasʃa	إتعشّى
to have lunch	etɣadda	إتغدّى
to hear (vt)	semeʿ	سمع
to help (vt)	sāʿed	ساعد
to hide (vt)	χabba	خبّأ
to hope (vi, vt)	tamanna	تمنّى
to hunt (vi, vt)	es̩t̩ād	اصطاد
to hurry (vi)	estaʿgel	إستعجل

10. The most important verbs. Part 3

to inform (vt)	'āl ly	قال لي
to insist (vi, vt)	as̩arr	أصرّ
to insult (vt)	ahān	أهان
to invite (vt)	ʿazam	عزم
to joke (vi)	hazzar	هزّر
to keep (vt)	h̩afaz̩	حفظ
to keep silent, to hush	seket	سكت
to kill (vt)	'atal	قتل
to know (sb)	ʿeref	عرف
to know (sth)	ʿeref	عرف
to laugh (vi)	d̩eh̩ek	ضحك
to liberate (city, etc.)	h̩arrar	حرّر
to look for ... (search)	dawwar ʿala	دوّر على
to love (sb)	h̩abb	حبّ
to make a mistake	ɣelet̩	غلط
to manage, to run	adār	أدار
to mean (signify)	'as̩ad	قصد
to mention (talk about)	zakar	ذكر

to miss (school, etc.)	ɣāb	غاب
to notice (see)	lāḥaẓ	لاحظ
to object (vi, vt)	e'tarad̩	إعترض
to observe (see)	rāqab	راقب
to open (vt)	fataḥ	فتح
to order (meal, etc.)	ṭalab	طلب
to order (mil.)	amar	أمر
to own (possess)	malak	ملك
to participate (vi)	ʃārek	شارك
to pay (vi, vt)	dafa'	دفع
to permit (vt)	samaḥ	سمح
to plan (vt)	χaṭṭeṭ	خطّط
to play (children)	le'eb	لعب
to pray (vi, vt)	ṣalla	صلّى
to prefer (vt)	faḍḍal	فضّل
to promise (vt)	wa'ad	وعد
to pronounce (vt)	naṭa'	نطق
to propose (vt)	'araḍ	عرض
to punish (vt)	'āqab	عاقب

11. The most important verbs. Part 4

to read (vi, vt)	'ara	قرأ
to recommend (vt)	naṣaḥ	نصح
to refuse (vi, vt)	rafaḍ	رفض
to regret (be sorry)	nedem	ندم
to rent (sth from sb)	est'gar	إستأجر
to repeat (say again)	karrar	كرّر
to reserve, to book	ḥagaz	حجز
to run (vi)	gery	جري
to save (rescue)	anqaz	أنقذ
to say (~ thank you)	'āl	قال
to scold (vt)	wabbeχ	وبّخ
to see (vt)	ʃāf	شاف
to sell (vt)	bā'	باع
to send (vt)	arsal	أرسل
to shoot (vi)	ḍarab bel nār	ضرب بالنار
to shout (vi)	ṣarraχ	صرّخ
to show (vt)	warra	ورّى
to sign (document)	waqqa'	وقّع
to sit down (vi)	'a'ad	قعد
to smile (vi)	ebtasam	إبتسم
to speak (vi, vt)	kallem	كلّم
to steal (money, etc.)	sara'	سرق
to stop (for pause, etc.)	wa''af	وقّف
to stop (please ~ calling me)	baṭṭal	بطّل
to study (vt)	daras	درس

to swim (vi)	ʿām	عام
to take (vt)	aχad	أخد
to think (vi, vt)	fakkar	فكّر
to threaten (vt)	hadded	هدّد
to touch (with hands)	lamas	لمس
to translate (vt)	targem	ترجم
to trust (vt)	wasaq	وثق
to try (attempt)	ḥāwel	حاول
to turn (e.g., ~ left)	ḥād	حاد
to underestimate (vt)	estaχaff	إستخفّ
to understand (vt)	fehem	فهم
to unite (vt)	waḥḥed	وحّد
to wait (vt)	estanna	إستنّى
to want (wish, desire)	ʿāyez	عايز
to warn (vt)	ḥazzar	حذّر
to work (vi)	eʃtaɣal	إشتغل
to write (vt)	katab	كتب
to write down	katab	كتب

12. Colours

colour	lone (m)	لون
shade (tint)	daraget el lōn (m)	درجة اللون
hue	ṣabɣet lōn (f)	صبغة اللون
rainbow	qose qozaḥ (m)	قوس قزح
white (adj)	abyaḍ	أبيض
black (adj)	aswad	أسود
grey (adj)	romādy	رمادي
green (adj)	aχḍar	أخضر
yellow (adj)	aṣfar	أصفر
red (adj)	aḥmar	أحمر
blue (adj)	azraʾ	أزرق
light blue (adj)	azraʾ fāteḥ	أزرق فاتح
pink (adj)	wardy	وردي
orange (adj)	bortoqāly	برتقاليّ
violet (adj)	banaffsegy	بنفّسجي
brown (adj)	bonny	بنّي
golden (adj)	dahaby	ذهبي
silvery (adj)	feḍḍy	فضّي
beige (adj)	bɛːʒ	بيج
cream (adj)	ʿāgy	عاجيّ
turquoise (adj)	fayrūzy	فيروزي
cherry red (adj)	aḥmar karazy	أحمر كرزي
lilac (adj)	laylaky	ليّلكي
crimson (adj)	qormozy	قرمزي
light (adj)	fāteḥ	فاتح

dark (adj)	ɣāme'	غامق
bright, vivid (adj)	zāhy	زاهي
coloured (pencils)	melawwen	ملوّن
colour (e.g. ~ film)	melawwen	ملوّن
black-and-white (adj)	abyaḍ we aswad	أبيض وأسوّد
plain (one-coloured)	sāda	سادة
multicoloured (adj)	mota'added el alwān	متعددّ الألوان

13. Questions

Who?	mīn?	مين؟
What?	eyh?	ايه؟
Where? (at, in)	feyn?	فين؟
Where (to)?	feyn?	فين؟
From where?	meneyn?	منين؟
When?	emta	امتى؟
Why? (What for?)	'aʃān eyh?	عشان ايه؟
Why? (~ are you crying?)	leyh?	ليه؟
What for?	l eyh?	لـ ليه؟
How? (in what way)	ezāy?	إزاي؟
What? (What kind of ...?)	eyh?	ايه؟
Which?	ayī?	أيّ؟
To whom?	le mīn?	لمين؟
About whom?	'an mīn?	عن مين؟
About what?	'an eyh?	عن ايه؟
With whom?	ma' mīn?	مع مين؟
How many? How much?	kām?	كام؟
Whose?	betā'et mīn?	بتاعت مين؟

14. Function words. Adverbs. Part 1

Where? (at, in)	feyn?	فين؟
here (adv)	hena	هنا
there (adv)	henāk	هناك
somewhere (to be)	fe makānen ma	في مكان ما
nowhere (not in any place)	meʃ fi ayī makān	مش في أيّ مكان
by (near, beside)	ganb	جنب
by the window	ganb el ʃebbāk	جنب الشبّاك
Where (to)?	feyn?	فين؟
here (e.g. come ~!)	hena	هنا
there (e.g. to go ~)	henāk	هناك
from here (adv)	men hena	من هنا
from there (adv)	men henāk	من هناك
close (adv)	'arīb	قريب
far (adv)	be'īd	بعيد

near (e.g. ~ Paris)	ʿand	عند
nearby (adv)	ʾarīb	قريب
not far (adv)	meʃ beʿīd	مش بعيد
left (adj)	el ʃemāl	الشمال
on the left	ʿalal ʃemāl	على الشمال
to the left	lel ʃemāl	للشمال
right (adj)	el yemīn	اليمين
on the right	ʿalal yemīn	على اليمين
to the right	lel yemīn	لليمين
in front (adv)	ʾoddām	قدّام
front (as adj)	amāmy	أمامي
ahead (the kids ran ~)	ela el amām	إلى الأمام
behind (adv)	waraʾ	وراء
from behind	men wara	من ورّا
back (towards the rear)	le wara	لورّا
middle	wasaṭ (m)	وسط
in the middle	fel wasat	في الوسط
at the side	ʿala ganb	على جنب
everywhere (adv)	fe kol makān	في كل مكان
around (in all directions)	ḥawaleyn	حوالين
from inside	men gowwah	من جوّه
somewhere (to go)	le ʾayī makān	لأي مكان
straight (directly)	ʿala ṭūl	على طول
back (e.g. come ~)	rogūʿ	رجوع
from anywhere	men ayī makān	من أيّ مكان
from somewhere	men makānen mā	من مكان ما
firstly (adv)	awwalan	أوّلاً
secondly (adv)	sāneyan	ثانياً
thirdly (adv)	sālesan	ثالثاً
suddenly (adv)	fagʾa	فجأة
at first (in the beginning)	fel bedāya	في البداية
for the first time	le ʾawwel marra	لأوّل مرّة
long before ...	ʾabl ... be modda ṭawīla	قبل... بمدة طويلة
anew (over again)	men gedīd	من جديد
for good (adv)	lel abad	للأبد
never (adv)	abadan	أبداً
again (adv)	tāny	تاني
now (at present)	delwaʾty	دلوقتي
often (adv)	ketīr	كثير
then (adv)	waʾtaha	وقتها
urgently (quickly)	ʿala ṭūl	على طول
usually (adv)	ʿādatan	عادةً
by the way, ...	ʿala fekra ...	على فكرة...
possibly	momken	ممكن

probably (adv)	momken	ممكن
maybe (adv)	momken	ممكن
besides …	bel eḍāfa ela …	بالإضافة إلى…
that's why …	ʿaʃān keda	عشان كده
in spite of …	bel raɣm men …	بالرغم من…
thanks to …	be faḍl …	بفضل…
what (pron.)	elly	إللي
that (conj.)	ennu	إنّه
something	ḥāga (f)	حاجة
anything (something)	ayī ḥāga (f)	أيّ حاجة
nothing	wala ḥāga	ولا حاجة
who (pron.)	elly	إللي
someone	ḥadd	حدّ
somebody	ḥadd	حدّ
nobody	wala ḥadd	ولا حدّ
nowhere (a voyage to ~)	meʃ le wala makān	مش لـ ولا مكان
nobody's	wala ḥadd	ولا حدّ
somebody's	le ḥadd	لحدّ
so (I'm ~ glad)	geddan	جداً
also (as well)	kamān	كمان
too (as well)	kamān	كمان

15. Function words. Adverbs. Part 2

Why?	leyh?	ليه؟
for some reason	le sabeben ma	لسبب ما
because …	ʿaʃān …	… عشان
for some purpose	le hadafen mā	لهدف ما
and	w	و
or	walla	ولّا
but	bass	بسّ
for (e.g. ~ me)	ʿaʃān	عشان
too (excessively)	ketīr geddan	كتير جدّاً
only (exclusively)	bass	بسّ
exactly (adv)	bel ḍabṭ	بالضبط
about (more or less)	naḥw	نحو
approximately (adv)	naḥw	نحو
approximate (adj)	taqrīby	تقريبي
almost (adv)	taʾrīban	تقريباً
the rest	el bāʾy (m)	الباقي
each (adj)	koll	كلّ
any (no matter which)	ayī	أيّ
many, much (a lot of)	ketīr	كتير
many people	nās ketīr	ناس كتير
all (everyone)	koll el nās	كلّ الناس
in return for …	fi moqābel …	… في مقابل

in exchange (adv)	fe moqābel	في مقابل
by hand (made)	bel yad	باليد
hardly (negative opinion)	bel kād	بالكاد
probably (adv)	momken	ممكن
on purpose (intentionally)	bel ʾaṣd	بالقصد
by accident (adv)	bel ṣodfa	بالصدفة
very (adv)	ʾawy	قويّ
for example (adv)	masalan	مثلاً
between	beyn	بين
among	wesṭ	وسط
so much (such a lot)	ketīr	كتير
especially (adv)	χāṣṣa	خاصّة

Basic concepts. Part 2

16. Opposites

rich (adj)	ɣany	غني
poor (adj)	fa'īr	فقير
ill, sick (adj)	marīḍ	مريض
well (not sick)	salīm	سليم
big (adj)	kebīr	كبير
small (adj)	ṣaɣīr	صغير
quickly (adv)	bosor'a	بسرعة
slowly (adv)	bo boṭ'	ببطء
fast (adj)	saree'	سريع
slow (adj)	baṭī'	بطيء
glad (adj)	farḥān	فرحان
sad (adj)	ḥazīn	حزين
together (adv)	ma' ba'ḍ	مع بعض
separately (adv)	le waḥdo	لوحده
aloud (to read)	beṣote 'āly	بصوت عالي
silently (to oneself)	beṣamt	بصمت
tall (adj)	'āly	عالي
low (adj)	wāṭy	واطي
deep (adj)	'amīq	عميق
shallow (adj)	ḍaḥl	ضحل
yes	aywa	أيوه
no	la'	لأ
distant (in space)	be'īd	بعيد
nearby (adj)	'arīb	قريب
far (adv)	be'īd	بعيد
nearby (adv)	'arīb	قريب
long (adj)	ṭawīl	طويل
short (adj)	'aṣīr	قصير
good (kindhearted)	ṭayeb	طيّب
evil (adj)	ʃerrīr	شرير

married (adj)	metgawwez	متجوّز
single (adj)	a'zab	أعزب
to forbid (vt)	mana'	منع
to permit (vt)	samaḥ	سمح
end	nehāya (f)	نهاية
beginning	bedāya (f)	بداية
left (adj)	el ʃemāl	الشمال
right (adj)	el yemīn	اليمين
first (adj)	awwel	أوّل
last (adj)	'āχer	آخر
crime	garīma (f)	جريمة
punishment	'eqāb (m)	عقاب
to order (vt)	amar	أمر
to obey (vi, vt)	ṭā'	طاع
straight (adj)	mostaqīm	مستقيم
curved (adj)	monḥany	منحني
paradise	el ganna (f)	الجنّة
hell	el gaḥīm (f)	الجحيم
to be born	etwalad	إتولّد
to die (vi)	māt	مات
strong (adj)	'awy	قوّي
weak (adj)	ḍa'īf	ضعيف
old (adj)	'agūz	عجوز
young (adj)	ʃāb	شاب
old (adj)	'adīm	قديم
new (adj)	gedīd	جديد
hard (adj)	ṣalb	صلب
soft (adj)	ṭary	طري
warm (tepid)	dāfy	دافي
cold (adj)	bāred	بارد
fat (adj)	teχīn	تخين
thin (adj)	rofaya'	رفيّع
narrow (adj)	ḍaye'	ضيّق
wide (adj)	wāse'	واسع
good (adj)	kewayes	كويّس
bad (adj)	weḥeʃ	وحش
brave (adj)	ʃogā'	شجاع
cowardly (adj)	gabān	جبان

17. Weekdays

Monday	el etneyn (m)	الإتنين
Tuesday	el talāt (m)	التلات
Wednesday	el arbe'ā' (m)	الأربعاء
Thursday	el χamīs (m)	الخميس
Friday	el gom'a (m)	الجمعة
Saturday	el sabt (m)	السبت
Sunday	el aḥad (m)	الأحد
today (adv)	el naharda	النهارده
tomorrow (adv)	bokra	بكرة
the day after tomorrow	ba'd bokra (m)	بعد بكرة
yesterday (adv)	embāreḥ	امبارح
the day before yesterday	awwel embāreḥ	أوّل امبارح
day	yome (m)	يوم
working day	yome 'amal (m)	يوم عمل
public holiday	agāza rasmiya (f)	أجازة رسميّة
day off	yome el agāza (m)	يوم أجازة
weekend	nehāyet el osbū' (f)	نهاية الأسبوع
all day long	ṭūl el yome	طول اليوم
the next day (adv)	fel yome elly ba'dīh	في اليوم اللي بعديه
two days ago	men yomeyn	من يومين
the day before	fel yome elly 'ablo	في اليوم اللي قبله
daily (adj)	yawmy	يومي
every day (adv)	yawmiyan	يومياً
week	osbū' (m)	أسبوع
last week (adv)	el esbū' elly fāt	الأسبوع اللي فات
next week (adv)	el esbū' elly gayī	الأسبوع اللي جاي
weekly (adj)	osbū'y	أسبوعي
every week (adv)	osbū'iyan	أسبوعياً
twice a week	marreteyn fel osbū'	مرّتين في الأسبوع
every Tuesday	koll solasā'	كلّ ثلاثاء

18. Hours. Day and night

morning	ṣobḥ (m)	صبح
in the morning	fel ṣobḥ	في الصبح
noon, midday	ẓohr (m)	ظهر
in the afternoon	ba'd el ḍohr	بعد الظهر
evening	leyl (m)	ليل
in the evening	bel leyl	بالليل
night	leyl (m)	ليل
at night	bel leyl	بالليل
midnight	noṣṣ el leyl (m)	نصّ الليل
second	sanya (f)	ثانية
minute	deTa (f)	دقيقة
hour	sā'a (f)	ساعة

half an hour	noṣṣ sāʿa (m)	نصّ ساعة
a quarter-hour	robʿ sāʿa (f)	ربع ساعة
fifteen minutes	χamastāʃer deʾīʾa	خمستاشر دقيقة
24 hours	arbaʿa we ʿeʃrīn sāʿa	أربعة وعشرين ساعة
sunrise	ʃorūʾ el ʃams (m)	شروق الشمس
dawn	fagr (m)	فجر
early morning	ṣobḥ badry (m)	صبح بدري
sunset	ɣorūb el ʃams (m)	غروب الشمس
early in the morning	el ṣobḥ badry	الصبح بدري
this morning	el naharda el ṣobḥ	النهاردة الصبح
tomorrow morning	bokra el ṣobḥ	بكرة الصبح
this afternoon	el naharda baʿd el ḍohr	النهاردة بعد الظهر
in the afternoon	baʿd el ḍohr	بعد الظهر
tomorrow afternoon	bokra baʿd el ḍohr	بكرة بعد الظهر
tonight (this evening)	el naharda bel leyl	النهاردة بالليل
tomorrow night	bokra bel leyl	بكرة بالليل
at 3 o'clock sharp	es sāʿa talāta bel ḍabṭ	الساعة تلاتة بالضبط
about 4 o'clock	es sāʿa arbaʿa taʾrīban	الساعة أربعة تقريبا
by 12 o'clock	ḥatt es sāʿa etnāʃar	حتى الساعة إتناشر
in 20 minutes	fe χelāl ʿeʃrīn deʿeeʿa	في خلال عشرين دقيقة
in an hour	fe χelāl sāʿa	في خلال ساعة
on time (adv)	fe mawʿedo	في موعده
a quarter to …	ella robʿ	إلّا ربع
within an hour	χelāl sāʿa	خلال ساعة
every 15 minutes	koll robʿ sāʿa	كلّ ربع ساعة
round the clock	leyl nahār	ليل نهار

19. Months. Seasons

January	yanāyer (m)	يناير
February	febrāyer (m)	فبراير
March	māres (m)	مارس
April	ebrīl (m)	إبريل
May	māyo (m)	مايو
June	yonyo (m)	يونيو
July	yolyo (m)	يوليو
August	oɣosṭos (m)	أغسطس
September	sebtamber (m)	سبتمبر
October	oktober (m)	أكتوبر
November	november (m)	نوفمبر
December	desember (m)	ديسمبر
spring	rabeeʿ (m)	ربيع
in spring	fel rabeeʿ	في الربيع
spring (as adj)	rabeeʿy	ربيعي
summer	ṣeyf (m)	صيف
in summer	fel ṣeyf	في الصيف

summer (as adj)	ṣeyfy	صيفي
autumn	χarīf (m)	خريف
in autumn	fel χarīf	في الخريف
autumn (as adj)	χarīfy	خريفي
winter	ʃetā' (m)	شتاء
in winter	fel ʃetā'	في الشتاء
winter (as adj)	ʃetwy	شتوّي
month	ʃahr (m)	شهر
this month	fel ʃahr da	في الشهر ده
next month	el ʃahr el gayī	الشهر الجايّ
last month	el ʃahr elly fāt	الشهر اللي فات
a month ago	men ʃahr	من شهر
in a month (a month later)	ba'd ʃahr	بعد شهر
in 2 months (2 months later)	ba'd ʃahreyn	بعد شهرين
the whole month	el ʃahr kollo	الشهر كلّه
all month long	ṭawāl el ʃahr	طوال الشهر
monthly (~ magazine)	ʃahry	شهري
monthly (adv)	ʃahry	شهري
every month	koll ʃahr	كلّ شهر
twice a month	marreteyn fel ʃahr	مرّتين في الشهر
year	sana (f)	سنة
this year	el sana di	السنة دي
next year	el sana el gaya	السنة الجايّة
last year	el sana elly fātet	السنة اللي فاتت
a year ago	men sana	من سنة
in a year	ba'd sana	بعد سنة
in two years	ba'd sanateyn	بعد سنتين
the whole year	el sana kollaha	السنة كلّها
all year long	ṭūl el sana	طول السنة
every year	koll sana	كلّ سنة
annual (adj)	sanawy	سنوّي
annually (adv)	koll sana	كلّ سنة
4 times a year	arba' marrāt fel sana	أربع مرات في السنة
date (e.g. today's ~)	tarīχ (m)	تاريخ
date (e.g. ~ of birth)	tarīχ (m)	تاريخ
calendar	natīga (f)	نتيجة
half a year	noṣṣ sana	نصّ سنة
six months	settet aʃ-hor (f)	ستّة أشهر
season (summer, etc.)	faṣl (m)	فصل
century	qarn (m)	قرن

20. Time. Miscellaneous

time	wa't (m)	وقت
moment	laḥza (f)	لحظة

instant (n)	laḥza (f)	لحظة
instant (adj)	laḥza	لحظة
lapse (of time)	fatra (f)	فترة
life	ḥayah (f)	حياة
eternity	abadiya (f)	أبديّة
epoch	ʿahd (m)	عهد
era	ʿaṣr (m)	عصر
cycle	dawra (f)	دوّرة
period	fatra (f)	فترة
term (short-~)	fatra (f)	فترة
the future	el mostaqbal (m)	المستقبل
future (as adj)	elly gayī	اللّي جاي
next time	el marra el gaya	المرّة الجايّة
the past	el māḍy (m)	الماضي
past (recent)	elly fāt	اللّي فات
last time	el marra elly fātet	المرّة اللّي فاتت
later (adv)	baʿdeyn	بعدين
after (prep.)	baʿd	بعد
nowadays (adv)	el ayām di	الأيام دي
now (at this moment)	delwaʾty	دلوّقتي
immediately (adv)	ḥālan	حالاً
soon (adv)	ʾarīb	قريب
in advance (beforehand)	moʾaddaman	مقدّماً
a long time ago	men zamān	من زمان
recently (adv)	men ʾorayeb	من قريّب
destiny	maṣīr (m)	مصير
recollections	zekra (f)	زكرى
archives	arʃīf (m)	أرشيف
during …	esnāʾ…	إثناء...
long, a long time (adv)	modda ṭawīla	مدّة طويلة
not long (adv)	le fatra ʾaṣīra	لفترة قصيرة
early (in the morning)	badry	بدري
late (not early)	metʾakχer	متأخّر
forever (for good)	lel abad	للأبد
to start (begin)	badaʾ	بدأ
to postpone (vt)	aggel	أجّل
at the same time	fe nafs el waqt	في نفس الوقت
permanently (adv)	be ʃakl dāʾem	بشكل دائم
constant (noise, pain)	mostamerr	مستمرّ
temporary (adj)	moʾakkatan	مؤقتّاً
sometimes (adv)	saʿāt	ساعات
rarely (adv)	nāderan	نادراً
often (adv)	ketīr	كثير

21. Lines and shapes

square	morabbaʿ (m)	مربّع
square (as adj)	morabbaʿ	مربع

circle	dayra (f)	دايرة
round (adj)	medawwar	مدوّر
triangle	mosallas (m)	مثلّث
triangular (adj)	mosallasy el ʃakl	مثلّثي الشكل
oval	baydawy (m)	بيضوّي
oval (as adj)	baydawy	بيضوي
rectangle	mostaṭīl (m)	مستطيل
rectangular (adj)	mostaṭīly	مستطيلي
pyramid	haram (m)	هرم
rhombus	moʿayen (m)	معيّن
trapezium	ʃebh el monḥaref (m)	شبه المنحرف
cube	mokaʿab (m)	مكعّب
prism	manʃūr (m)	منشور
circumference	moḥīṭ monḥany moɣlaq (m)	محيط منحنى مغلق
sphere	kora (f)	كرة
ball (solid sphere)	kora (f)	كرة
diameter	qaṭr (m)	قطر
radius	noṣṣ qaṭr (m)	نصّ قطر
perimeter (circle's ~)	moḥīṭ (m)	محيط
centre	wasaṭ (m)	وسط
horizontal (adj)	ofoqy	أفقي
vertical (adj)	ʿamūdy	عمودي
parallel (n)	motawāz (m)	متواز
parallel (as adj)	motawāzy	متوازي
line	χaṭṭ (m)	خطّ
stroke	ḥaraka (m)	حركة
straight line	χaṭṭ mostaqīm (m)	خطّ مستقيم
curve (curved line)	χaṭṭ monḥany (m)	خطّ منحني
thin (line, etc.)	rofayaʿ	رفيّع
contour (outline)	kontūr (m)	كنتور
intersection	taqāṭoʿ (m)	تقاطع
right angle	zawya mostaqīma (f)	زاوية مستقيمة
segment	ʾeṭʿa (f)	قطعة
sector (circular ~)	qaṭāʿ (m)	قطاع
side (of a triangle)	gāneb (m)	جانب
angle	zawya (f)	زاوية

22. Units of measurement

weight	wazn (m)	وزن
length	ṭūl (m)	طول
width	ʿarḍ (m)	عرض
height	ertefāʿ (m)	إرتفاع
depth	ʿomq (m)	عمق
volume	ḥagm (m)	حجم
area	mesāḥa (f)	مساحة
gram	gram (m)	جرام
milligram	milligrām (m)	ملّيغرام

kilogram	kilogrām (m)	كيلوغرام
ton	ṭenn (m)	طنّ
pound	reṭl (m)	رطل
ounce	onṣa (f)	أونصة
metre	metr (m)	متر
millimetre	millimetr (m)	ملّيمتر
centimetre	santimetr (m)	سنتيمتر
kilometre	kilometr (m)	كيلومتر
mile	mīl (m)	ميل
inch	boṣa (f)	بوصة
foot	'adam (m)	قدم
yard	yarda (f)	ياردة
square metre	metr morabbaʿ (m)	متر مربّع
hectare	hektār (m)	هكتار
litre	litre (m)	لتر
degree	daraga (f)	درجة
volt	volt (m)	فولت
ampere	ambere (m)	أمبير
horsepower	ḥoṣān (m)	حصان
quantity	kemiya (f)	كميّة
a little bit of …	ʃewayet …	شويّة...
half	noṣṣ (m)	نصّ
dozen	desta (f)	دستة
piece (item)	waḥda (f)	وحدة
size	ḥagm (m)	حجم
scale (map ~)	me'yās (m)	مقياس
minimal (adj)	el adna	الأدنى
the smallest (adj)	el aṣɣar	الأصغر
medium (adj)	motawasseṭ	متوّسط
maximal (adj)	el aqṣa	الأقصى
the largest (adj)	el akbar	الأكبر

23. Containers

canning jar (glass ~)	barṭamān (m)	برطمان
tin, can	kanz (m)	كانز
bucket	gardal (m)	جردل
barrel	barmīl (m)	برميل
wash basin (e.g., plastic ~)	ḥoḍe lel ɣasīl (m)	حوض للغسيل
tank (100L water ~)	χazzān (m)	خزّان
hip flask	zamzamiya (f)	زمزميّة
jerrycan	ʒerken (m)	جركن
tank (e.g., tank car)	χazzān (m)	خزّان
mug	mugg (m)	ماجّ
cup (of coffee, etc.)	fengān (m)	فنجان

saucer	ṭaba' fengān (m)	طبق فنجان
glass (tumbler)	kobbāya (f)	كوبّاية
wine glass	kāsa (f)	كاسة
stock pot (soup pot)	ḥalla (f)	حلّة
bottle (~ of wine)	ezāza (f)	إزازة
neck (of the bottle, etc.)	'onq (m)	عنق
carafe (decanter)	dawra' zogāgy (m)	دورق زجاجي
pitcher	ebrī' (m)	إبريق
vessel (container)	we'ā' (m)	وعاء
pot (crock, stoneware ~)	aṣīṣ (m)	أصيص
vase	vāza (f)	فازة
flacon, bottle (perfume ~)	ezāza (f)	إزازة
vial, small bottle	ezāza (f)	إزازة
tube (of toothpaste)	anbūba (f)	أنبوبة
sack (bag)	kīs (m)	كيس
bag (paper ~, plastic ~)	kīs (m)	كيس
packet (of cigarettes, etc.)	'elba (f)	علبة
box (e.g. shoebox)	'elba (f)	علبة
crate	ṣandū' (m)	صندوق
basket	salla (f)	سلّة

24. Materials

material	madda (f)	مادّة
wood (n)	χaʃab (m)	خشب
wood-, wooden (adj)	χaʃaby	خشبي
glass (n)	ezāz (m)	إزاز
glass (as adj)	ezāz	إزاز
stone (n)	ḥagar (m)	حجر
stone (as adj)	ḥagary	حجري
plastic (n)	blastik (m)	بلاستيك
plastic (as adj)	men el blastik	من البلاستيك
rubber (n)	maṭṭāṭ (m)	مطّاط
rubber (as adj)	maṭṭāṭy	مطّاطي
cloth, fabric (n)	'omāʃ (m)	قماش
fabric (as adj)	men el 'omāʃ	من القماش
paper (n)	wara' (m)	ورق
paper (as adj)	wara'y	ورقي
cardboard (n)	kartōn (m)	كرتون
cardboard (as adj)	kartony	كرتوني
polyethylene	bolyetylen (m)	بولي ايثيلين
cellophane	sellofān (m)	سيلوفان

plywood	ablakāʃ (m)	أبلكاش
porcelain (n)	borsalīn (m)	بورسلين
porcelain (as adj)	men el borsalīn	من البورسلين
clay (n)	ṭīn (m)	طين
clay (as adj)	fokχāry	فخّاري
ceramic (n)	seramīk (m)	سيراميك
ceramic (as adj)	men el seramik	من السيراميك

25. Metals

metal (n)	maʿdan (m)	معدن
metal (as adj)	maʿdany	معدني
alloy (n)	sebīka (f)	سبيكة
gold (n)	dahab (m)	ذهب
gold, golden (adj)	dahaby	ذهبي
silver (n)	faḍḍa (f)	فضّة
silver (as adj)	feḍḍy	فضّي
iron (n)	ḥadīd (m)	حديد
iron-, made of iron (adj)	ḥadīdy	حديدي
steel (n)	fulāz (m)	فولاذ
steel (as adj)	folāzy	فولاذي
copper (n)	neḥās (m)	نحاس
copper (as adj)	neḥāsy	نحاسي
aluminium (n)	aluminyum (m)	الومينيوم
aluminium (as adj)	aluminyum	الومينيوم
bronze (n)	bronze (m)	برونز
bronze (as adj)	bronzy	برونزي
brass	neḥās aṣfar (m)	نحاس أصفر
nickel	nikel (m)	نيكل
platinum	blatīn (m)	بلاتين
mercury	zeʾbaq (m)	زئبق
tin	ʾaṣdīr (m)	قصدير
lead	roṣāṣ (m)	رصاص
zinc	zink (m)	زنك

HUMAN BEING

Human being. The body

26. Humans. Basic concepts

human being	ensān (m)	إنسان
man (adult male)	rāgel (m)	راجل
woman	set (f)	ست
child	ṭefl (m)	طفل
girl	bent (f)	بنت
boy	walad (m)	ولد
teenager	morāheq (m)	مراهق
old man	ʿagūz (m)	عجوز
old woman	ʿagūza (f)	عجوزة

27. Human anatomy

organism (body)	ʿoḍw (m)	عضو
heart	ʾalb (m)	قلب
blood	damm (m)	دم
artery	ʃeryān (m)	شريان
vein	ʿerʾ (m)	عرق
brain	mokχ (m)	مخّ
nerve	ʿaṣab (m)	عصب
nerves	aʿṣāb (pl)	أعصاب
vertebra	faqra (f)	فقرة
spine (backbone)	ʿamūd faqry (m)	عمود فقري
stomach (organ)	meʿda (f)	معدة
intestines, bowels	amʿāʾ (pl)	أمعاء
intestine (e.g. large ~)	maʿy (m)	معى
liver	kebd (f)	كبد
kidney	kelya (f)	كلية
bone	ʿaḍm (m)	عظم
skeleton	haykal ʿazmy (m)	هيكل عظمي
rib	ḍelʿ (m)	ضلع
skull	gomgoma (f)	جمجمة
muscle	ʿaḍala (f)	عضلة
biceps	biseps (f)	بايسبس
triceps	triseps (f)	ترايسبس
tendon	watar (m)	وتر
joint	mefṣal (m)	مفصل

lungs	reʾateyn (du)	رئتين
genitals	aʿḍāʾ tanasoliya (pl)	أعضاء تناسلية
skin	boʃra (m)	بشرة

28. Head

head	raʾs (m)	رأس
face	weʃ (m)	وش
nose	manaχīr (m)	مناخير
mouth	boʾ (m)	بوء
eye	ʿeyn (f)	عين
eyes	ʿoyūn (pl)	عيون
pupil	ḥadʾa (f)	حدقة
eyebrow	ḥāgeb (m)	حاجب
eyelash	remʃ (m)	رمش
eyelid	gefn (m)	جفن
tongue	lesān (m)	لسان
tooth	senna (f)	سنّة
lips	ʃafāyef (pl)	شفايف
cheekbones	ʿaḍmet el χadd (f)	عضمة الخدّ
gum	lassa (f)	لثّة
palate	ḥanak (m)	حنك
nostrils	manaχer (pl)	مناخر
chin	daʾʾn (m)	دقن
jaw	fakk (m)	فكّ
cheek	χadd (m)	خدّ
forehead	gabha (f)	جبهة
temple	ṣedɣ (m)	صدغ
ear	wedn (f)	ودن
back of the head	ʾafa (m)	قفا
neck	raʾaba (f)	رقبة
throat	zore (m)	زور
hair	ʃaʿr (m)	شعر
hairstyle	tasrīḥa (f)	تسريحة
haircut	tasrīḥa (f)	تسريحة
wig	barūka (f)	باروكة
moustache	ʃanab (pl)	شنب
beard	leḥya (f)	لحية
to have (a beard, etc.)	ʿando	عنده
plait	ḍefīra (f)	ضفيرة
sideboards	sawālef (pl)	سوالف
red-haired (adj)	aḥmar el ʃaʿr	أحمر الشعر
grey (hair)	ʃaʿr abyaḍ	شعر أبيض
bald (adj)	aṣlaʿ	أصلع
bald patch	ṣalaʿ (m)	صلع
ponytail	deyl ḥoṣān (m)	ديل حصان
fringe	ʾoṣṣa (f)	قصّة

29. Human body

hand	yad (m)	يد
arm	derāʿ (f)	دراع
finger	ṣobāʿ (m)	صباع
toe	ṣobāʿ el ʾadam (m)	صباع القدم
thumb	ebhām (m)	إبهام
little finger	χonṣor (m)	خنصر
nail	ḍefr (m)	ضفر
fist	qabḍa (f)	قبضة
palm	kaff (f)	كفّ
wrist	meʿṣam (m)	معصم
forearm	sāʿed (m)	ساعد
elbow	kūʿ (m)	كوع
shoulder	ketf (f)	كتف
leg	regl (f)	رجل
foot	qadam (f)	قدم
knee	rokba (f)	ركبة
calf	semmāna (f)	سمّانة
hip	faχd (f)	فخد
heel	kaʿb (m)	كعب
body	gesm (m)	جسم
stomach	baṭn (m)	بطن
chest	ṣedr (m)	صدر
breast	sady (m)	ثدي
flank	ganb (m)	جنب
back	ḍahr (m)	ضهر
lower back	asfal el ḍahr (m)	أسفل الضهر
waist	wesṭ (f)	وسط
navel (belly button)	sorra (f)	سرّة
buttocks	ardāf (pl)	أرداف
bottom	debr (m)	دبر
beauty spot	ʃāma (f)	شامة
birthmark (café au lait spot)	waḥma	وحمة
tattoo	waʃm (m)	وشم
scar	nadba (f)	ندبة

Clothing & Accessories

30. Outerwear. Coats

clothes	malābes (pl)	ملابس
outerwear	malābes fo'aniya (pl)	ملابس فوقانيّة
winter clothing	malābes ʃetwiya (pl)	ملابس شتويّة
coat (overcoat)	balṭo (m)	بالطو
fur coat	balṭo farww (m)	بالطو فروّ
fur jacket	ʒaket farww (m)	جاكيت فروّ
down coat	balṭo maḥʃy rīʃ (m)	بالطو محشي ريش
jacket (e.g. leather ~)	ʒæket (m)	جاكيت
raincoat (trenchcoat, etc.)	ʒæket lel maṭar (m)	جاكيت للمطر
waterproof (adj)	wāqy men el maya	واقي من الميّة

31. Men's & women's clothing

shirt (button shirt)	'amīṣ (m)	قميص
trousers	banṭalone (f)	بنطلون
jeans	ʒeans (m)	جينز
suit jacket	ʒæket (f)	جاكت
suit	badla (f)	بدلة
dress (frock)	fostān (m)	فستان
skirt	ʒība (f)	جيبة
blouse	bloza (f)	بلوزة
knitted jacket (cardigan, etc.)	kardigan (m)	كارديجن
jacket (of a woman's suit)	ʒæket (m)	جاكيت
T-shirt	ti ʃirt (m)	تي شيرت
shorts (short trousers)	ʃort (m)	شورت
tracksuit	treneng (m)	تريننج
bathrobe	robe el ḥammām (m)	روب حمّام
pyjamas	beʒāma (f)	بيجاما
jumper (sweater)	blover (f)	بلوفر
pullover	blover (m)	بلوفر
waistcoat	vest (m)	فيست
tailcoat	badlet sahra ṭawīla (f)	بدلة سهرة طويلة
dinner suit	badla (f)	بدلة
uniform	zayī muwaḥḥad (m)	زيّ موحّد
workwear	lebs el ʃoɣl (m)	لبس الشغل
boiler suit	overall (m)	اوفر اول
coat (e.g. doctor's smock)	balṭo (m)	بالطو

32. Clothing. Underwear

underwear	malābes dāχeliya (pl)	ملابس داخلية
pants	sirwāl dāχly rigāly (m)	سروال داخلي رجاليّ
panties	sirwāl dāχly nisā'y (m)	سروال داخلي نسائيّ
vest (singlet)	fanella (f)	فانلّا
socks	ʃarāb (m)	شراب
nightdress	'amīṣ nome (m)	قميص نوم
bra	setyāna (f)	ستيانة
knee highs (knee-high socks)	ʃarabāt ṭawīla (pl)	شرابات طويلة
tights	klone (m)	كلون
stockings (hold ups)	gawāreb (pl)	جوارب
swimsuit, bikini	mayo (m)	مايّوه

33. Headwear

hat	ṭa'iya (f)	طاقيّة
trilby hat	borneyṭa (f)	برنيطة
baseball cap	base bāl kāb (m)	بيس بول كاب
flatcap	ṭa'iya mosaṭṭaḥa (f)	طاقيّة مسطحة
beret	bereyh (m)	بيريه
hood	ɣaṭa' (f)	غطاء
panama hat	qobba'et banama (f)	قبّعة بناما
knit cap (knitted hat)	ays kāb (m)	آيس كاب
headscarf	eʃarb (m)	إيشارب
women's hat	borneyṭa (f)	برنيطة
hard hat	χawza (f)	خوذة
forage cap	kāb (m)	كاب
helmet	χawza (f)	خوذة
bowler	qobba'a (f)	قبّعة
top hat	qobba'a rasmiya (f)	قبّعة رسمية

34. Footwear

footwear	gezam (pl)	جزم
shoes (men's shoes)	gazma (f)	جزمة
shoes (women's shoes)	gazma (f)	جزمة
boots (e.g., cowboy ~)	būt (m)	بوت
carpet slippers	ʃebʃeb (m)	شبشب
trainers	kotʃy tennis (m)	كوتشي تنس
trainers	kotʃy (m)	كوتشي
sandals	ṣandal (pl)	صندل
cobbler (shoe repairer)	eskāfy (m)	إسكافي
heel	ka'b (m)	كعب

pair (of shoes)	goze (m)	جوز
lace (shoelace)	ʃerīṭ (m)	شريط
to lace up (vt)	rabaṭ	ربط
shoehorn	labbāsa el gazma (f)	لبّاسة الجزمة
shoe polish	warnīʃ el gazma (m)	ورنيش الجزمة

35. Textile. Fabrics

cotton (n)	ʾoṭn (m)	قطن
cotton (as adj)	ʾoṭny	قطني
flax (n)	kettān (m)	كتّان
flax (as adj)	men el kettān	من الكتّان
silk (n)	ḥarīr (m)	حرير
silk (as adj)	ḥarīry	حريري
wool (n)	ṣūf (m)	صوف
wool (as adj)	ṣūfiya	صوفية
velvet	moχmal (m)	مخمل
suede	geld mazʾabar (m)	جلد مزأبر
corduroy	ʾoṭṭn ʾaṭīfa (f)	قطن قطيفة
nylon (n)	nylon (m)	نايلون
nylon (as adj)	men el naylon	من النيلون
polyester (n)	bolyester (m)	بوليستر
polyester (as adj)	men el bolyastar	من البوليستر
leather (n)	geld (m)	جلد
leather (as adj)	men el geld	من الجلد
fur (n)	farww (m)	فروّ
fur (e.g. ~ coat)	men el farww	من الفروّ

36. Personal accessories

gloves	gwanty (m)	جوانتي
mittens	gwanty men ɣeyr aṣābeʿ (m)	جوانتي من غير أصابع
scarf (muffler)	skarf (m)	سكارف
glasses	naḍḍāra (f)	نظّارة
frame (eyeglass ~)	eṭār (m)	إطار
umbrella	ʃamsiya (f)	شمسيّة
walking stick	ʿaṣāya (f)	عصاية
hairbrush	forʃet ʃaʿr (f)	فرشة شعر
fan	marwaḥa (f)	مروّحة
tie (necktie)	karavetta (f)	كرافتة
bow tie	bebyona (m)	بيبيونة
braces	ḥammala (f)	حمّالة
handkerchief	mandīl (m)	منديل
comb	meʃṭ (m)	مشط
hair slide	dabbūs (m)	دبّوس

hairpin	bensa (m)	بنسة
buckle	bokla (f)	بكلة
belt	ḥezām (m)	حزام
shoulder strap	ḥammalet el ketf (f)	حمّالة الكتف
bag (handbag)	ʃanṭa (f)	شنطة
handbag	ʃanṭet yad (f)	شنطة يد
rucksack	ʃanṭet ḍahr (f)	شنطة ظهر

37. Clothing. Miscellaneous

fashion	mūḍa (f)	موضة
in vogue (adj)	fel moḍa	في الموضة
fashion designer	moṣammem azyāʾ (m)	مصمّم أزياء
collar	yāʾa (f)	ياقة
pocket	geyb (m)	جيب
pocket (as adj)	geyb	جيب
sleeve	komm (m)	كمّ
hanging loop	ʿelāqa (f)	علّاقة
flies (on trousers)	lesān (m)	لسان
zip (fastener)	sosta (f)	سوستة
fastener	maʃbak (m)	مشبك
button	zerr (m)	زرّ
buttonhole	ʿarwa (f)	عروة
to come off (ab. button)	weʾeʿ	وقع
to sew (vi, vt)	χayaṭ	خيّط
to embroider (vi, vt)	ṭarraz	طرّز
embroidery	taṭrīz (m)	تطريز
sewing needle	ebra (f)	إبرة
thread	χeyṭ (m)	خيط
seam	derz (m)	درز
to get dirty (vi)	ettwassaχ	إتّوسّخ
stain (mark, spot)	boʾʿa (f)	بقعة
to crease, to crumple	takarmaʃ	تكرمش
to tear, to rip (vt)	ʾaṭaʿ	قطع
clothes moth	ʿetta (f)	عثّة

38. Personal care. Cosmetics

toothpaste	maʿgūn asnān (m)	معجون أسنان
toothbrush	forʃet senān (f)	فرشة أسنان
to clean one's teeth	naḍḍaf el asnān	نظّف الأسنان
razor	mūs (m)	موس
shaving cream	krīm ḥelāʾa (m)	كريم حلاقة
to shave (vi)	ḥalaʾ	حلق
soap	ṣabūn (m)	صابون

shampoo	ʃambū (m)	شامبو
scissors	ma'aṣ (m)	مقص
nail file	mabrad (m)	مبرد
nail clippers	mel'aṭ (m)	ملقط
tweezers	mel'aṭ (m)	ملقط
cosmetics	mawād tagmīl (pl)	مواد تجميل
face mask	mask (m)	ماسك
manicure	monekīr (m)	مونيكير
to have a manicure	'amal monikīr	عمل مونيكير
pedicure	badikīr (m)	باديكير
make-up bag	ʃanṭet mekyāʒ (f)	شنطة مكياج
face powder	bodret weʃ (f)	بودرة وش
powder compact	'elbet bodra (f)	علبة بودرة
blusher	aḥmar χodūd (m)	أحمر خدود
perfume (bottled)	barfān (m)	بارفان
toilet water (lotion)	kolonya (f)	كولونيا
lotion	loʃion (m)	لوشن
cologne	kolonya (f)	كولونيا
eyeshadow	eyeʃadow (m)	ايّ شادو
eyeliner	koḥl (m)	كحل
mascara	maskara (f)	ماسكارا
lipstick	rūʒ (m)	روج
nail polish	monekīr (m)	مونيكير
hair spray	mosabbet el ʃa'r (m)	مثبّت الشعر
deodorant	mozīl 'ara' (m)	مزيل عرق
cream	krīm (m)	كريم
face cream	krīm lel weʃ (m)	كريم للوش
hand cream	krīm eyd (m)	كريم أيد
anti-wrinkle cream	krīm moḍād lel taga'īd (m)	كريم مضاد للتجاعيد
day cream	krīm en nahār (m)	كريم النهار
night cream	krīm el leyl (m)	كريم الليل
day (as adj)	nahāry	نهاري
night (as adj)	layly	ليّلي
tampon	tambon (m)	تانبون
toilet paper (toilet roll)	wara' twalet (m)	ورق تواليت
hair dryer	seʃwār (m)	سشوار

39. Jewellery

jewellery, jewels	mogawharāt (pl)	مجوّهرات
precious (e.g. ~ stone)	ɣāly	غالي
hallmark stamp	damɣa (f)	دمغة
ring	χātem (m)	خاتم
wedding ring	deblet el faraḥ (m)	دبلة الفرح
bracelet	eswera (m)	إسوّرة
earrings	ḥala' (m)	حلق

necklace (~ of pearls)	ʿoʾd (m)	عقد
crown	tāg (m)	تاج
bead necklace	ʿoʾd χaraz (m)	عقد خرز
diamond	almāz (m)	ألماز
emerald	zomorrod (m)	زمرّد
ruby	yaʾūt aḥmar (m)	ياقوت أحمر
sapphire	yaʾūt azraʾ (m)	ياقوت أزرق
pearl	loʾloʾ (m)	لؤلؤ
amber	kahramān (m)	كهرمان

40. Watches. Clocks

watch (wristwatch)	sāʿa (f)	ساعة
dial	wag-h el sāʿa (m)	وجه الساعة
hand (clock, watch)	ʿaʾrab el sāʿa (m)	عقرب الساعة
metal bracelet	ʃerīṭ sāʿa maʿdaniya (m)	شريط ساعة معدنية
watch strap	ʃerīṭ el sāʿa (m)	شريط الساعة
battery	baṭṭariya (f)	بطّاريّة
to be flat (battery)	χelṣet	خلصت
to change a battery	ɣayar el baṭṭariya	غيّر البطّاريّة
to run fast	sabaʾ	سبق
to run slow	taʾakχar	تأخّر
wall clock	sāʿet ḥeyṭa (f)	ساعة حيطة
hourglass	sāʿa ramliya (f)	ساعة رمليّة
sundial	sāʿa ʃamsiya (f)	ساعة شمسيّة
alarm clock	monabbeh (m)	منبّه
watchmaker	saʿāty (m)	ساعاتي
to repair (vt)	ṣallaḥ	صلّح

Food. Nutricion

41. Food

meat	laḥma (f)	لحمة
chicken	ferāχ (m)	فراخ
poussin	farrūg (m)	فرّوج
duck	baṭṭa (f)	بطّة
goose	wezza (f)	وزّة
game	ṣeyd (m)	صيد
turkey	dīk rūmy (m)	ديك رومي
pork	laḥm el χanazīr (m)	لحم الخنزير
veal	laḥm el ʿegl (m)	لحم العجل
lamb	laḥm ḍāny (m)	لحم ضاني
beef	laḥm baqary (m)	لحم بقري
rabbit	laḥm arāneb (m)	لحم أرانب
sausage (bologna, etc.)	sogo'' (m)	سجق
vienna sausage (frankfurter)	sogo'' (m)	سجق
bacon	bakon (m)	بيكون
ham	hām(m)	هام
gammon	faχd χanzīr (m)	فخد خنزير
pâté	maʿgūn laḥm (m)	معجون لحم
liver	kebda (f)	كبدة
mince (minced meat)	hamburger (m)	هامبورجر
tongue	lesān (m)	لسان
egg	beyḍa (f)	بيضة
eggs	beyḍ (m)	بيض
egg white	bayāḍ el beyḍ (m)	بياض البيض
egg yolk	ṣafār el beyḍ (m)	صفار البيض
fish	samak (m)	سمك
seafood	sīfūd (pl)	سي فود
caviar	kaviar (m)	كافيار
crab	kaboria (m)	كابوريا
prawn	gammbary (m)	جمبري
oyster	maḥār (m)	محار
spiny lobster	estakoza (m)	استاكوزا
octopus	aχṭabūṭ (m)	أخطبوط
squid	kalmāry (m)	كالماري
sturgeon	samak el ḥafʃ (m)	سمك الحفش
salmon	salamon (m)	سلمون
halibut	samak el halbūt (m)	سمك الهلبوت
cod	samak el qadd (m)	سمك القد
mackerel	makerel (m)	ماكريل

tuna	tuna (f)	تونة
eel	ḥankalīs (m)	حنكليس
trout	salamon mera''aṭ (m)	سلمون مرقّط
sardine	sardīn (m)	سردين
pike	samak el karāky (m)	سمك الكراكي
herring	renga (f)	رنجة
bread	ʿeyʃ (m)	عيش
cheese	gebna (f)	جبنة
sugar	sokkar (m)	سكّر
salt	melḥ (m)	ملح
rice	rozz (m)	رزّ
pasta (macaroni)	makaruna (f)	مكرونة
noodles	nūdles (f)	نودلز
butter	zebda (f)	زبدة
vegetable oil	zeyt (m)	زيت
sunflower oil	zeyt ʿabbād el ʃams (m)	زيت عبّاد الشمس
margarine	margarīn (m)	مارجرين
olives	zaytūn (m)	زيتون
olive oil	zeyt el zaytūn (m)	زيت الزيتون
milk	laban (m)	لبن
condensed milk	ḥalīb mokassaf (m)	حليب مكثّف
yogurt	zabādy (m)	زبادي
soured cream	kreyma ḥamḍa (f)	كريمة حامضة
cream (of milk)	krīma (f)	كريمة
mayonnaise	mayonnɛ:z (m)	مايونيز
buttercream	krīmet zebda (f)	كريمة زبدة
groats (barley ~, etc.)	ḥobūb 'amḥ (pl)	حبوب قمح
flour	de'ī' (m)	دقيق
tinned food	moʿallabāt (pl)	معلّبات
cornflakes	korn fleks (m)	كورن فليكس
honey	ʿasal (m)	عسل
jam	mrabba (m)	مربّى
chewing gum	lebān (m)	لبان

42. Drinks

water	meyāh (f)	مياه
drinking water	mayet ʃorb (m)	ميّة شرب
mineral water	maya maʿdaniya (f)	ميّة معدنية
still (adj)	rakeda	راكدة
carbonated (adj)	kanz	كانز
sparkling (adj)	kanz	كانز
ice	talg (m)	ثلج
with ice	bel talg	بالتلج

non-alcoholic (adj)	men ɣeyr koḥūl	من غير كحول
soft drink	maʃrūb ɣāzy (m)	مشروب غازي
refreshing drink	ḥāga sa''a (f)	حاجة ساقعة
lemonade	limonāta (f)	ليموناتة
spirits	maʃrūbāt koḥūliya (pl)	مشروبات كحولية
wine	χamra (f)	خمرة
white wine	nebīz abyaḍ (m)	نبيذ أبيض
red wine	nebī aḥmar (m)	نبيذ أحمر
liqueur	liqure (m)	ليكيور
champagne	ʃambania (f)	شمبانيا
vermouth	vermote (m)	فيرموت
whisky	wiski (m)	ويسكي
vodka	vodka (f)	فودكا
gin	ʒin (m)	جين
cognac	konyāk (m)	كونياك
rum	rum (m)	رم
coffee	'ahwa (f)	قهوة
black coffee	'ahwa sāda (f)	قهوة سادة
white coffee	'ahwa bel ḥalīb (f)	قهوة بالحليب
cappuccino	kaputʃino (m)	كابتشينو
instant coffee	neskafe (m)	نيسكافيه
milk	laban (m)	لبن
cocktail	koktayl (m)	كوكتيل
milkshake	milk ʃejk (m)	ميلك شيك
juice	'aṣīr (m)	عصير
tomato juice	'aṣīr ṭamāṭem (m)	عصير طماطم
orange juice	'aṣīr bortoqāl (m)	عصير برتقال
freshly squeezed juice	'aṣīr freʃ (m)	عصير فريش
beer	bīra (f)	بيرة
lager	bīra χafīfa (f)	بيرة خفيفة
bitter	bīra ɣam'a (f)	بيرة غامقة
tea	ʃāy (m)	شاي
black tea	ʃāy aḥmar (m)	شاي أحمر
green tea	ʃāy aχḍar (m)	شاي أخضر

43. Vegetables

vegetables	χoḍār (pl)	خضار
greens	χoḍrawāt waraqiya (pl)	خضروات ورقية
tomato	ṭamāṭem (f)	طماطم
cucumber	χeyār (m)	خيار
carrot	gazar (m)	جزر
potato	baṭāṭes (f)	بطاطس
onion	baṣal (m)	بصل
garlic	tūm (m)	ثوم

cabbage	koronb (m)	كرنب
cauliflower	ʾarnabīṭ (m)	قرنبيط
Brussels sprouts	koronb broksel (m)	كرنب بروكسل
broccoli	brokkoli (m)	بركولي
beetroot	bangar (m)	بنجر
aubergine	bātengān (m)	باذنجان
courgette	kōsa (f)	كوسة
pumpkin	qarʿ ʿasaly (m)	قرع عسلي
turnip	left (m)	لفت
parsley	baʾdūnes (m)	بقدونس
dill	ʃabat (m)	شبت
lettuce	χass (m)	خسّ
celery	karfas (m)	كرفس
asparagus	helione (m)	هليون
spinach	sabāneχ (m)	سبانخ
pea	besella (f)	بسلّة
beans	fūl (m)	فول
maize	dora (f)	ذرة
kidney bean	faṣolya (f)	فاصوليا
sweet paper	felfel (m)	فلفل
radish	fegl (m)	فجل
artichoke	χarʃūf (m)	خرشوف

44. Fruits. Nuts

fruit	faχa (f)	فاكهة
apple	toffāḥa (f)	تفّاحة
pear	komettra (f)	كمّثرى
lemon	lymūn (m)	ليمون
orange	bortoqāl (m)	برتقال
strawberry (garden ~)	farawla (f)	فراولة
tangerine	yosfy (m)	يوسفي
plum	barʾūʾ (m)	برقوق
peach	χawχa (f)	خوخة
apricot	meʃmeʃ (f)	مشمش
raspberry	tūt el ʿalīʾ el aḥmar (m)	توت العليق الأحمر
pineapple	ananās (m)	أناناس
banana	moze (m)	موز
watermelon	baṭṭīχ (m)	بطّيخ
grape	ʿenab (m)	عنب
cherry	karaz (m)	كرز
melon	ʃammām (f)	شمّام
grapefruit	grabe frūt (m)	جريب فروت
avocado	avokado (f)	افوكاتو
papaya	babāya (m)	ببايا
mango	manga (m)	مانجة
pomegranate	rommān (m)	رمان

redcurrant	keʃmeʃ aḥmar (m)	كشمش أحمر
blackcurrant	keʃmeʃ aswad (m)	كشمش أسود
gooseberry	ʿenab el saʿlab (m)	عنب الثعلب
bilberry	ʿenab al aḥrāg (m)	عنب الأحراج
blackberry	tūt aswad (m)	توت أسود
raisin	zebīb (m)	زبيب
fig	tīn (m)	تين
date	tamr (m)	تمر
peanut	fūl sudāny (m)	فول سوداني
almond	loze (m)	لوز
walnut	ʿeyn gamal (f)	عين الجمل
hazelnut	bondoʾ (m)	بندق
coconut	goze el hend (m)	جوز هند
pistachios	fostoʾ (m)	فستق

45. Bread. Sweets

bakers' confectionery (pastry)	ḥalawīāt (pl)	حلويّات
bread	ʿeyʃ (m)	عيش
biscuits	baskawīt (m)	بسكويت
chocolate (n)	ʃokolāta (f)	شكولاتة
chocolate (as adj)	bel ʃokolāṭa	بالشكولاتة
candy (wrapped)	bonbony (m)	بونبوني
cake (e.g. cupcake)	keyka (f)	كيكة
cake (e.g. birthday ~)	torta (f)	تورتة
pie (e.g. apple ~)	feṭīra (f)	فطيرة
filling (for cake, pie)	ḥaʃwa (f)	حشوة
jam (whole fruit jam)	mrabba (m)	مربّى
marmalade	marmalād (f)	مرملاد
wafers	waffles (pl)	وافلز
ice-cream	ʾays krīm (m)	آيس كريم
pudding (Christmas ~)	būding (m)	بودنج

46. Cooked dishes

course, dish	wagba (f)	وجبة
cuisine	maṭbaχ (m)	مطبخ
recipe	waṣfa (f)	وصفة
portion	naṣīb (m)	نصيب
salad	solṭa (f)	سلطة
soup	ʃorba (f)	شوربة
clear soup (broth)	maraʾa (m)	مرقة
sandwich (bread)	sandawitʃ (m)	ساندويتش
fried eggs	beyḍ maʾly (m)	بيض مقلي
hamburger (beefburger)	hamburger (m)	هامبورجر

beefsteak	steak laḥm (m)	ستيك لحم
side dish	ṭaba' gāneby (m)	طبق جانبي
spaghetti	spaɣetti (m)	سباجيتي
mash	baṭāṭes mahrūsa (f)	بطاطس مهروسة
pizza	bītza (f)	بيتزا
porridge (oatmeal, etc.)	ʿaṣīda (f)	عصيدة
omelette	omlette (m)	اومليت
boiled (e.g. ~ beef)	maslū'	مسلوق
smoked (adj)	modakχen	مدخّن
fried (adj)	ma'ly	مقلي
dried (adj)	mogaffaf	مجفّف
frozen (adj)	mogammad	مجمّد
pickled (adj)	meχallel	مخلّل
sweet (sugary)	mesakkar	مسكّر
salty (adj)	māleḥ	مالح
cold (adj)	bāred	بارد
hot (adj)	soχn	سخن
bitter (adj)	morr	مرّ
tasty (adj)	ḥelw	حلو
to cook in boiling water	sala'	سلق
to cook (dinner)	ḥaḍḍar	حضّر
to fry (vt)	'ala	قلى
to heat up (food)	sakχan	سخّن
to salt (vt)	rasʃ malḥ	رشّ ملح
to pepper (vt)	rasʃ felfel	رشّ فلفل
to grate (vt)	baraʃ	برش
peel (n)	'eʃra (f)	قشرة
to peel (vt)	'asʃar	قشّر

47. Spices

salt	melḥ (m)	ملح
salty (adj)	māleḥ	مالح
to salt (vt)	rasʃ malḥ	رشّ ملح
black pepper	felfel aswad (m)	فلفل أسوّد
red pepper (milled ~)	felfel aḥmar (m)	فلفل أحمر
mustard	mosṭarda (m)	مسطردة
horseradish	fegl ḥār (m)	فجل حار
condiment	bahār (m)	بهار
spice	bahār (m)	بهار
sauce	ṣalṣa (f)	صلصة
vinegar	χall (m)	خلّ
anise	yansūn (m)	ينسون
basil	rīḥān (m)	ريحان
cloves	'oronfol (m)	قرنفل
ginger	zangabīl (m)	زنجبيل
coriander	kozbora (f)	كزبرة

cinnamon	ʾerfa (f)	قرفة
sesame	semsem (m)	سمسم
bay leaf	waraʾ el ɣār (m)	ورق الغار
paprika	babrika (f)	بابريكا
caraway	karawya (f)	كراوية
saffron	zaʿfarān (m)	زعفران

48. Meals

food	akl (m)	أكل
to eat (vi, vt)	akal	أكل
breakfast	foṭūr (m)	فطور
to have breakfast	feṭer	فطر
lunch	ɣadaʾ (m)	غداء
to have lunch	etɣadda	إتغدّى
dinner	ʿaʃāʾ (m)	عشاء
to have dinner	etʿasʃa	إتعشّى
appetite	ʃahiya (f)	شهيّة
Enjoy your meal!	bel hana wel ʃefa!	!بالهنا والشفا
to open (~ a bottle)	fataḥ	فتح
to spill (liquid)	dalaʾ	دلق
to spill out (vi)	dalaʾ	دلق
to boil (vi)	ɣely	غلى
to boil (vt)	ɣely	غلى
boiled (~ water)	maɣly	مغلي
to chill, cool down (vt)	barrad	برّد
to chill (vi)	barrad	برّد
taste, flavour	ṭaʿm (m)	طعم
aftertaste	ṭaʿm ma baʿd el mazāq (m)	طعم ما بعد المذاق
to slim down (lose weight)	χass	خسّ
diet	reʒīm (m)	رجيم
vitamin	vitamīn (m)	فيتامين
calorie	soʿra ḥarāriya (f)	سعرة حراريّة
vegetarian (n)	nabāty (m)	نباتي
vegetarian (adj)	nabāty	نباتي
fats (nutrient)	dohūn (pl)	دهون
proteins	brotenāt (pl)	بروتينات
carbohydrates	naʃawīāt (pl)	نشويّات
slice (of lemon, ham)	ʃarīḥa (f)	شريحة
piece (of cake, pie)	ʾeṭʿa (f)	قطعة
crumb (of bread, cake, etc.)	fattāta (f)	فتاتة

49. Table setting

spoon	maʿlaʾa (f)	معلقة
knife	sekkīna (f)	سكّينة

fork	ʃawka (f)	شوكة
cup (e.g., coffee ~)	fengān (m)	فنجان
plate (dinner ~)	ṭabaʾ (m)	طبق
saucer	ṭabaʾ fengān (m)	طبق فنجان
serviette	mandīl waraʾ (m)	منديل ورق
toothpick	χallet senān (f)	خلة سنان

50. Restaurant

restaurant	maṭʿam (m)	مطعم
coffee bar	ʾahwa (f), kaféih (m)	قهوة, كافيه
pub, bar	bār (m)	بار
tearoom	ṣalone ʃāy (m)	صالون شاي
waiter	garsone (m)	جرسون
waitress	garsona (f)	جرسونة
barman	bārman (m)	بارمان
menu	qāʾemet el ṭaʿām (f)	قائمة طعام
wine list	qāʾemet el χomūr (f)	قائمة خمور
to book a table	ḥagaz sofra	حجز سفرة
course, dish	wagba (f)	وجبة
to order (meal)	ṭalab	طلب
to make an order	ṭalab	طلب
aperitif	ʃarāb (m)	شراب
starter	moqabbelāt (pl)	مقبّلات
dessert, pudding	ḥalawīāt (pl)	حلويّات
bill	ḥesāb (m)	حساب
to pay the bill	dafaʿ el ḥesāb	دفع الحساب
to give change	edda el bāʾy	ادّي الباقي
tip	baʾʃīʃ (m)	بقشيش

Family, relatives and friends

51. Personal information. Forms

name (first name)	esm (m)	اسم
surname (last name)	esm el ʿaʾela (m)	اسم العائلة
date of birth	tarīχ el melād (m)	تاريخ الميلاد
place of birth	makān el melād (m)	مكان الميلاد
nationality	gensiya (f)	جنسيّة
place of residence	maqarr el eqāma (m)	مقرّ الإقامة
country	balad (m)	بلد
profession (occupation)	mehna (f)	مهنة
gender, sex	ginss (m)	جنس
height	ṭūl (m)	طول
weight	wazn (m)	وزن

52. Family members. Relatives

mother	walda (f)	والدة
father	wāled (m)	والد
son	walad (m)	ولد
daughter	bent (f)	بنت
younger daughter	el bent el saɣīra (f)	البنت الصغيرة
younger son	el ebn el saɣīr (m)	الابن الصغير
eldest daughter	el bent el kebīra (f)	البنت الكبيرة
eldest son	el ebn el kabīr (m)	الابن الكبير
brother	aχ (m)	أخ
elder brother	el aχ el kibīr (m)	الأخ الكبير
younger brother	el aχ el ṣoɣeyyir (m)	الأخ الصغير
sister	uχt (f)	أخت
elder sister	el uχt el kibīra (f)	الأخت الكبيرة
younger sister	el uχt el ṣoɣeyyira (f)	الأخت الصغيرة
cousin (masc.)	ibn ʿamm (m), ibn χāl (m)	إبن عمّ, إبن خال
cousin (fem.)	bint ʿamm (f), bint χāl (f)	بنت عمّ, بنت خال
mummy	mama (f)	ماما
dad, daddy	baba (m)	بابا
parents	waldeyn (du)	والدين
child	ṭefl (m)	طفل
children	aṭfāl (pl)	أطفال
grandmother	gedda (f)	جدّة
grandfather	gadd (m)	جدّ
grandson	ḥafīd (m)	حفيد

granddaughter	ḥafīda (f)	حفيدة
grandchildren	aḥfād (pl)	أحفاد
uncle	ʿamm (m), χāl (m)	عمّ, خال
aunt	ʿamma (f), χāla (f)	عمّة, خالة
nephew	ibn el aχ (m), ibn el uχt (m)	إبن الأخ, إبن الأخت
niece	bint el aχ (f), bint el uχt (f)	بنت الأخ, بنت الأخت
mother-in-law (wife's mother)	ḥamah (f)	حماة
father-in-law (husband's father)	ḥama (m)	حما
son-in-law (daughter's husband)	goze el bent (m)	جوز البنت
stepmother	merāt el abb (f)	مرات الأب
stepfather	goze el omm (m)	جوز الأم
infant	ṭefl raḍeeʿ (m)	طفل رضيع
baby (infant)	mawlūd (m)	موّلود
little boy, kid	walad ṣaɣīr (m)	ولد صغير
wife	goza (f)	جوزة
husband	goze (m)	جوز
spouse (husband)	goze (m)	جوز
spouse (wife)	goza (f)	جوزة
married (masc.)	metgawwez	متجوّز
married (fem.)	metgawweza	متجوّزة
single (unmarried)	aʿzab	أعزب
bachelor	aʿzab (m)	أعزب
divorced (masc.)	moṭallaq (m)	مطلّق
widow	armala (f)	أرملة
widower	armal (m)	أرمل
relative	ʾarīb (m)	قريب
close relative	nesīb ʾarīb (m)	نسيب قريب
distant relative	nesīb beʿīd (m)	نسيب بعيد
relatives	aqāreb (pl)	أقارب
orphan (boy or girl)	yatīm (m)	يتيم
guardian (of a minor)	walyī amr (m)	وليّ أمر
to adopt (a boy)	tabanna	تبنّى
to adopt (a girl)	tabanna	تبنّى

53. Friends. Colleagues

friend (masc.)	ṣadīq (m)	صديق
friend (fem.)	ṣadīqa (f)	صديقة
friendship	ṣadāqa (f)	صداقة
to be friends	ṣādaq	صادق
pal (masc.)	ṣāḥeb (m)	صاحب
pal (fem.)	ṣaḥba (f)	صاحبة
partner	rafīʾ (m)	رفيق
chief (boss)	raʾīs (m)	رئيس

superior (n)	el arfaʿ maqāman (m)	الأرفع مقاماً
owner, proprietor	ṣāḥib (m)	صاحب
subordinate (n)	tābeʿ (m)	تابع
colleague	zamīl (m)	زميل
acquaintance (person)	maʿrefa (m)	معرفة
fellow traveller	rafīʾ safar (m)	رفيق سفر
classmate	zamīl fel ṣaff (m)	زميل في الصفّ
neighbour (masc.)	gār (m)	جار
neighbour (fem.)	gāra (f)	جارة
neighbours	gerān (pl)	جيران

54. Man. Woman

woman	set (f)	ست
girl (young woman)	bent (f)	بنت
bride	ʿarūsa (f)	عروسة
beautiful (adj)	gamīla	جميلة
tall (adj)	ṭawīla	طويلة
slender (adj)	raʃīqa	رشيقة
short (adj)	ʾaṣīra	قصيرة
blonde (n)	ʃaʾra (f)	شقراء
brunette (n)	zāt al ʃaʿr el dāken (f)	ذات الشعر الداكن
ladies' (adj)	sayedāt	سيّدات
virgin (girl)	ʿazrāʾ (f)	عذراء
pregnant (adj)	ḥāmel	حامل
man (adult male)	rāgel (m)	راجل
blonde haired man	aʃʾar (m)	أشقر
dark haired man	zu el ʃaʿr el dāken (m)	ذو الشعر الداكن
tall (adj)	ṭawīl	طويل
short (adj)	ʾaṣīr	قصير
rude (rough)	waqeḥ	وقح
stocky (adj)	malyān	مليان
robust (adj)	matīn	متين
strong (adj)	ʾawy	قويّ
strength	ʾowwa (f)	قوّة
plump, fat (adj)	teχīn	تخين
swarthy (dark-skinned)	asmar	أسمر
slender (well-built)	raʃīq	رشيق
elegant (adj)	anīq	أنيق

55. Age

age	ʿomr (m)	عمر
youth (young age)	ʃabāb (m)	شباب

young (adj)	ʃāb	شاب
younger (adj)	aṣɣar	أصغر
older (adj)	akbar	أكبر
young man	ʃāb (m)	شاب
teenager	morāheq (m)	مراهق
guy, fellow	ʃāb (m)	شاب
old man	ʿagūz (m)	عجوز
old woman	ʿagūza (f)	عجوزة
adult (adj)	rāʃed (m)	راشد
middle-aged (adj)	fe montaṣaf el ʿomr	في منتصف العمر
elderly (adj)	ʿagūz	عجوز
old (adj)	ʿagūz	عجوز
retirement	maʿāʃ (m)	معاش
to retire (from job)	oḥīl ʿala el maʿāʃ	أحيل على المعاش
retiree, pensioner	motaqāʿed (m)	متقاعد

56. Children

child	ṭefl (m)	طفل
children	aṭfāl (pl)	أطفال
twins	tawʾam (du)	توأم
cradle	mahd (m)	مهد
rattle	χoʃχeyʃa (f)	خشخيشة
nappy	bambarz, ḥaffāḍ (m)	بامبرز, حفاض
dummy, comforter	bazzāza (f)	بزّازة
pram	ʿarabet aṭfāl (f)	عربة أطفال
nursery	rawḍet aṭfāl (f)	روضة أطفال
babysitter	dāda (f)	دادة
childhood	ṭofūla (f)	طفولة
doll	ʿarūsa (f)	عروسة
toy	leʿba (f)	لعبة
construction set (toy)	mokaʿʿabāt (pl)	مكعّبات
well-bred (adj)	moʾaddab	مؤدّب
ill-bred (adj)	ʾalīl el adab	قليل الأدب
spoilt (adj)	metdallaʿ	متدلّع
to be naughty	ʃefy	شقي
mischievous (adj)	laʿūb	لعوب
mischievousness	ezʿāg (m)	إزعاج
mischievous child	ṭefl laʿūb (m)	طفل لعوب
obedient (adj)	moṭeeʿ	مطيع
disobedient (adj)	ʿāq	عاقّ
docile (adj)	ʿāʾel	عاقل
clever (intelligent)	zaky	ذكي
child prodigy	ṭefl moʿgeza (m)	طفل معجزة

57. Married couples. Family life

to kiss (vt)	bās	باس
to kiss (vi)	bās	باس
family (n)	ʿeyla (f)	عيلة
family (as adj)	ʿāʾely	عائلي
couple	gozeyn (du)	جوزين
marriage (state)	gawāz (m)	جواز
hearth (home)	beyt (m)	بيت
dynasty	solāla ḥākema (f)	سلالة حاكمة
date	mawʿed (m)	موّعد
kiss	bosa (f)	بوسة
love (for sb)	ḥobb (m)	حبّ
to love (sb)	ḥabb	حبّ
beloved	ḥabīb	حبيب
tenderness	ḥanān (m)	حنان
tender (affectionate)	ḥanūn	حنون
faithfulness	el eχlāṣ (m)	الإخلاص
faithful (adj)	moχleṣ	مخلص
care (attention)	ʿenāya (f)	عناية
caring (~ father)	mohtamm	مهتمّ
newlyweds	ʿarūseyn (du)	عروسين
honeymoon	ʃahr el ʿasal (m)	شهر العسل
to get married (ab. woman)	tagawwaz	تجوّز
to get married (ab. man)	tagawwaz	تجوّز
wedding	faraḥ (m)	فرح
golden wedding	el zekra el χamsīn lel gawāz (f)	الذكرى الخمسين للجواز
anniversary	zekra sanawiya (f)	ذكرى سنوية
lover (masc.)	ḥabīb (m)	حبيب
mistress (lover)	ḥabība (f)	حبيبة
adultery	χeyāna zawgiya (f)	خيانة زوّجية
to cheat on ... (commit adultery)	χān	خان
jealous (adj)	ɣayūr	غيّور
to be jealous	ɣār	غار
divorce	ṭalāʾ (m)	طلاق
to divorce (vi)	ṭallaʾ	طلّق
to quarrel (vi)	etχāneʾ	إتخانق
to be reconciled (after an argument)	taṣālaḥ	تصالح
together (adv)	maʿ baʿḍ	مع بعض
sex	ginss (m)	جنس
happiness	saʿāda (f)	سعادة
happy (adj)	saʿīd	سعيد
misfortune (accident)	moṣība (m)	مصيبة
unhappy (adj)	taʿīs	تعيس

Character. Feelings. Emotions

58. Feelings. Emotions

feeling (emotion)	ʃoʿūr (m)	شعور
feelings	maʃāʿer (pl)	مشاعر
to feel (vt)	ʃaʿar	شعر
hunger	gūʿ (m)	جوع
to be hungry	ʿāyez ʾākol	عايز آكل
thirst	ʿaṭaʃ (m)	عطش
to be thirsty	ʿāyez aʃrab	عايز أشرب
sleepiness	neʿās (m)	نعاس
to feel sleepy	neʿes	نعس
tiredness	taʿab (m)	تعب
tired (adj)	taʿbān	تعبان
to get tired	teʿeb	تعب
mood (humour)	mazāg (m)	مزاج
boredom	malal (m)	ملل
to be bored	zeheʾ	زهق
seclusion	ʿozla (f)	عزلة
to seclude oneself	ʿazal	عزل
to worry (make anxious)	aʾlaʾ	أقلق
to be worried	ʾeleʾ	قلق
worrying (n)	ʾalaʾ (m)	قلق
anxiety	ʾalaʾ (m)	قلق
preoccupied (adj)	maʃɣūl el bāl	مشغول البال
to be nervous	etwattar	إتوّتر
to panic (vi)	etχaḍḍ	إتخضّ
hope	amal (m)	أمل
to hope (vi, vt)	tamanna	تمنّى
certainty	yaqīn (m)	يقين
certain, sure (adj)	motaʾakked	متأكّد
uncertainty	ʿadam el taʾakkod (m)	عدم التأكّد
uncertain (adj)	meʃ motaʾakked	مش متأكّد
drunk (adj)	sakrān	سكران
sober (adj)	ṣāḥy	صاحي
weak (adj)	ḍaʿīf	ضعيف
happy (adj)	saʿīd	سعيد
to scare (vt)	χawwef	خوّف
fury (madness)	ɣaḍab ʃedīd (m)	غضب شديد
rage (fury)	ɣaḍab (m)	غضب
depression	ekteʾāb (m)	إكتئاب
discomfort (unease)	ʿadam erteyāḥ (m)	عدم إرتياح

comfort	rāḥa (f)	راحة
to regret (be sorry)	nedem	ندم
regret	nadam (m)	ندم
bad luck	sū' ḥazẓ (m)	سوء حظ
sadness	ḥozn (f)	حزن
shame (remorse)	χagal (m)	خجل
gladness	faraḥ (m)	فرح
enthusiasm, zeal	ḥamās (m)	حماس
enthusiast	motaḥammes (m)	متحمّس
to show enthusiasm	taḥammas	تحمّس

59. Character. Personality

character	ʃaχṣiya (f)	شخصية
character flaw	ʿeyb (m)	عيب
mind, reason	ʿaʾl (m)	عقل
conscience	ḍamīr (m)	ضمير
habit (custom)	ʿāda (f)	عادة
ability (talent)	qodra (f)	قدرة
can (e.g. ~ swim)	ʿeref	عرف
patient (adj)	ṣabūr	صبور
impatient (adj)	ʾalīl el ṣabr	قليل الصبر
curious (inquisitive)	foḍūly	فضولي
curiosity	foḍūl (m)	فضول
modesty	tawāḍoʿ (m)	تواضع
modest (adj)	motawāḍeʿ	متواضع
immodest (adj)	meʃ motawāḍeʿ	مش متواضع
laziness	kasal (m)	كسل
lazy (adj)	kaslān	كسلان
lazy person (masc.)	kaslān (m)	كسلان
cunning (n)	makr (m)	مكر
cunning (as adj)	makkār	مكّار
distrust	ʿadam el seqa (m)	عدم الثقة
distrustful (adj)	ʃakkāk	شكّاك
generosity	karam (m)	كرم
generous (adj)	karīm	كريم
talented (adj)	mawhūb	موهوب
talent	mawheba (f)	موهبة
courageous (adj)	ʃogāʿ	شجاع
courage	ʃagāʿa (f)	شجاعة
honest (adj)	amīn	أمين
honesty	amāna (f)	أمانة
careful (cautious)	ḥazer	حذر
brave (courageous)	ʃogāʿ	شجاع
serious (adj)	gād	جاد

strict (severe, stern)	ṣārem	صارم
decisive (adj)	ḥāsem	حاسم
indecisive (adj)	motaradded	متردّد
shy, timid (adj)	χagūl	خجول
shyness, timidity	χagal (m)	خجل
confidence (trust)	seqa (f)	ثقة
to believe (trust)	wasaq	وثق
trusting (credulous)	saree' el taṣdīq	سريع التصديق
sincerely (adv)	beṣarāḥa	بصراحة
sincere (adj)	moχleṣ	مخلص
sincerity	eχlāṣ (m)	إخلاص
open (person)	ṣarīḥ	صريح
calm (adj)	hady	هادئ
frank (sincere)	ṣarīḥ	صريح
naïve (adj)	sāzeg	ساذج
absent-minded (adj)	ʃāred el fekr	شارد الفكر
funny (odd)	moḍḥek	مضحك
greed, stinginess	boχl (m)	بخل
greedy, stingy (adj)	ṭammā'	طماع
stingy (adj)	baχīl	بخيل
evil (adj)	ʃerrīr	شرير
stubborn (adj)	'anīd	عنيد
unpleasant (adj)	karīh	كريه
selfish person (masc.)	anāny (m)	أناني
selfish (adj)	anāny	أناني
coward	gabān (m)	جبان
cowardly (adj)	gabān	جبان

60. Sleep. Dreams

to sleep (vi)	nām	نام
sleep, sleeping	nome (m)	نوم
dream	ḥelm (m)	حلم
to dream (in sleep)	ḥelem	حلم
sleepy (adj)	na'sān	نعسان
bed	serīr (m)	سرير
mattress	martaba (f)	مرتبة
blanket (eiderdown)	baṭṭaniya (f)	بطّانيّة
pillow	maχadda (f)	مخدّة
sheet	melāya (f)	ملاية
insomnia	araq (m)	أرق
sleepless (adj)	bodūn nome	بدون نوم
sleeping pill	monawwem (m)	منوّم
to take a sleeping pill	aχad monawwem	اخد منوّم
to feel sleepy	ne'es	نعس
to yawn (vi)	ettāweb	إتّاوب

to go to bed	rāḥ lel serīr	راح للسرير
to make up the bed	waḍḍab el serīr	وضّب السرير
to fall asleep	nām	نام
nightmare	kabūs (m)	كابوس
snore, snoring	ʃeχīr (m)	شخير
to snore (vi)	ʃakχar	شخّر
alarm clock	monabbeh (m)	منبّه
to wake (vt)	ṣaḥḥa	صحّى
to wake up	ṣeḥy	صحي
to get up (vi)	ʾām	قام
to have a wash	ɣasal	غسل

61. Humour. Laughter. Gladness

humour (wit, fun)	hezār (m)	هزار
sense of humour	ḥess fokāhy (m)	حسّ فكاهي
to enjoy oneself	estamtaʿ	إستمتع
cheerful (merry)	farḥān	فرحان
merriment (gaiety)	bahga (f)	بهجة
smile	ebtesāma (f)	إبتسامة
to smile (vi)	ebtasam	إبتسم
to start laughing	badaʾ yeḍḥak	بدأ يضحك
to laugh (vi)	ḍeḥek	ضحك
laugh, laughter	ḍeḥka (f)	ضحكة
anecdote	ḥekāya (f)	حكاية
funny (anecdote, etc.)	moḍḥek	مضحك
funny (odd)	moḍḥek	مضحك
to joke (vi)	hazzar	هزّر
joke (verbal)	nokta (f)	نكتة
joy (emotion)	saʿāda (f)	سعادة
to rejoice (vi)	mereḥ	مرح
joyful (adj)	saʿīd	سعيد

62. Discussion, conversation. Part 1

communication	tawāṣol (m)	تواصل
to communicate	tawāṣal	تواصل
conversation	moḥadsa (f)	محادثة
dialogue	ḥewār (m)	حوار
discussion (discourse)	monaʾʃa (f)	مناقشة
dispute (debate)	χelāf (m)	خلاف
to dispute, to debate	χālef	خالف
interlocutor	muḥāwer (m)	محاوّر
topic (theme)	mawḍūʿ (m)	موضوع
point of view	weg-het naẓar (f)	وجهة نظر

opinion (point of view)	ra'yī (m)	رأي
speech (talk)	χeṭāb (m)	خطاب
discussion (of a report, etc.)	mona'ʃa (f)	مناقشة
to discuss (vt)	nā'eʃ	ناقش
talk (conversation)	ḥadīs (m)	حديث
to talk (to chat)	dardeʃ	دردش
meeting (encounter)	leqā' (m)	لقاء
to meet (vi, vt)	'ābel	قابل
proverb	masal (m)	مثل
saying	maqūla (f)	مقولة
riddle (poser)	loɣz (m)	لغز
to pose a riddle	toʃakkel loɣz	تشكّل لغز
password	kelmet el morūr (f)	كلمة مرور
secret	serr (m)	سرّ
oath (vow)	qasam (m)	قسم
to swear (an oath)	aqsam	أقسم
promise	wa'd (m)	وعد
to promise (vt)	wa'ad	وعد
advice (counsel)	naṣīḥa (f)	نصيحة
to advise (vt)	naṣaḥ	نصح
to follow one's advice	tatabba' naṣīḥa	تتبّع نصيحة
to listen to … (obey)	aṭā'	أطاع
news	aχbār (m)	أخبار
sensation (news)	ḍagga (f)	ضجّة
information (report)	ma'lumāt (pl)	معلومات
conclusion (decision)	estentāg (f)	إستنتاج
voice	ṣote (m)	صوت
compliment	madḥ (m)	مدح
kind (nice)	laṭīf	لطيف
word	kelma (f)	كلمة
phrase	'ebāra (f)	عبارة
answer	gawāb (m)	جواب
truth	ḥa'ī'a (f)	حقيقة
lie	kezb (m)	كذب
thought	fekra (f)	فكرة
idea (inspiration)	fekra (f)	فكرة
fantasy	χayāl (m)	خيال

63. Discussion, conversation. Part 2

respected (adj)	moḥtaram	محترم
to respect (vt)	eḥtaram	إحترم
respect	eḥterām (m)	إحترام
Dear … (letter)	'azīzy …	عزيزي…
to introduce (sb to sb)	'arraf	عرّف
to make acquaintance	ta'arraf	تعرّف

intention	niya (f)	نيّة
to intend (have in mind)	nawa	نوى
wish	omniya (f)	أمنية
to wish (~ good luck)	tamanna	تمنّى
surprise (astonishment)	mofag'a (f)	مفاجأة
to surprise (amaze)	fāga'	فاجئ
to be surprised	etfāge'	إتفاجئ
to give (vt)	edda	أدّى
to take (get hold of)	aχad	أخد
to give back	radd	ردّ
to return (give back)	ragga'	رجّع
to apologize (vi)	e'tazar	إعتذر
apology	e'tezār (m)	إعتذار
to forgive (vt)	'afa	عفا
to talk (speak)	etkallem	إتكلّم
to listen (vi)	seme'	سمع
to hear out	seme'	سمع
to understand (vt)	fehem	فهم
to show (to display)	'araḍ	عرض
to look at …	baṣṣ	بصّ
to call (yell for sb)	nāda	نادى
to distract (disturb)	ʃaɣal	شغل
to disturb (vt)	az'ag	أزعج
to pass (to hand sth)	sallem	سلّم
demand (request)	ṭalab (m)	طلب
to request (ask)	ṭalab	طلب
demand (firm request)	maṭlab (m)	مطلب
to demand (request firmly)	ṭāleb	طالب
to tease (call names)	ɣāẓ	غاظ
to mock (make fun of)	saχar	سخر
mockery, derision	soχreya (f)	سخرية
nickname	esm el ʃohra (m)	اسم الشهرة
insinuation	talmīḥ (m)	تلميح
to insinuate (imply)	lammaḥ	لمّح
to mean (vt)	'aṣad	قصد
description	waṣf (m)	وصف
to describe (vt)	waṣaf	وصف
praise (compliments)	madḥ (m)	مدح
to praise (vt)	madaḥ	مدح
disappointment	χeybet amal (f)	خيبة أمل
to disappoint (vt)	χayab	خيّب
to be disappointed	χābet 'āmalo	خابت آماله
supposition	efterāḍ (m)	إفتراض
to suppose (assume)	eftaraḍ	إفترض
warning (caution)	taḥzīr (m)	تحذير
to warn (vt)	ḥazzar	حذّر

64. Discussion, conversation. Part 3

to talk into (convince)	aqnaʿ	أقنع
to calm down (vt)	ṭamʾan	طمأن
silence (~ is golden)	sokūt (m)	سكوت
to be silent (not speaking)	seket	سكت
to whisper (vi, vt)	hamas	همس
whisper	hamsa (f)	همسة
frankly, sincerely (adv)	beṣarāḥa	بصراحة
in my opinion ...	fi raʾyi ...	... في رأيي
detail (of the story)	tafṣīl (m)	تفصيل
detailed (adj)	mofaṣṣal	مفصّل
in detail (adv)	bel tafṣīl	بالتفصيل
hint, clue	talmīḥ (m)	تلميح
to give a hint	edda lamḥa	أدى لمحة
look (glance)	naẓra (f)	نظرة
to have a look	alqa nazra	ألقى نظرة
fixed (look)	sābet	ثابت
to blink (vi)	ramaʃ	رمش
to wink (vi)	ɣamaz	غمز
to nod (in assent)	haz rāso	هزّ رأسه
sigh	tanhīda (f)	تنهيدة
to sigh (vi)	tanahhad	تنهّد
to shudder (vi)	ertaʿaʃ	ارتعش
gesture	eʃāret yad (f)	إشارة يد
to touch (one's arm, etc.)	lamas	لمس
to seize (e.g., ~ by the arm)	mesek	مسك
to tap (on the shoulder)	ḥazz	حزّ
Look out!	χally bālak!	!خللي بالك
Really?	feʿlan	فعلاً؟
Are you sure?	enta motaʾakked?	أنت متأكّد؟
Good luck!	bel tawfīʾ!	!بالتوفيق
I see!	wāḍeḥ!	!واضح
What a pity!	ya χesāra!	!يا خسارة

65. Agreement. Refusal

consent	mowafʾa (f)	موافقة
to consent (vi)	wāfeʾ	وافق
approval	ʾobūl (m)	قبول
to approve (vt)	ʾabal	قبل
refusal	rafḍ (m)	رفض
to refuse (vi, vt)	rafaḍ	رفض
Great!	ʿazīm!	!عظيم
All right!	tamām!	!تمام

Okay! (I agree)	ettafa'na!	إتّفقنا!
forbidden (adj)	mamnū'	ممنوع
it's forbidden	mamnū'	ممنوع
it's impossible	moṣtaḥīl	مستحيل
incorrect (adj)	ɣeleṭ	غلط
to reject (~ a demand)	rafaḍ	رفض
to support (cause, idea)	ayed	أيّد
to accept (~ an apology)	'abal	قبل
to confirm (vt)	akkad	أكّد
confirmation	ta'kīd (m)	تأكيد
permission	samāḥ (m)	سماح
to permit (vt)	samaḥ	سمح
decision	qarār (m)	قرار
to say nothing (hold one's tongue)	ṣamt	صمت
condition (term)	ʃarṭ (m)	شرط
excuse (pretext)	'ozr (m)	عذر
praise (compliments)	madḥ (m)	مدح
to praise (vt)	madaḥ	مدح

66. Success. Good luck. Failure

success	nagāḥ (m)	نجاح
successfully (adv)	be nagāḥ	بنجاح
successful (adj)	nāgeḥ	ناجح
luck (good luck)	ḥazz (m)	حظّ
Good luck!	bel tawfī'!	بالتوفيق!
lucky (e.g. ~ day)	maḥẓūẓ	محظوظ
lucky (fortunate)	maḥẓūẓ	محظوظ
failure	faʃal (m)	فشل
misfortune	sū' el ḥazz (m)	سوء الحظّ
bad luck	sū' el ḥazz (m)	سوء الحظّ
unsuccessful (adj)	ɣayr nāgeḥ	غير ناجح
catastrophe	karsa (f)	كارثة
pride	faχr (m)	فخر
proud (adj)	faχūr	فخور
to be proud	eftaχar	إفتخر
winner	fā'ez (m)	فائز
to win (vi)	fāz	فاز
to lose (not win)	χeser	خسر
try	moḥawla (f)	محاولة
to try (vi)	ḥāwel	حاول
chance (opportunity)	forṣa (f)	فرصة

67. Quarrels. Negative emotions

shout (scream)	ṣarχa (f)	صرخة
to shout (vi)	ṣarraχ	صرّخ
to start to cry out	ṣarraχ	صرّخ
quarrel	χenā'a (f)	خناقة
to quarrel (vi)	etχāne'	إتخانق
fight (squabble)	χenā'a (f)	خناقة
to make a scene	taʃāgar	تشاجر
conflict	χelāf (m)	خلاف
misunderstanding	sū' tafāhom (m)	سوء تفاهم
insult	ehāna (f)	إهانة
to insult (vt)	ahān	أهان
insulted (adj)	mohān	مهان
resentment	esteyā' (m)	إستياء
to offend (vt)	ahān	أهان
to take offence	estā'	إستاء
indignation	saχṭ (m)	سخط
to be indignant	estā'	إستاء
complaint	ʃakwa (f)	شكوَى
to complain (vi, vt)	ʃaka	شكا
apology	e'tezār (m)	إعتذار
to apologize (vi)	e'tazar	إعتذر
to beg pardon	e'tazar	إعتذر
criticism	naqd (m)	نقد
to criticize (vt)	naqad	نقد
accusation (charge)	ettehām (m)	إتّهام
to accuse (vt)	ettaham	إتّهم
revenge	enteqām (m)	إنتقام
to avenge (get revenge)	entaqam	إنتقم
to pay back	radd	ردّ
disdain	ezderā' (m)	إزدراء
to despise (vt)	eḥtaqar	إحتقر
hatred, hate	korh (f)	كره
to hate (vt)	kereh	كره
nervous (adj)	'aṣaby	عصبي
to be nervous	etwattar	إتوّتر
angry (mad)	ɣaḍbān	غضبان
to make angry	narfez	نرفز
humiliation	ezlāl (m)	إذلال
to humiliate (vt)	zallel	ذلّل
to humiliate oneself	tazallal	تذلّل
shock	ṣadma (f)	صدمة
to shock (vt)	ṣadam	صدم
trouble (e.g. serious ~)	moʃkela (f)	مشكلة

unpleasant (adj)	karīh	كريه
fear (dread)	χofe (m)	خوف
terrible (storm, heat)	ʃedīd	شديد
scary (e.g. ~ story)	moχīf	مخيف
horror	roʿb (m)	رعب
awful (crime, news)	baʃeʿ	بشع
to begin to tremble	ertaʿaʃ	إرتعش
to cry (weep)	baka	بكى
to start crying	badaʾ yebky	بدأ يبكي
tear	damaʿa (f)	دمعة
fault	ɣalṭa (f)	غلطة
guilt (feeling)	zanb (m)	ذنب
dishonor (disgrace)	ʿār (m)	عار
protest	eḥtegāg (m)	إحتجاج
stress	tawattor (m)	توتّر
to disturb (vt)	azʿag	أزعج
to be furious	ɣeḍeb	غضب
angry (adj)	ɣaḍbān	غضبان
to end (~ a relationship)	anha	أنهى
to swear (at sb)	ʃatam	شتم
to scare (become afraid)	χāf	خاف
to hit (strike with hand)	ḍarab	ضرب
to fight (street fight, etc.)	χāneʾ	خانق
to settle (a conflict)	sawwa	سوّى
discontented (adj)	meʃ rāḍy	مش راضي
furious (adj)	ɣaḍbān	غضبان
It's not good!	keda meʃ kwayes!	!كده مش كويّس
It's bad!	keda weḥeʃ!	كده وحش!

Medicine

68. Diseases

illness	maraḍ (m)	مرض
to be ill	mereḍ	مرض
health	ṣeḥḥa (f)	صحّة
runny nose (coryza)	raʃ-ḥ fel anf (m)	رشح في الأنف
tonsillitis	eltehāb el lawzateyn (m)	إلتهاب اللوزتين
cold (illness)	zokām (m)	زكام
to catch a cold	gālo bard	جاله برد
bronchitis	eltehāb ʃoʿaby (m)	إلتهاب شعبيّ
pneumonia	eltehāb raʾawy (m)	إلتهاب رئوي
flu, influenza	influenza (f)	إنفلونزا
shortsighted (adj)	ʾaṣīr el naẓar	قصير النظر
longsighted (adj)	beʿīd el naẓar	بعيد النظر
strabismus (crossed eyes)	ḥawal (m)	حوّل
squint-eyed (adj)	aḥwal	أحوّل
cataract	katarakt (f)	كاتاراكت
glaucoma	glawkoma (f)	جلوكوما
stroke	sakta (f)	سكتة
heart attack	azma ʾalbiya (f)	أزمة قلبية
myocardial infarction	nawba ʾalbiya (f)	نوبة قلبية
paralysis	ʃalal (m)	شلل
to paralyse (vt)	ʃall	شلّ
allergy	ḥasasiya (f)	حساسيّة
asthma	rabw (m)	ربو
diabetes	dāʾ el sokkary (m)	داء السكّري
toothache	alam asnān (m)	ألم الأسنان
caries	naχr el asnān (m)	نخر الأسنان
diarrhoea	es-hāl (m)	إسهال
constipation	emsāk (m)	إمساك
stomach upset	edṭrāb el meʿda (m)	إضطراب المعدة
food poisoning	tasammom (m)	تسمّم
to get food poisoning	etsammem	إتسمّم
arthritis	eltehāb el mafāṣel (m)	إلتهاب المفاصل
rickets	kosāḥ el aṭfāl (m)	كساح الأطفال
rheumatism	rheumatism (m)	روماتزم
atherosclerosis	taṣṣallob el ʃarayīn (m)	تصلّب الشرايين
gastritis	eltehāb el meʿda (m)	إلتهاب المعدة
appendicitis	eltehāb el zayda el dūdiya (m)	إلتهاب الزائدة الدودية

cholecystitis	eltehāb el marāra (m)	إلتهاب المرارة
ulcer	qorḥa (f)	قرحة
measles	maraḍ el ḥaṣba (m)	مرض الحصبة
rubella (German measles)	el ḥaṣba el almaniya (f)	الحصبة الألمانية
jaundice	yaraqān (m)	يرقان
hepatitis	eltehāb el kabed el vayrūsy (m)	إلتهاب الكبد الفيروسي
schizophrenia	fuṣām (m)	فصام
rabies (hydrophobia)	dā' el kalb (m)	داء الكلب
neurosis	eḍṭrāb 'aṣaby (m)	إضطراب عصبي
concussion	ertegāg el moχ (m)	إرتجاج المخ
cancer	saraṭān (m)	سرطان
sclerosis	taṣṣallob (m)	تصلّب
multiple sclerosis	taṣṣallob mota'added (m)	تصلّب متعدّد
alcoholism	edmān el χamr (m)	إدمان الخمر
alcoholic (n)	modmen el χamr (m)	مدمن الخمر
syphilis	syfilis el zehry (m)	سفلس الزهري
AIDS	el eydz (m)	الايدز
tumour	waram (m)	ورم
malignant (adj)	χabīs	خبيث
benign (adj)	ḥamīd (m)	حميد
fever	ḥomma (f)	حمّى
malaria	malaria (f)	ملاريا
gangrene	ɣanɣarīna (f)	غنغرينا
seasickness	dawār el baḥr (m)	دوار البحر
epilepsy	maraḍ el ṣara' (m)	مرض الصرع
epidemic	wabā' (m)	وباء
typhus	tyfus (m)	تيفوس
tuberculosis	maraḍ el soll (m)	مرض السلّ
cholera	kōlīra (f)	كوليرا
plague (bubonic ~)	ṭa'ūn (m)	طاعون

69. Symptoms. Treatments. Part 1

symptom	'araḍ (m)	عرض
temperature	ḥarāra (f)	حرارة
high temperature (fever)	ḥomma (f)	حمّى
pulse (heartbeat)	nabḍ (m)	نبض
dizziness (vertigo)	dawχa (f)	دوخة
hot (adj)	soχn	سخن
shivering	ra'ʃa (f)	رعشة
pale (e.g. ~ face)	aṣfar	أصفر
cough	koḥḥa (f)	كحّة
to cough (vi)	kaḥḥ	كحّ
to sneeze (vi)	'aṭas	عطس

faint	dawχa (f)	دوخة
to faint (vi)	oɣma ʿaleyh	أغمي عليه
bruise (hématome)	kadma (f)	كدمة
bump (lump)	tawarrom (m)	تورّم
to bang (bump)	etχabaṭ	إتخبط
contusion (bruise)	raḍḍa (f)	رضّة
to get a bruise	etkadam	إتكدم
to limp (vi)	ʿarag	عرج
dislocation	χalʿ (m)	خلع
to dislocate (vt)	χalaʿ	خلع
fracture	kasr (m)	كسر
to have a fracture	enkasar	إنكسر
cut (e.g. paper ~)	garḥ (m)	جرح
to cut oneself	garaḥ nafsoh	جرح نفسه
bleeding	nazīf (m)	نزيف
burn (injury)	ḥarʾ (m)	حرق
to get burned	et-ḥaraʾ	إتحرق
to prick (vt)	waχaz	وخز
to prick oneself	waχaz nafso	وخز نفسه
to injure (vt)	aṣāb	أصاب
injury	eṣāba (f)	إصابة
wound	garḥ (m)	جرح
trauma	ṣadma (f)	صدمة
to be delirious	haza	هذى
to stutter (vi)	talaʿsam	تلعثم
sunstroke	ḍarabet ʃams (f)	ضربة شمس

70. Symptoms. Treatments. Part 2

pain, ache	alam (m)	ألم
splinter (in foot, etc.)	ʃazya (f)	شظية
sweat (perspiration)	ʿerʾ (m)	عرق
to sweat (perspire)	ʿereʾ	عرق
vomiting	targeeʿ (m)	ترجيع
convulsions	taʃonnogāt (pl)	تشنّجات
pregnant (adj)	ḥāmel	حامل
to be born	etwalad	اتولّد
delivery, labour	welāda (f)	ولادة
to deliver (~ a baby)	walad	ولد
abortion	eg-hāḍ (m)	إجهاض
breathing, respiration	tanaffos (m)	تنفّس
in-breath (inhalation)	estenʃāq (m)	إستنشاق
out-breath (exhalation)	zafīr (m)	زفير
to exhale (breathe out)	zafar	زفر
to inhale (vi)	estanʃaq	إستنشق

disabled person	moʿāq (m)	معاق
cripple	moqʿad (m)	مقعد
drug addict	modmen moχaddarāt (m)	مدمن مخدّرات
deaf (adj)	aṭraʃ	أطرش
mute (adj)	aχras	أخرس
deaf mute (adj)	aṭraʃ aχras	أطرش أخرس
mad, insane (adj)	magnūn	مجنون
madman (demented person)	magnūn (m)	مجنون
madwoman	magnūna (f)	مجنونة
to go insane	etgannen	اتجنّن
gene	ʒīn (m)	جين
immunity	manāʿa (f)	مناعة
hereditary (adj)	werāsy	وراثي
congenital (adj)	χolqy men el welāda	خلقي من الولادة
virus	virūs (m)	فيروس
microbe	mikrūb (m)	ميكروب
bacterium	garsūma (f)	جرثومة
infection	ʿadwa (f)	عدوى

71. Symptoms. Treatments. Part 3

hospital	mostaʃfa (m)	مستشفى
patient	marīḍ (m)	مريض
diagnosis	taʃχīṣ (m)	تشخيص
cure	ʃefāʾ (m)	شفاء
medical treatment	ʿelāg ṭebby (m)	علاج طبي
to get treatment	etʿāleg	اتعالج
to treat (~ a patient)	ʿālag	عالج
to nurse (look after)	marraḍ	مرّض
care (nursing ~)	ʿenāya (f)	عناية
operation, surgery	ʿamaliya grāḥiya (f)	عمليّة جراحية
to bandage (head, limb)	ḍammad	ضمّد
bandaging	taḍmīd (m)	تضميد
vaccination	talqīḥ (m)	تلقيح
to vaccinate (vt)	laqqaḥ	لقّح
injection	ḥoʾna (f)	حقنة
to give an injection	ḥaʾan ebra	حقن إبرة
attack	nawba (f)	نوبة
amputation	batr (m)	بتر
to amputate (vt)	batr	بتر
coma	ɣaybūba (f)	غيبوبة
to be in a coma	kān fi ḥālet ɣaybūba	كان في حالة غيبوبة
intensive care	el ʿenāya el morakkaza (f)	العناية المركّزة
to recover (~ from flu)	ʃefy	شفي
condition (patient's ~)	ḥāla (f)	حالة

consciousness	waʿy (m)	وعي
memory (faculty)	zākera (f)	ذاكرة
to pull out (tooth)	χalaʿ	خلع
filling	ḥaʃww (m)	حشو
to fill (a tooth)	ḥaʃa	حشا
hypnosis	el tanwīm el meɣnaṭīsy (m)	التنويم المغناطيسي
to hypnotize (vt)	nawwem	نوّم

72. Doctors

doctor	doktore (m)	دكتور
nurse	momarreḍa (f)	ممرّضة
personal doctor	doktore ʃaχṣy (m)	دكتور شخصي
dentist	doktore asnān (m)	دكتور أسنان
optician	doktore el ʿoyūn (m)	دكتور العيون
general practitioner	ṭabīb baṭna (m)	طبيب باطنة
surgeon	garrāḥ (m)	جرّاح
psychiatrist	doktore nafsāny (m)	دكتور نفساني
paediatrician	doktore aṭfāl (m)	دكتور أطفال
psychologist	aχeṣāʾy ʿelm el nafs (m)	أخصائي علم النفس
gynaecologist	doktore nesa (m)	دكتور نسا
cardiologist	doktore ʾalb (m)	دكتور قلب

73. Medicine. Drugs. Accessories

medicine, drug	dawāʾ (m)	دواء
remedy	ʿelāg (m)	علاج
to prescribe (vt)	waṣaf	وصف
prescription	waṣfa (f)	وصفة
tablet, pill	ʾorṣ (m)	قرص
ointment	marham (m)	مرهم
ampoule	ambūla (f)	أمبولة
mixture, solution	dawāʾ ʃorb (m)	دواء شراب
syrup	ʃarāb (m)	شراب
capsule	ḥabba (f)	حبّة
powder	zorūr (m)	ذرور
gauze bandage	ḍammāda ʃāʃ (f)	ضمادة شاش
cotton wool	ʾoṭn (m)	قطن
iodine	yūd (m)	يود
plaster	blaster (m)	بلاستر
eyedropper	ʾaṭṭāra (f)	قطّارة
thermometer	termometr (m)	ترمومتر
syringe	serennga (f)	سرنّجة
wheelchair	korsy motaḥarrek (m)	كرسي متحرك
crutches	ʿokkāz (m)	عكّاز

painkiller	mosakken (m)	مسكّن
laxative	molayen (m)	مليّن
spirits (ethanol)	etanol (m)	إيثانول
medicinal herbs	a'ʃāb ṭebbiya (pl)	أعشاب طبّية
herbal (~ tea)	'oʃby	عشبي

74. Smoking. Tobacco products

tobacco	tabɣ (m)	تبغ
cigarette	segāra (f)	سيجارة
cigar	segār (m)	سيجار
pipe	ɣelyone (m)	غليون
packet (of cigarettes)	'elba (f)	علبة
matches	kebrīt (m)	كبريت
matchbox	'elbet kebrīt (f)	علبة كبريت
lighter	wallā'a (f)	ولّاعة
ashtray	ṭa'ṭū'a (f)	طقطوقة
cigarette case	'elbet sagāyer (f)	علبة سجائر
cigarette holder	ḥamelet segāra (f)	حاملة سيجارة
filter (cigarette tip)	filter (m)	فلتر
to smoke (vi, vt)	dakχen	دخّن
to light a cigarette	walla' segāra	ولّع سيجارة
smoking	tadχīn (m)	تدخين
smoker	modakχen (m)	مدخّن
cigarette end	'aqab segāra (m)	عقب سيجارة
smoke, fumes	dokχān (m)	دخّان
ash	ramād (m)	رماد

HUMAN HABITAT

City

75. City. Life in the city

city, town	madīna (f)	مدينة
capital city	ʿāṣema (f)	عاصمة
village	qarya (f)	قرية
city map	χarīṭet el madinah (f)	خريطة المدينة
city centre	wesṭ el balad (m)	وسط البلد
suburb	ḍāḥeya (f)	ضاحية
suburban (adj)	el ḍawāḥy	الضواحي
outskirts	aṭrāf el madīna (pl)	أطراف المدينة
environs (suburbs)	ḍawāḥy el madīna (pl)	ضواحي المدينة
city block	ḥayī (m)	حي
residential block (area)	ḥayī sakany (m)	حي سكني
traffic	ḥaraket el morūr (f)	حركة المرور
traffic lights	eʃārāt el morūr (pl)	إشارات المرور
public transport	wasāʾel el naʾl (pl)	وسائل النقل
crossroads	taqāṭoʿ (m)	تقاطع
zebra crossing	maʿbar (m)	معبر
pedestrian subway	nafaʾ moʃāh (m)	نفق مشاه
to cross (~ the street)	ʿabar	عبر
pedestrian	māʃy (m)	ماشي
pavement	raṣīf (m)	رصيف
bridge	kobry (m)	كبري
embankment (river walk)	korneyʃ (m)	كورنيش
fountain	nafūra (f)	نافورة
allée (garden walkway)	mamʃa (m)	ممشى
park	ḥadīqa (f)	حديقة
boulevard	bolvār (m)	بولفار
square	medān (m)	ميدان
avenue (wide street)	ʃāreʿ (m)	شارع
street	ʃāreʿ (m)	شارع
side street	zoʾāʾ (m)	زقاق
dead end	ṭarīʾ masdūd (m)	طريق مسدود
house	beyt (m)	بيت
building	mabna (m)	مبنى
skyscraper	nāṭeḥet sahāb (f)	ناطحة سحاب
facade	waɣa (f)	واجهة
roof	saʾf (m)	سقف

window	ʃebbāk (m)	شبّاك
arch	qose (m)	قوس
column	ʿamūd (m)	عمود
corner	zawya (f)	زاوية
shop window	vatrīna (f)	فترينة
signboard (store sign, etc.)	yafṭa, lāfeta (f)	لافتة, يافطة
poster (e.g., playbill)	boster (m)	بوستر
advertising poster	boster eʿlān (m)	بوستر إعلان
hoarding	lawḥet eʿlanāt (f)	لوحة إعلانات
rubbish	zebāla (f)	زبالة
rubbish bin	ṣandūʾ zebāla (m)	صندوق زبالة
to litter (vi)	rama zebāla	رمى زبالة
rubbish dump	mazbala (f)	مزبلة
telephone box	koʃk telefōn (m)	كشك تليفون
lamppost	ʿamūd nūr (m)	عمود نور
bench (park ~)	korsy (m)	كرسي
police officer	ʃorṭy (m)	شرطي
police	ʃorṭa (f)	شرطة
beggar	ʃaḥḥāt (m)	شحّات
homeless (n)	motaʃarred (m)	متشرّد

76. Urban institutions

shop	maḥal (m)	محل
chemist, pharmacy	ṣaydaliya (f)	صيدليّة
optician (spectacles shop)	maḥal naḍḍārāt (m)	محل نضّارات
shopping centre	mole (m)	مول
supermarket	subermarket (m)	سوبرماركت
bakery	maχbaz (m)	مخبز
baker	χabbāz (m)	خبّاز
cake shop	ḥalawāny (m)	حلواني
grocery shop	baʾʾāla (f)	بقّالة
butcher shop	gezāra (f)	جزارة
greengrocer	dokkān χoḍār (m)	دكّان خضار
market	sūʾ (f)	سوق
coffee bar	ʾahwa (f), kaféih (m)	قهوة, كافيه
restaurant	maṭʿam (m)	مطعم
pub, bar	bār (m)	بار
pizzeria	maḥal pizza (m)	محل بيتزا
hairdresser	ṣalone ḥelāʾa (m)	صالون حلاقة
post office	maktab el barīd (m)	مكتب البريد
dry cleaners	dray klīn (m)	دراي كلين
photo studio	estudio taṣwīr (m)	إستوديو تصوير
shoe shop	maḥal gezam (m)	محل جزم
bookshop	maḥal kotob (m)	محل كتب

sports shop	maḥal mostalzamāt reyaḍiya (m)	محل مستلزمات رياضية
clothes repair shop	maḥal χeyāṭet malābes (m)	محل خياطة ملابس
formal wear hire	ta'gīr malābes rasmiya (m)	تأجير ملابس رسمية
video rental shop	maḥal ta'gīr video (m)	محل تأجير فيديو
circus	serk (m)	سيرك
zoo	ḥadīqet el ḥayawān (f)	حديقة حيوان
cinema	sinema (f)	سينما
museum	mat-ḥaf (m)	متحف
library	maktaba (f)	مكتبة
theatre	masraḥ (m)	مسرح
opera (opera house)	obra (f)	أوبرا
nightclub	malha leyly (m)	ملهى ليّلي
casino	kazino (m)	كازينو
mosque	masged (m)	مسجد
synagogue	kenīs (m)	كنيس
cathedral	katedra'iya (f)	كاتدرائية
temple	ma'bad (m)	معبد
church	kenīsa (f)	كنيسة
college	kolliya (m)	كليّة
university	gam'a (f)	جامعة
school	madrasa (f)	مدرسة
prefecture	moqaṭ'a (f)	مقاطعة
town hall	baladiya (f)	بلديّة
hotel	fondo' (m)	فندق
bank	bank (m)	بنك
embassy	safāra (f)	سفارة
travel agency	ʃerket seyāḥa (f)	شركة سياحة
information office	maktab el este'lāmāt (m)	مكتب الإستعلامات
currency exchange	ṣarrāfa (f)	صرّافة
underground, tube	metro (m)	مترو
hospital	mostaʃfa (m)	مستشفى
petrol station	maḥaṭṭet banzīn (f)	محطّة بنزين
car park	maw'ef el 'arabeyāt (m)	موقف العربيات

77. Urban transport

bus, coach	buṣ (m)	باص
tram	trām (m)	ترام
trolleybus	trolly buṣ (m)	ترولي باص
route (bus ~)	χaṭṭ (m)	خطّ
number (e.g. bus ~)	raqam (m)	رقم
to go by ...	rāḥ be ...	... راح بـ
to get on (~ the bus)	rekeb	ركب
to get off ...	nezel men	نزل من

stop (e.g. bus ~)	maw'af (m)	موّقف
next stop	el maḥaṭṭa el gaya (f)	المحطة الجاية
terminus	'āχer maw'af (m)	آخر موقف
timetable	gadwal (m)	جدوَل
to wait (vt)	estanna	إستنّى
ticket	tazkara (f)	تذكرة
fare	ogra (f)	أجرة
cashier (ticket seller)	kaʃier (m)	كاشيير
ticket inspection	taftīʃ el tazāker (m)	تفتيش التذاكر
ticket inspector	mofatteʃ tazāker (m)	مفتّش تذاكر
to be late (for ...)	met'akχer	متأخّر
to miss (~ the train, etc.)	ta'akχar	تأخّر
to be in a hurry	mesta'gel	مستعجل
taxi, cab	taksi (m)	تاكسي
taxi driver	sawwā' taksi (m)	سوّاق تاكسي
by taxi	bel taksi	بالتاكسي
taxi rank	maw'ef taksi (m)	موّقف تاكسي
to call a taxi	kallem taksi	كلّم تاكسي
to take a taxi	aχad taksi	أخد تاكسي
traffic	ḥaraket el morūr (f)	حركة المرور
traffic jam	zaḥmet el morūr (f)	زحمة المرور
rush hour	sā'et el zorwa (f)	ساعة الذروة
to park (vi)	rakan	ركن
to park (vt)	rakan	ركن
car park	maw'ef el 'arabeyāt (m)	موقف العربيات
underground, tube	metro (m)	مترو
station	maḥaṭṭa (f)	محطّة
to take the tube	aχad el metro	أخد المترو
train	qeṭār, 'aṭṭr (m)	قطار
train station	maḥaṭṭet qeṭār (f)	محطّة قطار

78. Sightseeing

monument	temsāl (m)	تمثال
fortress	'al'a (f)	قلعة
palace	'aṣr (m)	قصر
castle	'al'a (f)	قلعة
tower	borg (m)	برج
mausoleum	ḍarīḥ (m)	ضريح
architecture	handasa me'māriya (f)	هندسة معمارية
medieval (adj)	men el qorūn el wosṭa	من القرون الوسطى
ancient (adj)	'atīq	عتيق
national (adj)	waṭany	وطني
famous (monument, etc.)	maʃ-hūr	مشهور
tourist	sā'eḥ (m)	سائح
guide (person)	morʃed (m)	مرشد

excursion, sightseeing tour	gawla (f)	جولة
to show (vt)	warra	ورّى
to tell (vt)	ʾāl	قال
to find (vt)	laʾa	لقى
to get lost (lose one's way)	ḍāʿ	ضاع
map (e.g. underground ~)	χarīṭa (f)	خريطة
map (e.g. city ~)	χarīṭa (f)	خريطة
souvenir, gift	tezkār (m)	تذكار
gift shop	maḥal hadāya (m)	محل هدايا
to take pictures	ṣawwar	صوّر
to have one's picture taken	etṣawwar	إتصوّر

79. Shopping

to buy (purchase)	eʃtara	إشترى
shopping	ḥāga (f)	حاجة
to go shopping	eʃtara	إشترى
shopping	ʃobbing (m)	شوبينج
to be open (ab. shop)	maftūḥ	مفتوح
to be closed	moɣlaq	مغلق
footwear, shoes	gezam (pl)	جزم
clothes, clothing	malābes (pl)	ملابس
cosmetics	mawād tagmīl (pl)	مواد تجميل
food products	akl (m)	أكل
gift, present	hediya (f)	هديّة
shop assistant (masc.)	bayāʿ (m)	بيّاع
shop assistant (fem.)	bayāʿa (f)	بيّاعة
cash desk	ṣandūʾ el dafʿ (m)	صندوق الدفع
mirror	merāya (f)	مراية
counter (shop ~)	manḍada (f)	منضدة
fitting room	ɣorfet el ʾeyās (f)	غرفة القياس
to try on	garrab	جرّب
to fit (ab. dress, etc.)	nāseb	ناسب
to fancy (vt)	ʿagab	عجب
price	seʿr (m)	سعر
price tag	tiket el seʿr (m)	تيكت السعر
to cost (vt)	kallef	كلّف
How much?	bekām?	بكام؟
discount	χaṣm (m)	خصم
inexpensive (adj)	meʃ ɣāly	مش غالي
cheap (adj)	reχīṣ	رخيص
expensive (adj)	ɣāly	غالي
It's expensive	da ɣāly	ده غالي
hire (n)	esteʾgār (m)	إستئجار
to hire (~ a dinner jacket)	estʾgar	إستأجر

credit (trade credit)	e'temān (m)	إئتمان
on credit (adv)	bel ta'seeṭ	بالتقسيط

80. Money

money	folūs (pl)	فلوس
currency exchange	taḥwīl 'omla (m)	تحويل عملة
exchange rate	se'r el ṣarf (m)	سعر الصرف
cashpoint	makinet ṣarrāf 'āly (f)	ماكينة صرّاف آلي
coin	'erʃ (m)	قرش
dollar	dolār (m)	دولار
euro	yoro (m)	يورو
lira	lira (f)	ليرة
Deutschmark	el mark el almāny (m)	المارك الألماني
franc	frank (m)	فرنك
pound sterling	geneyh esterlīny (m)	جنيه استرليني
yen	yen (m)	ين
debt	deyn (m)	دين
debtor	modīn (m)	مدين
to lend (money)	sallef	سلّف
to borrow (vi, vt)	estalaf	إستلف
bank	bank (m)	بنك
account	ḥesāb (m)	حساب
to deposit (vt)	awda'	أودع
to deposit into the account	awda' fel ḥesāb	أودع في الحساب
to withdraw (vt)	saḥab men el ḥesāb	سحب من الحساب
credit card	kredit kard (f)	كريدت كارد
cash	kæʃ (m)	كاش
cheque	ʃīk (m)	شيك
to write a cheque	katab ʃīk	كتب شيك
chequebook	daftar ʃikāt (m)	دفتر شيكات
wallet	maḥfaẓa (f)	محفظة
purse	maḥfazet fakka (f)	محفظة فكّة
safe	χazzāna (f)	خزّانة
heir	wāres (m)	وارث
inheritance	werāsa (f)	وراثة
fortune (wealth)	sarwa (f)	ثروّة
lease	'a'd el egār (m)	عقد الإيجار
rent (money)	ogret el sakan (f)	أجرة السكن
to rent (sth from sb)	est'gar	إستأجر
price	se'r (m)	سعر
cost	taman (m)	ثمن
sum	mablaɣ (m)	مبلغ
to spend (vt)	ṣaraf	صرف
expenses	maṣarīf (pl)	مصاريف

to economize (vi, vt)	waffar	وفّر
economical	mowaffer	موّفر
to pay (vi, vt)	dafaʿ	دفع
payment	dafʿ (m)	دفع
change (give the ~)	el bāʾy (m)	الباقي
tax	ḍarība (f)	ضريبة
fine	ɣarāma (f)	غرامة
to fine (vt)	faraḍ ɣarāma	فرض غرامة

81. Post. Postal service

post office	maktab el barīd (m)	مكتب البريد
post (letters, etc.)	el barīd (m)	البريد
postman	sāʿy el barīd (m)	ساعي البريد
opening hours	awʾāt el ʿamal (pl)	أوقات العمل
letter	resāla (f)	رسالة
registered letter	resāla mosaggala (f)	رسالة مسجّلة
postcard	kart barīdy (m)	كرت بريدي
telegram	barqiya (f)	برقيّة
parcel	ṭard (m)	طرد
money transfer	ḥewāla māliya (f)	حوالة مالية
to receive (vt)	estalam	إستلم
to send (vt)	arsal	أرسل
sending	ersāl (m)	إرسال
address	ʿenwān (m)	عنوان
postcode	raqam el barīd (m)	رقم البريد
sender	morsel (m)	مرسل
receiver	morsel elayh (m)	مرسل إليه
name (first name)	esm (m)	اسم
surname (last name)	esm el ʿaʾela (m)	اسم العائلة
postage rate	taʿrīfa (f)	تعريفة
standard (adj)	ʿādy	عادي
economical (adj)	mowaffer	موّفر
weight	wazn (m)	وزن
to weigh (~ letters)	wazan	وزن
envelope	ẓarf (m)	ظرف
postage stamp	ṭābeʿ (m)	طابع
to stamp an envelope	alṣaq ṭābeʿ	ألصق طابع

Dwelling. House. Home

82. House. Dwelling

house	beyt (m)	بيت
at home (adv)	fel beyt	في البيت
yard	sāḥa (f)	ساحة
fence (iron ~)	sūr (m)	سور
brick (n)	ṭūb (m)	طوب
brick (as adj)	men el ṭūb	من الطوب
stone (n)	ḥagar (m)	حجر
stone (as adj)	ḥagary	حجري
concrete (n)	χarasāna (f)	خرسانة
concrete (as adj)	χarasāny	خرساني
new (new-built)	gedīd	جديد
old (adj)	ʾadīm	قديم
decrepit (house)	ʾāayel lel soqūṭ	آيل للسقوط
modern (adj)	moʿāṣer	معاصر
multistorey (adj)	motaʿadded el ṭawābeq	متعدّد الطوابق
tall (~ building)	ʿāly	عالي
floor, storey	dore (m)	دور
single-storey (adj)	zu ṭābeq wāḥed	ذو طابق واحد
ground floor	el dore el awwal (m)	الدور الأوّل
top floor	ṭābeʾ ʿolwy (m)	طابق علوي
roof	saʾf (m)	سقف
chimney	madχana (f)	مدخنة
roof tiles	qarmīd (m)	قرميد
tiled (adj)	men el qarmīd	من القرميد
loft (attic)	ʿelya (f)	علية
window	ʃebbāk (m)	شبّاك
glass	ezāz (m)	إزاز
window ledge	ḥāfet el ʃebbāk (f)	حافة الشبّاك
shutters	ʃīʃ (m)	شيش
wall	ḥeyṭa (f)	حيطة
balcony	balakona (f)	بلكونة
downpipe	masūret el taṣrīf (f)	ماسورة التصريف
upstairs (to be ~)	foʾe	فوق
to go upstairs	ṭeleʿ	طلع
to come down (the stairs)	nezel	نزل
to move (to new premises)	naʾal	نقل

83. House. Entrance. Lift

entrance	madχal (m)	مدخل
stairs (stairway)	sellem (m)	سلّم
steps	daragāt (pl)	درجات
banisters	drabzīn (m)	درابزين
lobby (hotel ~)	ṣāla (f)	صالة
postbox	ṣandū' el barīd (m)	صندوق البريد
waste bin	ṣandū' el zebāla (m)	صندوق الزبالة
refuse chute	manfaz el zebāla (m)	منفذ الزبالة
lift	asanseyr (m)	اسانسير
goods lift	asanseyr el ʃaḥn (m)	اسانسير الشحن
lift cage	kabīna (f)	كابينة
to take the lift	rekeb el asanseyr	ركب الاسانسير
flat	ʃa''a (f)	شقّة
residents (~ of a building)	sokkān (pl)	سكّان
neighbour (masc.)	gār (m)	جار
neighbour (fem.)	gāra (f)	جارة
neighbours	gerān (pl)	جيران

84. House. Doors. Locks

door	bāb (m)	باب
gate (vehicle ~)	bawwāba (f)	بوّابة
handle, doorknob	okret el bāb (f)	اوكرة الباب
to unlock (unbolt)	fataḥ	فتح
to open (vt)	fataḥ	فتح
to close (vt)	'afal	قفل
key	meftāḥ (m)	مفتاح
bunch (of keys)	rabṭa (f)	ربطة
to creak (door, etc.)	ṣarr	صر
creak	ṣarīr (m)	صرير
hinge (door ~)	mafaṣṣla (f)	مفصّلة
doormat	seggādet bāb (f)	سجّادة باب
door lock	'efl el bāb (m)	قفل الباب
keyhole	χorm el meftāḥ (m)	خرم المفتاح
crossbar (sliding bar)	terbās (m)	ترباس
door latch	terbās (m)	ترباس
padlock	'efl (m)	قفل
to ring (~ the door bell)	rann	رنّ
ringing (sound)	ranīn (m)	رنين
doorbell	garas (m)	جرس
doorbell button	zerr (m)	زر
knock (at the door)	ṭar', da'' (m)	طرق, دقّ
to knock (vi)	χabbaṭ	خبّط

code	kōd (m)	كود
combination lock	kōd (m)	كود
intercom	garas el bāb (m)	جرس الباب
number (on the door)	raqam (m)	رقم
doorplate	lawḥa (f)	لوحة
peephole	el ʿeyn el seḥriya (m)	العين السحرية

85. Country house

village	qarya (f)	قرية
vegetable garden	bostān xoḍār (m)	بستان خضار
fence	sūr (m)	سور
picket fence	sūr (m)	سور
wicket gate	bawwāba farʿiya (f)	بوّابة فرعيّة
granary	ʃouna (f)	شونة
cellar	serdāb (m)	سرداب
shed (garden ~)	saʾīfa (f)	سقيفة
water well	bīr (m)	بير
stove (wood-fired ~)	forn (m)	فرن
to stoke the stove	awqad el botogāz	أوقد البوتاجاز
firewood	ḥaṭab (m)	حطب
log (firewood)	ʾeṭʿet ḥaṭab (f)	قطعة حطب
veranda	varannda (f)	فاراندة
deck (terrace)	ʃorfa (f)	شرفة
stoop (front steps)	sellem (m)	سلّم
swing (hanging seat)	morgeyḥa (f)	مرجيحة

86. Castle. Palace

castle	ʾalʿa (f)	قلعة
palace	ʾaṣr (m)	قصر
fortress	ʾalʿa (f)	قلعة
wall (round castle)	sūr (m)	سور
tower	borg (m)	برج
keep, donjon	borbg raʾīsy (m)	برج رئيسي
portcullis	bāb motaḥarrek (m)	باب متحرّك
subterranean passage	serdāb (m)	سرداب
moat	xondoq māʾy (m)	خندق مائي
chain	selsela (f)	سلسلة
arrow loop	mozɣal (m)	مزغل
magnificent (adj)	rāʾeʿ	رائع
majestic (adj)	mohīb	مهيب
impregnable (adj)	maneeʿ	منيع
medieval (adj)	men el qorūn el wosṭa	من القرون الوسطى

87. Flat

flat	ʃa’’a (f)	شقّة
room	oḍa (f)	أوضة
bedroom	oḍet el nome (f)	أوضة النوم
dining room	oḍet el sofra (f)	أوضة السفرة
living room	oḍet el esteqbāl (f)	أوضة الإستقبال
study (home office)	maktab (m)	مكتب
entry room	madχal (m)	مدخل
bathroom	ḥammām (m)	حمّام
water closet	ḥammām (m)	حمّام
ceiling	sa’f (m)	سقف
floor	arḍiya (f)	أرضية
corner	zawya (f)	زاوية

88. Flat. Cleaning

to clean (vi, vt)	naḍḍaf	نظّف
to put away (to stow)	ʃāl	شال
dust	ɣobār (m)	غبار
dusty (adj)	meɣabbar	مغبّر
to dust (vt)	masaḥ el ɣobār	مسح الغبار
vacuum cleaner	maknasa kahraba’iya (f)	مكنسة كهربائيّة
to vacuum (vt)	naḍḍaf be maknasa kahrabā’iya	نظّف بمكنسة كهربائيّة
to sweep (vi, vt)	kanas	كنس
sweepings	qomāma (f)	قمامة
order	nezām (m)	نظام
disorder, mess	fawḍa (m)	فوّضى
mop	ʃarʃūba (f)	شرشوبة
duster	mamsaḥa (f)	ممسحة
short broom	ma’sʃa (f)	مقشّة
dustpan	lammāma (f)	لمّامة

89. Furniture. Interior

furniture	asās (m)	أثاث
table	maktab (m)	مكتب
chair	korsy (m)	كرسي
bed	serīr (m)	سرير
sofa, settee	kanaba (f)	كنبة
armchair	korsy (m)	كرسي
bookcase	χazzānet kotob (f)	خزّانة كتب
shelf	raff (m)	رفّ
wardrobe	dolāb (m)	دولاب
coat rack (wall-mounted ~)	ʃammā‘a (f)	شمّاعة

coat stand	ʃammāʿa (f)	شمّاعة
chest of drawers	dolāb adrāg (m)	دولاب أدراج
coffee table	ṭarabeyzet el ʾahwa (f)	طرابيزة القهوة
mirror	merāya (f)	مراية
carpet	seggāda (f)	سجّادة
small carpet	seggāda (f)	سجّادة
fireplace	daffāya (f)	دفّاية
candle	ʃamʿa (f)	شمعة
candlestick	ʃamʿadān (m)	شمعدان
drapes	satāʾer (pl)	ستائر
wallpaper	waraʾ ḥāʾeṭ (m)	ورق حائط
blinds (jalousie)	satāʾer ofoqiya (pl)	ستائر أفقيّة
table lamp	abāʒūr (f)	اباجورة
wall lamp (sconce)	lammbet ḥāʾeṭ (f)	لمّبة حائط
standard lamp	meṣbāḥ arḍy (m)	مصباح أرضي
chandelier	nagafa (f)	نجفة
leg (of a chair, table)	regl (f)	رجل
armrest	masnad (m)	مسند
back (backrest)	masnad (m)	مسند
drawer	dorg (m)	درج

90. Bedding

bedclothes	bayāḍāt el serīr (pl)	بياضات السرير
pillow	maχadda (f)	مخدّة
pillowslip	kīs el maχadda (m)	كيس المخدّة
duvet	leḥāf (m)	لحاف
sheet	melāya (f)	ملاية
bedspread	ɣaṭāʾ el serīr (m)	غطاء السرير

91. Kitchen

kitchen	maṭbaχ (m)	مطبخ
gas	ɣāz (m)	غاز
gas cooker	botoɣāz (m)	بوتوغاز
electric cooker	forn kaharabāʾy (m)	فرن كهربائي
oven	forn (m)	فرن
microwave oven	mikroweyv (m)	ميكروويف
refrigerator	tallāga (f)	ثلاجة
freezer	freyzer (m)	فريزر
dishwasher	ɣassālet aṭbāʾ (f)	غسّالة أطباق
mincer	farrāmet laḥm (f)	فرّامة لحم
juicer	ʿaṣṣāra (f)	عصّارة
toaster	maḥmaṣet χobz (f)	محمصة خبز
mixer	χallāṭ (m)	خلّاط

coffee machine	makinet ṣonʿ el ʾahwa (f)	ماكينة صنع القهوة
coffee pot	ɣallāya kahrabaʾiya (f)	غلّاية القهوة
coffee grinder	maṭ-ḥanet ʾahwa (f)	مطحنة قهوة
kettle	ɣallāya (f)	غلّاية
teapot	barrād el ʃāy (m)	برّاد الشاي
lid	ɣaṭāʾ (m)	غطاء
tea strainer	maṣfāh el ʃāy (f)	مصفاة الشاي
spoon	maʿlaʾa (f)	معلقة
teaspoon	maʿlaʾet ʃāy (f)	معلقة شاي
soup spoon	maʿlaʾa kebīra (f)	ملعقة كبيرة
fork	ʃawka (f)	شوكة
knife	sekkīna (f)	سكّينة
tableware (dishes)	awāny (pl)	أواني
plate (dinner ~)	ṭabaʾ (m)	طبق
saucer	ṭabaʾ fengān (m)	طبق فنجان
shot glass	kāsa (f)	كاسة
glass (tumbler)	kobbāya (f)	كوبّاية
cup	fengān (m)	فنجان
sugar bowl	sokkariya (f)	سكّريّة
salt cellar	mamlaḥa (f)	مملحة
pepper pot	mobhera (f)	مبهرة
butter dish	ṭabaʾ zebda (m)	طبق زبدة
stock pot (soup pot)	ḥalla (f)	حلّة
frying pan (skillet)	ṭāsa (f)	طاسة
ladle	maɣrafa (f)	مغرفة
colander	maṣfāh (f)	مصفاه
tray (serving ~)	ṣeniya (f)	صينيّة
bottle	ezāza (f)	إزازة
jar (glass)	barṭamān (m)	برطمان
tin (can)	kanz (m)	كانز
bottle opener	fattāḥa (f)	فتّاحة
tin opener	fattāḥa (f)	فتّاحة
corkscrew	barrīma (f)	بريّمة
filter	filter (m)	فلتر
to filter (vt)	ṣaffa	صفّى
waste (food ~, etc.)	zebāla (f)	زبالة
waste bin (kitchen ~)	ṣandūʾ el zebāla (m)	صندوق الزبالة

92. Bathroom

bathroom	ḥammām (m)	حمّام
water	meyāh (f)	مياه
tap	ḥanafiya (f)	حنفيّة
hot water	maya soχna (f)	مايّة سخنة
cold water	maya barda (f)	مايّة باردة

toothpaste	maʿgūn asnān (m)	معجون أسنان
to clean one's teeth	naḍḍaf el asnān	نظّف الأسنان
toothbrush	forʃet senān (f)	فرشة أسنان
to shave (vi)	ḥala'	حلق
shaving foam	raɣwa lel ḥelā'a (f)	رغوة للحلاقة
razor	mūs (m)	موس
to wash (one's hands, etc.)	ɣasal	غسل
to have a bath	estaḥamma	إستحمّى
shower	doʃ (m)	دوش
to have a shower	aχad doʃ	أخد دوش
bath	banyo (m)	بانيو
toilet (toilet bowl)	twalet (m)	تواليت
sink (washbasin)	ḥoḍe (m)	حوض
soap	ṣabūn (m)	صابون
soap dish	ṣabbāna (f)	صبّانة
sponge	līfa (f)	ليفة
shampoo	ʃambū (m)	شامبو
towel	fūṭa (f)	فوطة
bathrobe	robe el ḥammām (m)	روب حمّام
laundry (laundering)	ɣasīl (m)	غسيل
washing machine	ɣassāla (f)	غسّالة
to do the laundry	ɣasal el malābes	غسل الملابس
washing powder	mas-ḥū' ɣasīl (m)	مسحوق غسيل

93. Household appliances

TV, telly	televizion (m)	تليفزيون
tape recorder	gehāz tasgīl (m)	جهاز تسجيل
video	'āla tasgīl video (f)	آلة تسجيل فيديو
radio	gehāz radio (m)	جهاز راديو
player (CD, MP3, etc.)	blayer (m)	بليير
video projector	gehāz ʿarḍ (m)	جهاز عرض
home cinema	sinema manzeliya (f)	سينما منزليّة
DVD player	dividī blayer (m)	دي في دي بليير
amplifier	mokabbaer el ṣote (m)	مكبّر الصوت
video game console	'ātāry (m)	أتاري
video camera	kamera video (f)	كاميرا فيديو
camera (photo)	kamera (f)	كاميرا
digital camera	kamera diʒital (f)	كاميرا ديجيتال
vacuum cleaner	maknasa kahraba'iya (f)	مكنسة كهربائيّة
iron (e.g. steam ~)	makwa (f)	مكواة
ironing board	lawḥet kayī (f)	لوحة كيّ
telephone	telefon (m)	تليفون
mobile phone	mobile (m)	موبايل

typewriter	'āla katba (f)	آلة كاتبة
sewing machine	makanet el χeyāṭa (f)	مكنة الخياطة
microphone	mikrofon (m)	ميكروفون
headphones	samma'āt ra'siya (pl)	سمّاعات رأسية
remote control (TV)	remowt kontrol (m)	ريموت كنترول
CD, compact disc	sidī (m)	سي دي
cassette, tape	kasett (m)	كاسيت
vinyl record	esṭewāna mūsīqa (f)	أسطوانة موسيقى

94. Repairs. Renovation

renovations	tagdīdāt (m)	تجديدات
to renovate (vt)	gadded	جدّد
to repair, to fix (vt)	ṣallaḥ	صلّح
to put in order	nazzam	نظّم
to redo (do again)	'ād	عاد
paint	dehān (m)	دهان
to paint (~ a wall)	dahhen	دهّن
house painter	dahhān (m)	دهّان
paintbrush	forʃet dehān (f)	فرشاة الدهان
whitewash	maḥlūl mobayeḍ (m)	محلول مبيّض
to whitewash (vt)	beyḍ	بيّض
wallpaper	wara' ḥā'eṭ (m)	ورق حائط
to wallpaper (vt)	laṣaq wara' el ḥā'eṭ	لصق ورق الحائط
varnish	warnīʃ (m)	ورنيش
to varnish (vt)	ṭala bel warnīʃ	طلى بالورنيش

95. Plumbing

water	meyāh (f)	مياه
hot water	maya soχna (f)	مايّة سخنة
cold water	maya barda (f)	مايّة باردة
tap	ḥanafiya (f)	حنفيّة
drop (of water)	'aṭra (f)	قطرة
to drip (vi)	'aṭṭar	قطّر
to leak (ab. pipe)	sarrab	سرّب
leak (pipe ~)	tasarrob (m)	تسرب
puddle	berka (f)	بركة
pipe	masūra (f)	ماسورة
valve (e.g., ball ~)	ṣamām (m)	صمام
to be clogged up	kān masdūd	كان مسدود
tools	adawāt (pl)	أدوات
adjustable spanner	el meftāḥ el englīzy (m)	المفتاح الإنجليزي
to unscrew (lid, filter, etc.)	fataḥ	فتح

to screw (tighten)	aḥkam el ʃadd	أحكم الشدّ
to unclog (vt)	sallek	سلّك
plumber	samkary (m)	سمكري
basement	badrome (m)	بدروم
sewerage (system)	ʃabaket el magāry (f)	شبكة المجاري

96. Fire. Conflagration

fire (accident)	ḥariʾ (m)	حريق
flame	lahab (m)	لهب
spark	ʃarāra (f)	شرارة
smoke (from fire)	dokχān (m)	دخّان
torch (flaming stick)	ʃoʿla (f)	شعلة
campfire	nār moχayem (m)	نار مخيّم
petrol	banzīn (m)	بنزين
paraffin	kerosīn (m)	كيروسين
flammable (adj)	qābel lel eḥterāq	قابل للإحتراق
explosive (adj)	māda motafaggera	مادة متفجّرة
NO SMOKING	mamnūʿ el tadχīn	ممنوع التدخين
safety	amn (m)	أمن
danger	χaṭar (m)	خطر
dangerous (adj)	χaṭīr	خطير
to catch fire	eʃtaʿal	إشتعل
explosion	enfegār (m)	إنفجار
to set fire	aʃʿal el nār	أشعل النار
arsonist	moʃʿel ḥarīq ʿan ʿamd (m)	مشعل حريق عن عمد
arson	eḥrāq el momtalakāt (m)	إحراق الممتلكات
to blaze (vi)	awhag	أوهج
to burn (be on fire)	et-ḥaraʾ	إتحرق
to burn down	et-ḥaraʾ	إتحرق
to call the fire brigade	kallim ʾism el ḥariʾ	كلّم قسم الحريق
firefighter, fireman	rāgel el maṭāfy (m)	راجل المطافي
fire engine	sayāret el maṭāfy (f)	سيّارة المطافي
fire brigade	ʾesm el maṭāfy (f)	قسم المطافي
fire engine ladder	sellem el maṭāfy (m)	سلّم المطافي
fire hose	χarṭūm el mayya (m)	خرطوم الميّة
fire extinguisher	ṭaffayet ḥariʾ (f)	طفّاية حريق
helmet	χawza (f)	خوذة
siren	sarīna (f)	سرينة
to cry (for help)	ṣarraχ	صرّخ
to call for help	estaɣās	إستغاث
rescuer	monqez (m)	منقذ
to rescue (vt)	anqaz	أنقذ
to arrive (vi)	weṣel	وصل
to extinguish (vt)	ṭaffa	طفّى
water	meyāh (f)	مياه

sand	raml (m)	رمل
ruins (destruction)	ḥeṭām (pl)	حطام
to collapse (building, etc.)	enhār	إنهار
to fall down (vi)	enhār	إنهار
to cave in (ceiling, floor)	enhār	إنهار
piece of debris	ʾeṭʿet ḥeṭām (f)	قطعة حطام
ash	ramād (m)	رماد
to suffocate (die)	eθχanaʾ	إتخنق
to be killed (perish)	māt	مات

HUMAN ACTIVITIES

Job. Business. Part 1

97. Banking

bank	bank (m)	بنك
branch (of a bank)	farʿ (m)	فرع
consultant	mowazzaf bank (m)	موظّف بنك
manager (director)	modīr (m)	مدير
bank account	ḥesāb bank (m)	حساب بنك
account number	raqam el ḥesāb (m)	رقم الحساب
current account	ḥesāb gāry (m)	حساب جاري
deposit account	ḥesāb tawfīr (m)	حساب توّفير
to open an account	fataḥ ḥesāb	فتح حساب
to close the account	ʾafal ḥesāb	قفل حساب
to deposit into the account	awdaʿ fel ḥesāb	أودع في الحساب
to withdraw (vt)	saḥab men el ḥesāb	سحب من الحساب
deposit	wadeeʿa (f)	وديعة
to make a deposit	awdaʿ	أودع
wire transfer	ḥewāla maṣrefiya (f)	حوالة مصرفيّة
to wire, to transfer	ḥawwel	حوّل
sum	mablaɣ (m)	مبلغ
How much?	kām?	كام؟
signature	tawqeeʿ (m)	توقيع
to sign (vt)	waqqaʿ	وقّع
credit card	kredit kard (f)	كريدت كارد
code (PIN code)	kōd (m)	كود
credit card number	raqam el kredit kard (m)	رقم الكريدت كارد
cashpoint	makinet ṣarrāf ʾāly (f)	ماكينة صرّاف آلي
cheque	ʃīk (m)	شيك
to write a cheque	katab ʃīk	كتب شيك
chequebook	daftar ʃikāt (m)	دفتر شيكات
loan (bank ~)	qarḍ (m)	قرض
to apply for a loan	ʾaddem ṭalab ʿala qarḍ	قدّم طلب على قرض
to get a loan	ḥaṣal ʿala qarḍ	حصل على قرض
to give a loan	edda qarḍ	ادّى قرض
guarantee	ḍamān (m)	ضمان

98. Telephone. Phone conversation

telephone	telefon (m)	تليفون
mobile phone	mobile (m)	موبايل
answerphone	gehāz radd ʿalal mokalmāt (m)	جهاز ردّ على المكالمات
to call (by phone)	ettaṣal	إتّصل
call, ring	mokalma telefoniya (f)	مكالمة تليفونية
to dial a number	ettaṣal be raqam	إتّصل برقم
Hello!	alo!	ألو!
to ask (vt)	saʾal	سأل
to answer (vi, vt)	radd	ردّ
to hear (vt)	semeʿ	سمع
well (adv)	kewayes	كويّس
not well (adv)	meʃ kowayīs	مش كويّس
noises (interference)	taʃwīʃ (m)	تشويش
receiver	sammāʿa (f)	سمّاعة
to pick up (~ the phone)	rafaʿ el sammāʿa	رفع السمّاعة
to hang up (~ the phone)	ʾafal el sammāʿa	قفل السمّاعة
busy (engaged)	maʃɣūl	مشغول
to ring (ab. phone)	rann	رنّ
telephone book	dalīl el telefone (m)	دليل التليفون
local (adj)	maḥalliya	ة محلّيّة
local call	mokalma maḥalliya (f)	مكالمة محلّيّة
trunk (e.g. ~ call)	biʿīd	بعيد
trunk call	mokalma biʿīda (f)	مكالمة بعيدة المدى
international (adj)	dowly	دوّلي
international call	mokalma dowliya (f)	مكالمة دوليّة

99. Mobile telephone

mobile phone	mobile (m)	موبايل
display	ʿarḍ (m)	عرض
button	zerr (m)	زرّ
SIM card	sim kard (m)	سيم كارد
battery	baṭṭariya (f)	بطّاريّة
to be flat (battery)	χelṣet	خلصت
charger	ʃāḥen (m)	شاحن
menu	qāʾema (f)	قائمة
settings	awḍāʿ (pl)	أوضاع
tune (melody)	naɣama (f)	نغمة
to select (vt)	eχtār	إختار
calculator	ʾāla ḥasba (f)	آلة حاسبة
voice mail	barīd ṣawty (m)	بريد صوتي
alarm clock	monabbeh (m)	منبّه

contacts	gehāt el etteṣāl (pl)	جهات الإتّصال
SMS (text message)	resāla 'aṣīra ɛsɛmɛs (f)	رسالة قصيرة sms
subscriber	moʃtarek (m)	مشترك

100. Stationery

ballpoint pen	'alam gāf (m)	قلم جاف
fountain pen	'alam rīʃa (m)	قلم ريشة
pencil	'alam roṣāṣ (m)	قلم رصاص
highlighter	markar (m)	ماركر
felt-tip pen	'alam fulumaster (m)	قلم فلوماستر
notepad	mozakkera (f)	مذكّرة
diary	gadwal el a'māl (m)	جدول الأعمال
ruler	masṭara (f)	مسطرة
calculator	'āla ḥasba (f)	آلة حاسبة
rubber	astīka (f)	استيكة
drawing pin	dabbūs (m)	دبّوس
paper clip	dabbūs wara' (m)	دبّوس ورق
glue	ṣamɣ (m)	صمغ
stapler	dabbāsa (f)	دبّاسة
hole punch	χarrāma (m)	خرّامة
pencil sharpener	barrāya (f)	برّاية

Job. Business. Part 2

101. Mass Media

newspaper	garīda (f)	جريدة
magazine	magalla (f)	مجلّة
press (printed media)	ṣaḥāfa (f)	صحافة
radio	radio (m)	راديو
radio station	maḥaṭṭet radio (f)	محطّة راديو
television	televizion (m)	تليفزيون
presenter, host	mo'addem (m)	مقدّم
newsreader	mozee' (m)	مذيع
commentator	mo'alleq (m)	معلّق
journalist	ṣaḥafy (m)	صحفي
correspondent (reporter)	morāsel (m)	مراسل
press photographer	moṣawwer ṣaḥafy (m)	مصوّر صحفي
reporter	ṣaḥafy (m)	صحفي
editor	moḥarrer (m)	محرّر
editor-in-chief	ra'īs taḥrīr (m)	رئيس تحرير
to subscribe (to ...)	eʃtarak	إشترك
subscription	eʃterāk (m)	إشتراك
subscriber	moʃtarek (m)	مشترك
to read (vi, vt)	'ara	قرأ
reader	qāre' (m)	قارئ
circulation (of a newspaper)	tadāwol (m)	تداول
monthly (adj)	ʃahry	شهري
weekly (adj)	osbū'y	أسبوعي
issue (edition)	'adad (m)	عدد
new (~ issue)	gedīd	جديد
headline	'enwān (m)	عنوان
short article	maqāla saɣīra (f)	مقالة قصيرة
column (regular article)	'amūd (m)	عمود
article	maqāla (f)	مقالة
page	ṣafḥa (f)	صفحة
reportage, report	rebortāʒ (m)	ريبورتاج
event (happening)	ḥadass (m)	حدث
sensation (news)	ḍagga (f)	ضجّة
scandal	feḍīḥa (f)	فضيحة
scandalous (adj)	fāḍeḥ	فاضح
great (~ scandal)	ʃahīr	شهير
programme (e.g. cooking ~)	barnāmeg (m)	برنامج
interview	leqā' ṣaḥafy (m)	لقاء صحفي

live broadcast	ezā'a mobāʃera (f)	إذاعة مباشرة
channel	qanah (f)	قناة

102. Agriculture

agriculture	zerā'a (f)	زراعة
peasant (masc.)	fallāḥ (m)	فلّاح
peasant (fem.)	fallāḥa (f)	فلّاحة
farmer	mozāre' (m)	مزارع
tractor	garrār (m)	جرّار
combine, harvester	ḥaṣṣāda (f)	حصّادة
plough	meḥrās (m)	محراث
to plough (vi, vt)	ḥaras	حرث
ploughland	ḥaql maḥrūθ (m)	حقل محروث
furrow (in field)	talem (m)	تلم
to sow (vi, vt)	bezr	بذر
seeder	bazzara (f)	بذّارة
sowing (process)	zar' (m)	زرع
scythe	meḥasʃ (m)	محشّ
to mow, to scythe	ḥasʃ	حشّ
spade (tool)	karīk (m)	كريك
to till (vt)	ḥaras	حرث
hoe	magrafa (f)	مجرفة
to hoe, to weed	est'ṣal nabatāt	إستأصل نباتات
weed (plant)	nabāt ṭafayly (m)	نبات طفيّلي
watering can	raʃāʃa (f)	رشّاشة
to water (plants)	sa'a	سقى
watering (act)	sa'y (m)	سقي
pitchfork	mazrāh (f)	مذراة
rake	madamma (f)	مدمّة
fertiliser	semād (m)	سماد
to fertilise (vt)	sammed	سمّد
manure (fertiliser)	semād (m)	سماد
field	ḥaql (m)	حقل
meadow	marag (m)	مرج
vegetable garden	bostān χoḍār (m)	بستان خضار
orchard (e.g. apple ~)	bostān (m)	بستان
to graze (vt)	ra'a	رعى
herdsman	rā'y (m)	راعي
pasture	mar'a (m)	مرعى
cattle breeding	tarbeya el mawāʃy (f)	تربية المواشي
sheep farming	tarbeya aɣnām (f)	تربية أغنام

plantation	mazraʿa (f)	مزرعة
row (garden bed ~s)	ḥoḍe (m)	حوض
hothouse	dafīʾa (f)	دفيئة
drought (lack of rain)	gafāf (m)	جفاف
dry (~ summer)	gāf	جاف
grain	ḥobūb (pl)	حبوب
cereal crops	maḥaṣīl el ḥubūb (pl)	محاصيل الحبوب
to harvest, to gather	ḥaṣad	حصد
miller (person)	ṭaḥḥān (m)	طحّان
mill (e.g. gristmill)	ṭaḥūna (f)	طاحونة
to grind (grain)	ṭaḥn el ḥobūb	طحن الحبوب
flour	deʾīʾ (m)	دقيق
straw	ʾaʃ (m)	قشّ

103. Building. Building process

building site	arḍ benāʾ (f)	أرض بناء
to build (vt)	bana	بنى
building worker	ʿāmel benāʾ (m)	عامل بناء
project	maʃrūʿ (m)	مشروع
architect	mohandes meʿmāry (m)	مهندس معماري
worker	ʿāmel (m)	عامل
foundations (of a building)	asās (m)	أساس
roof	saʾf (m)	سقف
foundation pile	kawmet el asās (f)	كومة الأساس
wall	ḥeyṭa (f)	حيطة
reinforcing bars	ḥadīd taslīḥ (m)	حديد تسليح
scaffolding	saʾʾāla (f)	سقّالة
concrete	χarasāna (f)	خرسانة
granite	granīt (m)	جرانيت
stone	ḥagar (m)	حجر
brick	ṭūb (m)	طوب
sand	raml (m)	رمل
cement	asmant (m)	إسمنت
plaster (for walls)	ṭalāʾ gaṣṣ (m)	طلاء جصّ
to plaster (vt)	ṭala bel gaṣṣ	طلى بالجصّ
paint	dehān (m)	دهان
to paint (~ a wall)	dahhen	دهّن
barrel	barmīl (m)	برميل
crane	rāfeʿa (f)	رافعة
to lift, to hoist (vt)	rafaʿ	رفع
to lower (vt)	nazzel	نزّل
bulldozer	bulldozer (m)	بولدوزر
excavator	ḥaffāra (f)	حفّارة

scoop, bucket	magrafa (f)	مجرفة
to dig (excavate)	ḥafar	حفر
hard hat	χawza (f)	خوذة

Professions and occupations

104. Job search. Dismissal

job	ʻamal (m)	عمل
staff (work force)	kawādir (pl)	كوادر
personnel	ṭāqem el ʻāmelīn (m)	طاقم العاملين
career	mehna (f)	مهنة
prospects (chances)	ʼāfāq (pl)	آفاق
skills (mastery)	maharāt (pl)	مهارات
selection (screening)	eχteyār (m)	إختيار
employment agency	wekālet tawẓīf (f)	وكالة توّظيف
curriculum vitae, CV	sīra zātiya (f)	سيرة ذاتيّة
job interview	moʼablet ʻamal (f)	مقابلة عمل
vacancy	wazīfa χaleya (f)	وظيفة خالية
salary, pay	morattab (m)	مرتّب
fixed salary	rāteb sābet (m)	راتب ثابت
pay, compensation	ogra (f)	أجرة
position (job)	manṣeb (m)	منصب
duty (of an employee)	wāgeb (m)	واجب
range of duties	magmūʻa men el wāgebāt (f)	مجموعة من الواجبات
busy (I'm ~)	maʃɣūl	مشغول
to fire (dismiss)	rafad	رفد
dismissal	eqāla (m)	إقالة
unemployment	baṭāla (f)	بطالة
unemployed (n)	ʻāṭel (m)	عاطل
retirement	maʻāʃ (m)	معاش
to retire (from job)	oḥīl ʻala el maʻāʃ	أحيل على المعاش

105. Business people

director	modīr (m)	مدير
manager (director)	modīr (m)	مدير
boss	raʼīs (m)	رئيس
superior	motafawweq (m)	متفوّق
superiors	roʼasāʼ (pl)	رؤساء
president	raʼīs (m)	رئيس
chairman	raʼīs (m)	رئيس
deputy (substitute)	nāʼeb (m)	نائب
assistant	mosāʻed (m)	مساعد

secretary	sekerteyr (m)	سكرتير
personal assistant	sekerteyr χāṣ (m)	سكرتير خاص
businessman	ragol a'māl (m)	رجل أعمال
entrepreneur	rā'ed a'māl (m)	رائد أعمال
founder	mo'asses (m)	مؤسّس
to found (vt)	asses	أسّس
founding member	mo'asses (m)	مؤسّس
partner	ʃerīk (m)	شريك
shareholder	mālek el as-hom (m)	مالك الأسهم
millionaire	millyonīr (m)	مليونير
billionaire	milliardīr (m)	مليادير
owner, proprietor	ṣāḥeb (m)	صاحب
landowner	ṣāḥeb el arḍ (m)	صاحب الأرض
client	'amīl (m)	عميل
regular client	'amīl dā'em (m)	عميل دائم
buyer (customer)	moʃtary (m)	مشتري
visitor	zā'er (m)	زائر
professional (n)	moḥtaref (m)	محترف
expert	χabīr (m)	خبير
specialist	motaχaṣṣeṣ (m)	متخصّص
banker	ṣāḥeb maṣraf (m)	صاحب مصرف
broker	semsār (m)	سمسار
cashier	'āmel kaʃier (m)	عامل كاشيير
accountant	muḥāseb (m)	محاسب
security guard	ḥāres amn (m)	حارس أمن
investor	mostasmer (m)	مستثمر
debtor	modīn (m)	مدين
creditor	dā'en (m)	دائن
borrower	moqtareḍ (m)	مقترض
importer	mostawred (m)	مستوّرد
exporter	moṣadder (m)	مصدّر
manufacturer	el ʃerka el moṣanne'a (f)	الشركة المصنّعة
distributor	mowazze' (m)	موزّع
middleman	wasīṭ (m)	وسيط
consultant	mostaʃār (m)	مستشار
sales representative	mandūb mabi'āt (m)	مندوب مبيعات
agent	wakīl (m)	وكيل
insurance agent	wakīl el ta'mīn (m)	وكيل التأمين

106. Service professions

cook	ṭabbāχ (m)	طبّاخ
chef (kitchen chef)	el ʃeyf (m)	الشيف

baker	χabbāz (m)	خبّاز
barman	bārman (m)	بارمان
waiter	garsone (m)	جرسون
waitress	garsona (f)	جرسونة
lawyer, barrister	muḥāmy (m)	محامي
lawyer (legal expert)	muḥāmy χabīr qanūny (m)	محامي خبير قانوني
notary public	mowassaq (m)	موثّق
electrician	kahrabā'y (m)	كهربائي
plumber	samkary (m)	سمكري
carpenter	naggār (m)	نجّار
masseur	modallek (m)	مدلّك
masseuse	modalleka (f)	مدلّكة
doctor	doktore (m)	دكتور
taxi driver	sawwā' taksi (m)	سوّاق تاكسي
driver	sawwā' (m)	سوّاق
delivery man	rāgel el delivery (m)	راجل الديلفري
chambermaid	'āmela tandīf ɣoraf (f)	عاملة تنظيف غرف
security guard	ḥāres amn (m)	حارس أمن
flight attendant (fem.)	moḍīfet ṭayarān (f)	مضيفة طيران
schoolteacher	modarres madrasa (m)	مدرّس مدرسة
librarian	amīn maktaba (m)	أمين مكتبة
translator	motargem (m)	مترجم
interpreter	motargem fawwry (m)	مترجم فوّري
guide	morʃed (m)	مرشد
hairdresser	ḥallā' (m)	حلاّق
postman	sā'y el barīd (m)	ساعي البريد
salesman (store staff)	bayā' (m)	بيّاع
gardener	bostāny (m)	بستاني
domestic servant	χādema (m)	خادمة
maid (female servant)	χadema (f)	خادمة
cleaner (cleaning lady)	'āmela tandīf (f)	عاملة تنظيف

107. Military professions and ranks

private	gondy (m)	جنّدي
sergeant	raqīb tāny (m)	رقيب تاني
lieutenant	molāzem tāny (m)	ملازم تاني
captain	naqīb (m)	نقيب
major	rā'ed (m)	رائد
colonel	'aqīd (m)	عقيد
general	ʒenerāl (m)	جنرال
marshal	marʃāl (m)	مارشال
admiral	amerāl (m)	أميرال
military (n)	'askary (m)	عسكري
soldier	gondy (m)	جنّدي

officer	ḍābeṭ (m)	ضابط
commander	qā'ed (m)	قائد
border guard	ḥaras ḥodūd (m)	حرس حدود
radio operator	'āmel lāselky (m)	عامل لاسلكي
scout (searcher)	rā'ed mostakʃef (m)	رائد مستكشف
pioneer (sapper)	mohandes 'askary (m)	مهندس عسكري
marksman	rāmy (m)	رامي
navigator	mallāḥ (m)	ملاّح

108. Officials. Priests

king	malek (m)	ملك
queen	maleka (f)	ملكة
prince	amīr (m)	أمير
princess	amīra (f)	أميرة
czar	qayṣar (m)	قيصر
czarina	qayṣara (f)	قيصرة
president	ra'īs (m)	رئيس
Secretary (minister)	wazīr (m)	وزير
prime minister	ra'īs wozarā' (m)	رئيس وزراء
senator	'oḍw magles el ʃoyūχ (m)	عضو مجلس الشيوخ
diplomat	deblomāsy (m)	دبلوماسي
consul	qonṣol (m)	قنصل
ambassador	safīr (m)	سفير
counselor (diplomatic officer)	mostaʃār (m)	مستشار
official, functionary (civil servant)	mowazzaf (m)	موظّف
prefect	ra'īs edāret el ḥayī (m)	رئيس إدارة الحي
mayor	ra'īs el baladiya (m)	رئيس البلديّة
judge	qāḍy (m)	قاضي
prosecutor	el na'eb el 'ām (m)	النائب العام
missionary	mobasʃer (m)	مبشّر
monk	rāheb (m)	راهب
abbot	ra'īs el deyr (m)	رئيس الدير
rabbi	ḥaχām (m)	حاخام
vizier	wazīr (m)	وزير
shah	ʃāh (m)	شاه
sheikh	ʃɛyχ (m)	شيخ

109. Agricultural professions

beekeeper	naḥḥāl (m)	نحّال
shepherd	rā'y (m)	راعي

agronomist	mohandes zerāʿy (m)	مهندس زراعي
cattle breeder	morabby el mawāʃy (m)	مربّي المواشي
veterinary surgeon	doktore beṭary (m)	دكتور بيطري
farmer	mozāreʿ (m)	مزارع
winemaker	ṣāneʿ el χamr (m)	صانع الخمر
zoologist	χabīr fe ʿelm el ḥayawān (m)	خبير في علم الحيوان
cowboy	rāʿy el baʾar (m)	راعي البقر

110. Art professions

actor	momassel (m)	ممثّل
actress	momassela (f)	ممثّلة
singer (masc.)	moṭreb (m)	مطرب
singer (fem.)	moṭreba (f)	مطربة
dancer (masc.)	rāqeṣ (m)	راقص
dancer (fem.)	raʾāṣa (f)	راقصة
performer (masc.)	fannān (m)	فنّان
performer (fem.)	fannāna (f)	فنّانة
musician	ʿāzef (m)	عازف
pianist	ʿāzef biano (m)	عازف بيانو
guitar player	ʿāzef guitar (m)	عازف جيتار
conductor (orchestra ~)	qāʾed orkestra (m)	قائد أوركسترا
composer	molaḥḥen (m)	ملحّن
impresario	modīr ferʾa (m)	مدير فرقة
film director	moχreg aflām (m)	مخرج أفلام
producer	monteg (m)	منتج
scriptwriter	kāteb senario (m)	كاتب سيناريو
critic	nāqed (m)	ناقد
writer	kāteb (m)	كاتب
poet	ʃāʿer (m)	شاعر
sculptor	naḥḥāt (m)	نحّات
artist (painter)	rassām (m)	رسّام
juggler	bahlawān (m)	بهلوان
clown	aragoze (m)	أراجوز
acrobat	bahlawān (m)	بهلوان
magician	sāḥer (m)	ساحر

111. Various professions

doctor	doktore (m)	دكتور
nurse	momarreḍa (f)	ممرّضة
psychiatrist	doktore nafsāny (m)	دكتور نفساني
dentist	doktore asnān (m)	دكتور أسنان

surgeon	garrāḥ (m)	جرّاح
astronaut	rā'ed faḍā' (m)	رائد فضاء
astronomer	'ālem falak (m)	عالم فلك
pilot	ṭayār (m)	طيّار
driver (of a taxi, etc.)	sawwā' (m)	سوّاق
train driver	sawwā' (m)	سوّاق
mechanic	mikanīky (m)	ميكانيكي
miner	'āmel mangam (m)	عامل منجم
worker	'āmel (m)	عامل
locksmith	'affāl (m)	قفّال
joiner (carpenter)	naggār (m)	نجّار
turner (lathe operator)	χarrāṭ (m)	خرّاط
building worker	'āmel benā' (m)	عامل بناء
welder	laḥḥām (m)	لحّام
professor (title)	brofessor (m)	بروفيسور
architect	mohandes me'māry (m)	مهندس معماري
historian	mo'arreχ (m)	مؤرّخ
scientist	'ālem (m)	عالم
physicist	fizyā'y (m)	فيزيائي
chemist (scientist)	kemyā'y (m)	كيميائي
archaeologist	'ālem'āsār (m)	عالم آثار
geologist	ʒeoloʒy (m)	جيولوجي
researcher (scientist)	bāḥes (m)	باحث
babysitter	dāda (f)	دادة
teacher, educator	mo'allem (m)	معلّم
editor	moḥarrer (m)	محرّر
editor-in-chief	ra'īs taḥrīr (m)	رئيس تحرير
correspondent	morāsel (m)	مراسل
typist (fem.)	kāteba 'ala el 'āla el kāteba (f)	كاتبة على الآلة الكاتبة
designer	moṣammem (m)	مصمّم
computer expert	motaχaṣṣeṣ bel kombuter (m)	متخصّص بالكمبيوتر
programmer	mobarmeg (m)	مبرمج
engineer (designer)	mohandes (m)	مهندس
sailor	baḥḥār (m)	بحّار
seaman	baḥḥār (m)	بحّار
rescuer	monqez (m)	منقذ
firefighter	rāgel el maṭāfy (m)	راجل المطافئ
police officer	ʃorṭy (m)	شرطي
watchman	ḥāres (m)	حارس
detective	moḥaqqeq (m)	محقّق
customs officer	mowazzaf el gamārek (m)	موظّف الجمارك
bodyguard	ḥāres ʃaχṣy (m)	حارس شخصي
prison officer	ḥāres segn (m)	حارس سجن
inspector	mofatteʃ (m)	مفتّش
sportsman	reyāḍy (m)	رياضي
trainer, coach	modarreb (m)	مدرّب

butcher	gazzār (m)	جزّار
cobbler (shoe repairer)	eskāfy (m)	إسكافي
merchant	tāger (m)	تاجر
loader (person)	ʃayāl (m)	شيّال
fashion designer	moṣammem azyā' (m)	مصمّم أزياء
model (fem.)	modeyl (f)	موديل

112. Occupations. Social status

schoolboy	talmīz (m)	تلميذ
student (college ~)	ṭāleb (m)	طالب
philosopher	faylasūf (m)	فيلسوف
economist	eqtiṣādy (m)	إقتصادي
inventor	moχtare' (m)	مخترع
unemployed (n)	'āṭel (m)	عاطل
retiree, pensioner	motaqā'ed (m)	متقاعد
spy, secret agent	gasūs (m)	جاسوس
prisoner	sagīn (m)	سجين
striker	moḍrab (m)	مضرب
bureaucrat	buroqrāṭy (m)	بيروقراطي
traveller (globetrotter)	raḥḥāla (m)	رحّالة
gay, homosexual (n)	ʃāz (m)	شاذ
hacker	haker (m)	هاكِر
hippie	hippi (m)	هيبي
bandit	qāṭe' ṭarī' (m)	قاطع طريق
hit man, killer	qātel ma'gūr (m)	قاتل مأجور
drug addict	modmen moχaddarāt (m)	مدمن مخدّرات
drug dealer	tāger moχaddarāt (m)	تاجر مخدّرات
prostitute (fem.)	mommos (f)	مومس
pimp	qawwād (m)	قوّاد
sorcerer	sāḥer (m)	ساحر
sorceress (evil ~)	sāḥera (f)	ساحرة
pirate	'orṣān (m)	قرصان
slave	'abd (m)	عبد
samurai	samuray (m)	ساموراي
savage (primitive)	motawaḥḥeʃ (m)	متوحّش

Sports

113. Kinds of sports. Sportspersons

sportsman	reyāḍy (m)	رياضي
kind of sport	nūʿ men el reyāḍa (m)	نوع من الرياضة
basketball	koret el salla (f)	كرة السلّة
basketball player	lāʿeb korat el salla (m)	لاعب كرة السلّة
baseball	baseball (m)	بيسبول
baseball player	lāʿeb basebāl (m)	لاعب بيسبول
football	koret el qadam (f)	كرة القدم
football player	lāʿeb korat qadam (m)	لاعب كرة القدم
goalkeeper	ḥāres el marma (m)	حارس المرمى
ice hockey	hoky (m)	هوكي
ice hockey player	lāʿeb hoky (m)	لاعب هوكي
volleyball	voliball (m)	فولي بول
volleyball player	lāʿeb volly bal (m)	لاعب فولي بول
boxing	molakma (f)	ملاكمة
boxer	molākem (m)	ملاكم
wrestling	moṣarʿa (f)	مصارعة
wrestler	moṣāreʿ (m)	مصارع
karate	karate (m)	كاراتيه
karate fighter	lāʿeb karateyh (m)	لاعب كاراتيه
judo	ʒudo (m)	جودو
judo athlete	lāʿeb ʒudo (m)	لاعب جودو
tennis	tennis (m)	تنسّ
tennis player	lāʿeb tennis (m)	لاعب تنس
swimming	sebāḥa (f)	سباحة
swimmer	sabbāḥ (m)	سبّاح
fencing	mobarza (f)	مبارزة
fencer	mobārez (m)	مبارز
chess	ʃaṭarang (m)	شطرنج
chess player	lāʿeb ʃaṭarang (m)	لاعب شطرنج
alpinism	tasalloq el gebāl (m)	تسلّق الجبال
alpinist	motasalleq el gebāl (m)	متسلّق الجبال
running	garyī (m)	جريّ

runner	ʻaddāʼ (m)	عدّاء
athletics	alʻāb el qowa (pl)	ألعاب القوى
athlete	lāʻeb reyāḍy (m)	لاعب رياضي
horse riding	reyāḍa el forūsiya (f)	رياضة الفروسيّة
horse rider	fāres (m)	فارس
figure skating	tazallog fanny ʻalal galīd (m)	تزلّج فنّي على الجليد
figure skater (masc.)	motazalleg rāqeṣ (m)	متزلّج راقص
figure skater (fem.)	motazallega rāqeṣa (f)	متزلّجة راقصة
powerlifting	rafʻ el asqāl (m)	رفع الأثقال
powerlifter	rāfeʻ el asqāl (m)	رافع الأثقال
car racing	sebāʼ el sayarāt (m)	سباق السيارات
racer (driver)	sawwāʼ sebāʼ (m)	سائق سباق
cycling	rokūb el darragāt (m)	ركوب الدرّاجات
cyclist	lāʻeb el darrāga (m)	لاعب الدرّاجة
long jump	el qafz el ʻāly (m)	القفز العالي
pole vaulting	el qafz bel ʻaṣa (m)	القفز بالعصا
jumper	qāfez (m)	قافز

114. Kinds of sports. Miscellaneous

American football	koret el qadam (f)	كرة القدم
badminton	el rīʃa (m)	الريشة
biathlon	el biatlon (m)	البياتلون
billiards	bilyardo (m)	بلياردو
bobsleigh	zalāga gamaʻiya (f)	زلاجة جماعية
bodybuilding	body building (m)	بادي بيلدنج
water polo	koret el maya (f)	كرة الميّة
handball	koret el yad (f)	كرة اليد
golf	golf (m)	جولف
rowing	tagdīf (m)	تجديف
scuba diving	ɣoṣe (m)	غوص
cross-country skiing	reyāḍa el ski (f)	رياضة الإسكي
table tennis (ping-pong)	koret el ṭawla (f)	كرة الطاولة
sailing	reyāḍa ebḥār el marākeb (f)	رياضة إبحارالمراكب
rally	sebāʼ el sayarāt (m)	سباق السيارات
rugby	rugby (m)	رجبي
snowboarding	el tazallog ʻlal galīd (m)	التزلّج على الجليد
archery	remāya (f)	رماية

115. Gym

barbell	bār ḥadīd (m)	بار حديد
dumbbells	dumbbells (m)	دمبلز

training machine	gehāz tadrīb (m)	جهاز تدريب
exercise bicycle	ʿagalet tadrīb (f)	عجلة تدريب
treadmill	trīdmil (f)	تريد ميل
horizontal bar	ʿoʾla (f)	عقلة
parallel bars	el motawaziyīn (pl)	المتوازيين
vault (vaulting horse)	manaṣṣet el qafz (f)	منصّة القفز
mat (exercise ~)	ḥaṣīra (f)	حصيرة
skipping rope	ḥabl el naṭṭ (m)	حبل النطّ
aerobics	aerobiks (m)	ايروبيكس
yoga	yoga (f)	يوجا

116. Sports. Miscellaneous

Olympic Games	alʿāb olombiya (pl)	ألعاب أولمبيّة
winner	fāʾez (m)	فائز
to be winning	fāz	فاز
to win (vi)	fāz	فاز
leader	zaʿīm (m)	زعيم
to lead (vi)	taʾaddam	تقدّم
first place	el martaba el ūla (f)	المرتبة الأولى
second place	el martaba el tanya (f)	المرتبة الثانية
third place	el martaba el talta (f)	المرتبة الثالثة
medal	medalya (f)	ميدالية
trophy	kaʾs (f)	كأس
prize cup (trophy)	kaʾs (f)	كأس
prize (in game)	gayza (f)	جائزة
main prize	akbar gayza (f)	أكبر جائزة
record	raqam qeyāsy (m)	رقم قياسي
to set a record	fāz be raqam qeyāsy	فاز برقم قياسي
final	mobarāh nehaʾiya (f)	مباراة نهائيّة
final (adj)	nehāʾy	نهائي
champion	baṭal (m)	بطل
championship	boṭūla (f)	بطولة
stadium	malʿab (m)	ملعب
terrace	modarrag (m)	مدرّج
fan, supporter	moʃaggeʿ (m)	مشجّع
opponent, rival	ʿadeww (m)	عدوّ
start (start line)	χaṭṭ el bedāya (m)	خطّ البداية
finish line	χaṭṭ el nehāya (m)	خطّ النهاية
defeat	hazīma (f)	هزيمة
to lose (not win)	χeser	خسر
referee	ḥakam (m)	حكم
jury (judges)	hayʾet el ḥokm (f)	هيئة الحكم

score	natīga (f)	نتيجة
draw	ta'ādol (m)	تعادل
to draw (vi)	ta'ādal	تعادل
point	no'ṭa (f)	نقطة
result (final score)	natīga neha'iya (f)	نتيجة نهائية
period	ʃoṭe (m)	شوط
half-time	beyn el ʃoṭeyn	بين الشوطين
doping	monasʃeṭāt (pl)	منشّطات
to penalise (vt)	'āqab	عاقب
to disqualify (vt)	ḥaram	حرم
apparatus	adah (f)	أداة
javelin	remḥ (m)	رمح
shot (metal ball)	kora ma'daniya (f)	كرة معدنية
ball (snooker, etc.)	kora (f)	كرة
aim (target)	hadaf (m)	هدف
target	hadaf (m)	هدف
to shoot (vi)	ḍarab bel nār	ضرب بالنار
accurate (~ shot)	maḍbūṭ	مضبوط
trainer, coach	modarreb (m)	مدرّب
to train (sb)	darrab	درّب
to train (vi)	etdarrab	إتدرّب
training	tadrīb (m)	تدريب
gym	gīm (m)	جيم
exercise (physical)	tamrīn (m)	تمرين
warm-up (athlete ~)	tasχīn (m)	تسخين

Education

117. School

school	madrasa (f)	مدرسة
headmaster	modīr el madrasa (m)	مدير المدرسة
student (m)	talmīz (m)	تلميذ
student (f)	telmīza (f)	تلميذة
schoolboy	talmīz (m)	تلميذ
schoolgirl	telmīza (f)	تلميذة
to teach (sb)	ʿallem	علّم
to learn (language, etc.)	taʿallam	تعلّم
to learn by heart	ḥafaẓ	حفظ
to learn (~ to count, etc.)	taʿallam	تعلّم
to be at school	daras	درس
to go to school	rāḥ el madrasa	راح المدرسة
alphabet	abgadiya (f)	أبجدية
subject (at school)	madda (f)	مادّة
classroom	faṣl (m)	فصل
lesson	dars (m)	درس
playtime, break	estrāḥa (f)	إستراحة
school bell	garas el madrasa (m)	جرس المدرسة
school desk	disk el madrasa (m)	ديسك المدرسة
blackboard	sabbūra (f)	سبّورة
mark	daraga (f)	درجة
good mark	daraga kewayesa (f)	درجة كويسة
bad mark	daraga meʃ kewayesa (f)	درجة مش كويسة
to give a mark	edda daraga	إدّى درجة
mistake, error	χaṭaʾ (m)	خطأ
to make mistakes	aχṭaʾ	أخطأ
to correct (an error)	ṣaḥḥaḥ	صحّح
crib	berʃām (m)	برشام
homework	wāgeb (m)	واجب
exercise (in education)	tamrīn (m)	تمرين
to be present	ḥaḍar	حضر
to be absent	ɣāb	غاب
to miss school	taɣeyyab ʿan el madrasa	تغيّب عن المدرسة
to punish (vt)	ʿāqab	عاقب
punishment	ʿeqāb (m)	عقاب
conduct (behaviour)	solūk (m)	سلوك

school report	el taqrīr el madrasy (m)	التقرير المدرسي
pencil	ʾalam roṣāṣ (m)	قلم رصاص
rubber	astīka (f)	استيكة
chalk	ṭabaʃīr (m)	طباشير
pencil case	maʾlama (f)	مقلمة
schoolbag	ʃanṭet el madrasa (f)	شنطة المدرسة
pen	ʾalam (m)	قلم
exercise book	daftar (m)	دفتر
textbook	ketāb taʿlīm (m)	كتاب تعليم
compasses	bargal (m)	برجل
to make technical drawings	rasam rasm teqany	رسم رسم تقني
technical drawing	rasm teqany (m)	رسم تقني
poem	ʾaṣīda (f)	قصيدة
by heart (adv)	ʿan ẓahr qalb	عن ظهر قلب
to learn by heart	ḥafaẓ	حفظ
school holidays	agāza (f)	أجازة
to be on holiday	ʿando agāza	عنده أجازة
to spend holidays	ʾaḍa el agāza	قضى الأجازة
test (at school)	emteḥān (m)	إمتحان
essay (composition)	enʃāʾ (m)	إنشاء
dictation	emlāʾ (m)	إملاء
exam (examination)	emteḥān (m)	إمتحان
to do an exam	ʿamal emteḥān	عمل إمتحان
experiment (e.g., chemistry ~)	tagreba (f)	تجربة

118. College. University

academy	akademiya (f)	أكاديميّة
university	gamʿa (f)	جامعة
faculty (e.g., ~ of Medicine)	kolliya (f)	كلّيّة
student (masc.)	ṭāleb (m)	طالب
student (fem.)	ṭāleba (f)	طالبة
lecturer (teacher)	muḥāḍer (m)	محاضر
lecture hall, room	modarrag (m)	مدرّج
graduate	motaχarreg (m)	متخرج
diploma	dibloma (f)	دبلومة
dissertation	resāla ʿelmiya (f)	رسالة علميّة
study (report)	derāsa (f)	دراسة
laboratory	moχtabar (m)	مختبر
lecture	moḥaḍra (f)	محاضرة
coursemate	zamīl fel ṣaff (m)	زميل في الصفّ
scholarship, bursary	menḥa derāsiya (f)	منحة دراسيّة
academic degree	daraga ʿelmiya (f)	درجة علميّة

119. Sciences. Disciplines

mathematics	reyāḍīāt (pl)	رياضيّات
algebra	el gabr (m)	الجبر
geometry	handasa (f)	هندسة
astronomy	ʿelm el falak (m)	علم الفلك
biology	al aḥya' (m)	الأحياء
geography	goɣrafia (f)	جغرافيا
geology	ʒeoloʒia (f)	جيولوجيا
history	tarīχ (m)	تاريخ
medicine	ṭebb (m)	طبّ
pedagogy	tarbeya (f)	تربية
law	qanūn (m)	قانون
physics	fezya' (f)	فيزياء
chemistry	kemya' (f)	كيمياء
philosophy	falsafa (f)	فلسفة
psychology	ʿelm el nafs (m)	علم النفس

120. Writing system. Orthography

grammar	el naḥw wel ṣarf (m)	النحو والصرف
vocabulary	mofradāt el loɣa (pl)	مفردات اللغة
phonetics	ṣawtīāt (pl)	صوتيات
noun	esm (m)	اسم
adjective	ṣefa (f)	صفة
verb	feʿl (m)	فعل
adverb	ẓarf (m)	ظرف
pronoun	ḍamīr (m)	ضمير
interjection	oslūb el taʿaggob (m)	أسلوب التعجّب
preposition	ḥarf el garr (m)	حرف الجرّ
root	gezr el kelma (m)	جذر الكلمة
ending	nehāya (f)	نهاية
prefix	sabaeqa (f)	سابقة
syllable	maqṭaʿ lafzy (m)	مقطع لفظي
suffix	lāḥeqa (f)	لاحقة
stress mark	nabra (f)	نبرة
apostrophe	ʿalāmet ḥazf (f)	علامة حذف
full stop	no'ṭa (f)	نقطة
comma	faṣla (f)	فاصلة
semicolon	no'ṭa w faṣla (f)	نقطة وفاصلة
colon	no'ṭeteyn (pl)	نقطتين
ellipsis	talat no'aṭ (pl)	ثلاث نقط
question mark	ʿalāmet estefhām (f)	علامة إستفهام
exclamation mark	ʿalāmet taʿaggob (f)	علامة تعجّب

inverted commas	ʿalamāt el eqtebās (pl)	علامات الإقتباس
in inverted commas	beyn ʿalamaty el eqtebās	بين علامتي الاقتباس
parenthesis	qoseyn (du)	قوسين
in parenthesis	beyn el qoseyn	بين القوسين
hyphen	ʿalāmet waṣl (f)	علامة وصل
dash	ʃorṭa (f)	شرطة
space (between words)	farāɣ (m)	فراغ
letter	ḥarf (m)	حرف
capital letter	ḥarf kebīr (m)	حرف كبير
vowel (n)	ḥarf ṣauty (m)	حرف صوتي
consonant (n)	ḥarf sāken (m)	حرف ساكن
sentence	gomla (f)	جملة
subject	fāʿel (m)	فاعل
predicate	mosnad (m)	مسند
line	saṭr (m)	سطر
on a new line	men bedāyet el saṭr	من بداية السطر
paragraph	faqra (f)	فقرة
word	kelma (f)	كلمة
group of words	magmūʿa men el kelamāt (pl)	مجموعة من الكلمات
expression	moṣṭalaḥ (m)	مصطلح
synonym	morādef (m)	مرادف
antonym	motaḍād loɣawy (m)	متضاد لغوي
rule	qaʿeda (f)	قاعدة
exception	estesnāʾ (m)	إستثناء
correct (adj)	ṣaḥīḥ	صحيح
conjugation	ṣarf (m)	صرف
declension	taṣrīf el asmāʾ (m)	تصريف الأسماء
nominal case	ḥāla esmiya (f)	حالة أسمية
question	soʾāl (m)	سؤال
to underline (vt)	ḥaṭṭ χaṭṭ taḥt	حطّ خطّ تحت
dotted line	χaṭṭ menaʾʾaṭ (m)	خطّ منقّط

121. Foreign languages

language	loɣa (f)	لغة
foreign (adj)	agnaby	أجنبيّ
foreign language	loɣa agnabiya (f)	لغة أجنبية
to study (vt)	daras	درس
to learn (language, etc.)	taʿallam	تعلّم
to read (vi, vt)	ʾara	قرأ
to speak (vi, vt)	kallem	كلّم
to understand (vt)	fehem	فهم
to write (vt)	katab	كتب
fast (adv)	bosorʿa	بسرعة
slowly (adv)	bo boṭʾ	ببطء

fluently (adv)	beṭalāqa	بطلاقة
rules	qawāʿed (pl)	قواعد
grammar	el naḥw wel ṣarf (m)	النحو والصرف
vocabulary	mofradāt el loɣa (pl)	مفردات اللغة
phonetics	ṣawtīāt (pl)	صوتيات
textbook	ketāb taʿlīm (m)	كتاب تعليم
dictionary	qamūs (m)	قاموس
teach-yourself book	ketāb taʿlīm zāty (m)	كتاب تعليم ذاتي
phrasebook	ketāb lel ʿebarāt el ʃāʾeʿa (m)	كتاب للعبارت الشائعة
cassette, tape	kasett (m)	كاسيت
videotape	ʃerīʾṭ video (m)	شريط فيديو
CD, compact disc	sidī (m)	سي دي
DVD	dividī (m)	دي في دي
alphabet	abgadiya (f)	أبجدية
to spell (vt)	tahagga	تهجّى
pronunciation	noṭʾ (m)	نطق
accent	lahga (f)	لهجة
with an accent	be lahga	بـ لهجة
without an accent	men ɣeyr lahga	من غير لهجة
word	kelma (f)	كلمة
meaning	maʿna (m)	معنى
course (e.g. a French ~)	dawra (f)	دورة
to sign up	saggel esmo	سجّل إسمه
teacher	modarres (m)	مدرّس
translation (process)	targama (f)	ترجمة
translation (text, etc.)	targama (f)	ترجمة
translator	motargem (m)	مترجم
interpreter	motargem fawwry (m)	مترجم فوّري
polyglot	ʿalīm beʿeddet loɣāt (m)	عليم بعدّة لغات
memory	zākera (f)	ذاكرة

122. Fairy tale characters

Father Christmas	baba neweyl (m)	بابا نويل
Cinderella	sindrīla	سيندريلا
mermaid	ʿarūset el baḥr (f)	عروسة البحر
Neptune	nibtūn (m)	نبتون
magician, wizard	sāḥer (m)	ساحر
fairy	genniya (f)	جنّيّة
magic (adj)	seḥry	سحري
magic wand	el ʿaṣāya el seḥriya (f)	العصاية السحرية
fairy tale	ḥekāya χayaliya (f)	حكاية خيالية
miracle	moʿgeza (f)	معجزة
dwarf	qazam (m)	قزم

to turn into ...	taḥawwal ela ...	تحوّل إلى...
ghost	ʃabaḥ (m)	شبح
phantom	ʃabaḥ (m)	شبح
monster	waḥʃ (m)	وحش
dragon	tennīn (m)	تنّين
giant	ʿemlāq (m)	عملاق

123. Zodiac Signs

Aries	borg el ḥaml (m)	برج الحمل
Taurus	borg el sore (m)	برج الثور
Gemini	borg el gawzāʾ (m)	برج الجوزاء
Cancer	borg el saraṭān (m)	برج السرطان
Leo	borg el asad (m)	برج الأسد
Virgo	borg el ʿazrāʾ (m)	برج العذراء
Libra	borg el mezān (m)	برج الميزان
Scorpio	borg el ʿaʾrab (m)	برج العقرب
Sagittarius	borg el qose (m)	برج القوس
Capricorn	borg el gady (m)	برج الجدي
Aquarius	borg el dalw (m)	برج الدلو
Pisces	borg el ḥūt (m)	برج الحوت
character	ʃaχṣiya (f)	شخصية
character traits	el ṣefāt el ʃaχṣiya (pl)	الصفات الشخصية
behaviour	solūk (m)	سلوك
to tell fortunes	ʾara el ṭāleʿ	قرأ الطالع
fortune-teller	ʿarrāfa (f)	عرّافة
horoscope	tawaqqoʿāt el abrāg (pl)	توقّعات الأبراج

Arts

124. Theatre

theatre	masraḥ (m)	مسرح
opera	obra (f)	أوبرا
operetta	obrette (f)	أوبريت
ballet	baleyh (m)	باليه
theatre poster	molṣaq (m)	ملصق
theatre company	fer'a (f)	فرقة
tour	gawlet fananīn (f)	جولة فنّانين
to be on tour	tagawwal	تجوّل
to rehearse (vi, vt)	'amal brova	عمل بروفة
rehearsal	brova (f)	بروفة
repertoire	barnāmeg el masraḥ (m)	برنامج المسرح
performance	adā' (m)	أداء
theatrical show	'arḍ masraḥy (m)	عرض مسرحي
play	masraḥiya (f)	مسرحيّة
ticket	tazkara (f)	تذكرة
booking office	ʃebbāk el tazāker (m)	شبّاك التذاكر
lobby, foyer	ṣāla (f)	صالة
coat check (cloakroom)	ɣorfet īdā' el ma'āṭef (f)	غرفة إيداع المعاطف
cloakroom ticket	beṭā'et edā' el ma'aṭef (f)	بطاقة إيداع المعاطف
binoculars	naḍḍāra mo'aẓẓema lel obera (f)	نظارة معظمة للأوبرا
usher	ḥāgeb el sinema (m)	حاجب السينما
stalls (orchestra seats)	karāsy el orkestra (pl)	كراسي الأوركسترا
balcony	balakona (f)	بلكونة
dress circle	ʃorfa (f)	شرفة
box	log (m)	لوج
row	ṣaff (m)	صفّ
seat	meq'ad (m)	مقعد
audience	gomhūr (m)	جمهور
spectator	moʃāhed (m)	مشاهد
to clap (vi, vt)	ṣaffa'	صفّق
applause	taṣfī' (m)	تصفيق
ovation	taṣfī' ḥār (m)	تصفيق حار
stage	χaʃabet el masraḥ (f)	خشبة المسرح
curtain	setāra (f)	ستارة
scenery	dekor (m)	ديكور
backstage	kawalīs (pl)	كواليس
scene (e.g. the last ~)	maʃ-had (m)	مشهد
act	faṣl (m)	فصل
interval	estrāḥa (f)	استراحة

125. Cinema

actor	momassel (m)	ممثّل
actress	momassela (f)	ممثّلة
cinema (industry)	el aflām (m)	الأفلام
film	film (m)	فيلم
episode	gozʾ (m)	جزء
detective film	film bolīsy (m)	فيلم بوليسي
action film	film akʃen (m)	فيلم أكشن
adventure film	film moɣamarāt (m)	فيلم مغامرات
science fiction film	film χayāl ʿelmy (m)	فيلم خيال علمي
horror film	film roʿb (m)	فيلم رعب
comedy film	film komedia (f)	فيلم كوميديا
melodrama	melodrama (m)	ميلودراما
drama	drama (f)	دراما
fictional film	film χayāly (m)	فيلم خيالي
documentary	film wasāʾeqy (m)	فيلم وثائقي
cartoon	kartōn (m)	كرتون
silent films	sinema ṣāmeta (f)	سينما صامتة
role (part)	dore (m)	دور
leading role	dore raʾīsy (m)	دور رئيسي
to play (vi, vt)	massel	مثّل
film star	negm senamāʾy (m)	نجم سينمائي
well-known (adj)	maʿrūf	معروف
famous (adj)	maʃ-hūr	مشهور
popular (adj)	maḥbūb	محبوب
script (screenplay)	senario (m)	سيناريو
scriptwriter	kāteb senario (m)	كاتب سيناريو
film director	moχreg (m)	مخرج
producer	monteg (m)	منتج
assistant	mosāʿed (m)	مساعد
cameraman	moṣawwer (m)	مصوّر
stuntman	moʾaddy maʃāhed χaṭīra (m)	مؤدي مشاهد خطيرة
double (body double)	momassel badīl (m)	ممثّل بديل
to shoot a film	ṣawwar film	صوّر فيلم
audition, screen test	tagreba adāʾ (f)	تجربة أداء
shooting	taṣwīr (m)	تصوير
film crew	ṭāqem el film (m)	طاقم الفيلم
film set	manteʾet taṣwīr (f)	منطقة التصوير
camera	kamera (f)	كاميرا
cinema	sinema (f)	سينما
screen (e.g. big ~)	ʃāʃa (f)	شاشة
to show a film	ʿaraḍ film	عرض فيلم
soundtrack	mosīqa taṣweriya (f)	موسيقي تصويرية
special effects	moʾasserāt χāṣa (pl)	مؤثّرات خاصّة

subtitles	targamet el ḥewār (f)	ترجمة الحوار
credits	ʃāret el nehāya (f)	شارة النهاية
translation	targama (f)	ترجمة

126. Painting

art	fann (m)	فنّ
fine arts	fonūn gamīla (pl)	فنون جميلة
art gallery	maʿraḍ fonūn (m)	معرض فنون
art exhibition	maʿraḍ fanny (m)	معرض فنّي
painting (art)	lawḥa (f)	لوحة
graphic art	fann taṣwīry (m)	فن تصويري
abstract art	fann tagrīdy (m)	فنّ تجريدي
impressionism	el enṭebāʿiya (f)	الإنطباعيّة
picture (painting)	lawḥa (f)	لوحة
drawing	rasm (m)	رسم
poster	boster (m)	بوستر
illustration (picture)	rasm tawḍīḥy (m)	رسم توضيحي
miniature	ṣūra moṣagɣara (f)	صورة مصغّرة
copy (of painting, etc.)	nosχa (f)	نسخة
reproduction	nosχa ṭebʾ el aṣl (f)	نسخة طبق الأصل
mosaic	fosayfesāʾ (f)	فسيفساء
stained glass window	ʃebbāk ʾezāz mlawwen (m)	شبّاك قزاز ملوّن
fresco	taṣwīr gaṣṣy (m)	تصوير جصي
engraving	naʾʃ (m)	نقش
bust (sculpture)	temsāl neṣfy (m)	تمثال نصفي
sculpture	naḥt (m)	نحت
statue	temsāl (m)	تمثال
plaster of Paris	gibss (m)	جيبس
plaster (as adj)	men el gebs	من الجيبس
portrait	bortreyh (m)	بورتريه
self-portrait	bortreyh ʃaχṣy (m)	بورتريه شخصي
landscape painting	lawḥet manzar ṭabeeʿy (f)	لوحة منظر طبيعي
still life	ṭabeeʿa ṣāmeta (f)	طبيعة صامتة
caricature	ṣūra karikatoriya (f)	صورة كاريكاتورية
sketch	rasm tamhīdy (m)	رسم تمهيدي
paint	lone (m)	لون
watercolor paint	alwān maya (m)	ألوان ميّة
oil (paint)	zeyt (m)	زيت
pencil	ʾalam roṣāṣ (m)	قلم رصاص
Indian ink	ḥebr hendy (m)	حبر هندي
charcoal	faḥm (m)	فحم
to draw (vi, vt)	rasam	رسم
to paint (vi, vt)	rasam	رسم
to pose (vi)	ʾaʿad	قعد
artist's model (masc.)	modeyl ḥayī amām el rassām (m)	موديل حيّ أمام الرسّام

artist's model (fem.)	modeyl ḥayī amām el rassām (m)	موديل حيّ أمام الرسّام
artist (painter)	rassām (m)	رسّام
work of art	ʿamal fanny (m)	عمل فنّي
masterpiece	toḥfa faniya (f)	تحفة فنية
studio (artist's workroom)	warʃa (f)	ورشة
canvas (cloth)	kanava (f)	كانفا
easel	masnad el loḥe (m)	مسند اللوح
palette	lawḥet el alwān (f)	لوحة الألوان
frame (picture ~, etc.)	eṭār (m)	إطار
restoration	tarmīm (m)	ترميم
to restore (vt)	rammem	رمّم

127. Literature & Poetry

literature	adab (m)	أدب
author (writer)	moʾallef (m)	مؤلّف
pseudonym	esm mostaʿār (m)	اسم مستعار
book	ketāb (m)	كتاب
volume	mogallad (m)	مجلّد
table of contents	gadwal el moḥtawayāt (m)	جدول المحتويات
page	ṣafḥa (f)	صفحة
main character	el ʃaχṣiya el raʾesiya (f)	الشخصية الرئيسية
autograph	tawqeeʿ el moʾallef (m)	توقيع المؤلّف
short story	qeṣṣa ʾaṣīra (f)	قصّة قصيرة
story (novella)	ʾoṣṣa (f)	قصّة
novel	rewāya (f)	رواية
work (writing)	moʾallef (m)	مؤلّف
fable	ḥekāya (f)	حكاية
detective novel	rewāya bolesiya (f)	رواية بوليسية
poem (verse)	ʾaṣīda (f)	قصيدة
poetry	ʃeʿr (m)	شعر
poem (epic, ballad)	ʾaṣīda (f)	قصيدة
poet	ʃāʿer (m)	شاعر
fiction	χayāl (m)	خيال
science fiction	χayāl ʿelmy (m)	خيال علمي
adventures	adab el moɣamrāt (m)	أدب المغامرات
educational literature	adab tarbawy (m)	أدب تربوّي
children's literature	adab el aṭfāl (m)	أدب الأطفال

128. Circus

circus	serk (m)	سيرك
travelling circus	serk motanaʾʾel (m)	سيرك متنقّل
programme	barnāmeg (m)	برنامج
performance	adāʾ (m)	أداء

act (circus ~)	ʿarḍ (m)	عرض
circus ring	ḥalabet el serk (f)	حلبة السيرك
pantomime (act)	momassel īmāʾy (m)	ممثّل إيمائي
clown	aragoze (m)	أراجوز
acrobat	bahlawān (m)	بهلوان
acrobatics	alʿab bahlawaniya (f)	ألعاب بهلوانية
gymnast	lāʿeb gombāz (m)	لاعب جمباز
acrobatic gymnastics	gombāz (m)	جمباز
somersault	ḥarakāt ʃaʾlaba (pl)	حركات شقلبة
strongman	el ragl el qawy (m)	الرجل القوي
tamer (e.g., lion ~)	morawweḍ (m)	مروّض
rider (circus horse ~)	fāres (m)	فارس
assistant	mosāʿed (m)	مساعد
stunt	ḥeyla (f)	حيلة
magic trick	χedʿa seḥriya (f)	خدعة سحرية
conjurer, magician	sāḥer (m)	ساحر
juggler	bahlawān (m)	بهلوان
to juggle (vi, vt)	leʿeb be korāt ʿadīda	لعب بكرات عديدة
animal trainer	modarreb ḥayawanāt (m)	مدرّب حيوانات
animal training	tadrīb el ḥayawanāt (m)	تدريب الحيوانات
to train (animals)	darrab	درّب

129. Music. Pop music

music	mosīqa (f)	موسيقى
musician	ʿāzef (m)	عازف
musical instrument	ʾāla moseqiya (f)	آلة موسيقيّة
to play ...	ʿazaf ...	عزف...
guitar	guitar (m)	جيتار
violin	kamān (m)	كمان
cello	el tʃello (m)	التشيلو
double bass	kamān kebīr (m)	كمان كبير
harp	qesār (m)	قيثار
piano	biano (m)	بيانو
grand piano	biano kebīr (m)	بيانو كبير
organ	arɣan (m)	أرغن
wind instruments	ʾālāt el nafχ (pl)	آلات النفخ
oboe	mezmār (m)	مزمار
saxophone	saksofon (m)	ساكسوفون
clarinet	klarinet (m)	كلارنيت
flute	flute (m)	فلوت
trumpet	būʾ (m)	بوق
accordion	okordiōn (m)	أكورديون
drum	ṭabla (f)	طبلة
duo	sonāʾy (m)	ثنائي

trio	solāsy (m)	ثلاثي
quartet	robāʿy (m)	رباعي
choir	korale (m)	كورال
orchestra	orkestra (f)	أوركسترا
pop music	mosīqa el bob (f)	موسيقى البوب
rock music	mosīqa el rok (f)	موسيقى الروك
rock group	ferʾet el rokk (f)	فرقة الروك
jazz	ʒāzz (m)	جاز
idol	maʿbūd (m)	معبود
admirer, fan	moʿgab (m)	معجب
concert	ḥafla mūsiqiya (f)	حفلة موسيقيّة
symphony	semfoniya (f)	سمفونيّة
composition	ʾeṭʿa mosiqiya (f)	قطعة موسيقيّة
to compose (write)	allaf	ألّف
singing (n)	ɣenāʾ (m)	غناء
song	oɣniya (f)	أغنيّة
tune (melody)	laḥn (m)	لحن
rhythm	eqāʿ (m)	إيقاع
blues	mosīqa el blues (f)	موسيقى البلوز
sheet music	notāt (pl)	نوتات
baton	ʿaṣa el maystro (m)	عصا المايسترو
bow	qose (m)	قوس
string	watar (m)	وتر
case (e.g. guitar ~)	ʃanṭa (f)	شنطة

Rest. Entertainment. Travel

130. Trip. Travel

tourism, travel	seyāḥa (f)	سياحة
tourist	sā'eḥ (m)	سائح
trip, voyage	reḥla (f)	رحلة
adventure	moɣamra (f)	مغامرة
trip, journey	reḥla (f)	رحلة
holiday	agāza (f)	أجازة
to be on holiday	kān fi agāza	كان في أجازة
rest	estrāḥa (f)	إستراحة
train	qeṭār, 'aṭṭr (m)	قطار
by train	bel qeṭār - bel aṭṭr	بالقطار
aeroplane	ṭayāra (f)	طيّارة
by aeroplane	bel ṭayāra	بالطيّارة
by car	bel sayāra	بالسيّارة
by ship	bel safīna	بالسفينة
luggage	el ʃonaṭ (pl)	الشنط
suitcase	ʃanṭa (f)	شنطة
luggage trolley	'arabet ʃonaṭ (f)	عربة شنط
passport	basbore (m)	باسبور
visa	ta'ʃīra (f)	تأشيرة
ticket	tazkara (f)	تذكرة
air ticket	tazkara ṭayarān (f)	تذكرة طيران
guidebook	dalīl (m)	دليل
map (tourist ~)	χarīṭa (f)	خريطة
area (rural ~)	mante'a (f)	منطقة
place, site	makān (m)	مكان
exotica (n)	ɣarāba (f)	غرابة
exotic (adj)	ɣarīb	غريب
amazing (adj)	mod-heʃ	مدهش
group	magmū'a (f)	مجموعة
excursion, sightseeing tour	gawla (f)	جولة
guide (person)	morʃed (m)	مرشد

131. Hotel

hotel	fondo' (m)	فندق
motel	motel (m)	موتيل
three-star (~ hotel)	talat nogūm	ثلاث نجوم

five-star	χamas nogūm	خمس نجوم
to stay (in a hotel, etc.)	nezel	نزل
room	oḍa (f)	أوضة
single room	owḍa le ʃaχṣ wāḥed (f)	أوضة لشخص واحد
double room	oḍa le ʃaχṣeyn (f)	أوضة لشخصين
to book a room	ḥagaz owḍa	حجز أوضة
half board	wagbeteyn fel yome (du)	وجبتين في اليوم
full board	talat wagabāt fel yome	ثلاث وجبات في اليوم
with bath	bel banyo	بـ البانيو
with shower	bel doʃ	بالدوش
satellite television	televizion be qanawāt faḍā'iya (m)	تليفزيون بقنوات فضائية
air-conditioner	takyīf (m)	تكييف
towel	fūṭa (f)	فوطة
key	meftāḥ (m)	مفتاح
administrator	modīr (m)	مدير
chambermaid	'āmela tandīf γoraf (f)	عاملة تنظيف غرف
porter	ʃayāl (m)	شيّال
doorman	bawwāb (m)	بوّاب
restaurant	maṭ'am (m)	مطعم
pub, bar	bār (m)	بار
breakfast	foṭūr (m)	فطور
dinner	'aʃā' (m)	عشاء
buffet	bofeyh (m)	بوفيه
lobby	rad-ha (f)	ردهة
lift	asanseyr (m)	اسانسير
DO NOT DISTURB	nargu 'adam el ez'āg	نرجو عدم الإزعاج
NO SMOKING	mamnū' el tadχīn	ممنوع التدخين

132. Books. Reading

book	ketāb (m)	كتاب
author	mo'allef (m)	مؤلّف
writer	kāteb (m)	كاتب
to write (~ a book)	allaf	ألّف
reader	qāre' (m)	قارئ
to read (vi, vt)	'ara	قرأ
reading (activity)	qerā'a (f)	قراءة
silently (to oneself)	beṣamt	بصمت
aloud (adv)	beṣote 'āly	بصوت عالي
to publish (vt)	naʃar	نشر
publishing (process)	naʃr (m)	نشر
publisher	nāʃer (m)	ناشر
publishing house	dar el ṭebā'a wel naʃr (f)	دار الطباعة والنشر

to come out (be released)	ṣadar	صدر
release (of a book)	ṣodūr (m)	صدور
print run	ʿadad el nosaχ (m)	عدد النسخ
bookshop	maḥal kotob (m)	محل كتب
library	maktaba (f)	مكتبة
story (novella)	ʾoṣṣa (f)	قصّة
short story	qeṣṣa ʾaṣīra (f)	قصّة قصيرة
novel	rewāya (f)	رواية
detective novel	rewāya bolesiya (f)	رواية بوليسية
memoirs	mozakkerāt (pl)	مذكّرات
legend	osṭūra (f)	أسطورة
myth	χorāfa (f)	خرافة
poetry, poems	ʃeʿr (m)	شعر
autobiography	sīret ḥayah (f)	سيرة حياة
selected works	muχtarāt (pl)	مختارات
science fiction	χayāl ʿelmy (m)	خيال علمي
title	ʿenwān (m)	عنوان
introduction	moqaddema (f)	مقدّمة
title page	ṣafḥet ʿenwān (f)	صفحة العنوان
chapter	faṣl (m)	فصل
extract	χolāṣa (f)	خلاصة
episode	maʃ-had (m)	مشهد
plot (storyline)	ḥabka (f)	حبكة
contents	moḥtawayāt (pl)	محتويات
table of contents	gadwal el moḥtawayāt (m)	جدوّل المحتويات
main character	el ʃaχṣiya el raʾesiya (f)	الشخصية الرئيسية
volume	mogallad (m)	مجلّد
cover	ɣelāf (m)	غلاف
binding	taglīd (m)	تجليد
bookmark	ʃerīʾṭ (m)	شريط
page	ṣafḥa (f)	صفحة
to page through	ʾalleb el ṣafaḥāt	قلّب الصفحات
margins	hāmeʃ (m)	هامش
annotation (marginal note, etc.)	molaḥza (f)	ملاحظة
footnote	molaḥza (f)	ملاحظة
text	noṣṣ (m)	نصّ
type, fount	nūʿ el χaṭṭ (m)	نوع الخطّ
misprint, typo	χaṭaʾ maṭbaʿy (m)	خطأ مطبعيّ
translation	targama (f)	ترجمة
to translate (vt)	targem	ترجم
original (n)	aṣliya (f)	أصلية
famous (adj)	maʃ-hūr	مشهور
unknown (not famous)	meʃ maʿrūf	مش معروف

interesting (adj)	moʃawweq	مشوّق
bestseller	aktar mabeeʿan (m)	أكثر مبيعاً
dictionary	qamūs (m)	قاموس
textbook	ketāb taʿlīm (m)	كتاب تعليم
encyclopedia	ensayklopedia (f)	إنسيكلوبيديا

133. Hunting. Fishing

hunting	ṣeyd (m)	صيد
to hunt (vi, vt)	eṣṭād	إصطاد
hunter	ṣayād (m)	صيّاد
to shoot (vi)	ḍarab bel nār	ضرب بالنار
rifle	bondoqiya (f)	بندقيّة
bullet (shell)	roṣāṣa (f)	رصاصة
shot (lead balls)	ʿeyār (m)	عيار
steel trap	maṣyada (f)	مصيّدة
snare (for birds, etc.)	fakχ (m)	فخّ
to fall into the steel trap	weʾeʿ fe fakχ	وقع في فخّ
to lay a steel trap	naṣb fakχ	نصب فخّ
poacher	sāreʾ el ṣeyd (m)	سارق الصيد
game (in hunting)	ṣeyd (m)	صيد
hound dog	kalb ṣeyd (m)	كلب صيد
safari	safāry (m)	سفاري
mounted animal	ḥayawān moḥannaṭ (m)	حيوان محنّط
fisherman	ṣayād el samak (m)	صيّاد السمك
fishing (angling)	ṣeyd el samak (m)	صيد السمك
to fish (vi)	eṣṭād samak	إصطاد سمك
fishing rod	ṣennāra (f)	صنّارة
fishing line	χeyṭ (m)	خيط
hook	ʃaṣ el garīma (m)	شص الصيد
float	ʿawwāma (f)	عوّامة
bait	ṭaʿm (m)	طعم
to cast a line	ṭaraḥ el ṣennāra	طرح الصنّارة
to bite (ab. fish)	ʿaḍḍ	عض
catch (of fish)	el samak el mosṭād (m)	السمك المصطاد
ice-hole	fat-ḥa fel galīd (f)	فتحة في الجليد
fishing net	ʃabaket el ṣeyd (f)	شبكة الصيد
boat	markeb (m)	مركب
to net (to fish with a net)	eṣṭād bel ʃabaka	إصطاد بالشبكة
to cast[throw] the net	rama ʃabaka	رمى شبكة
to haul the net in	aχrag ʃabaka	أخرج شبكة
to fall into the net	weʾeʿ fe ʃabaka	وقع في شبكة
whaler (person)	ṣayād el ḥūt (m)	صيّاد الحوت
whaleboat	safīna ṣeyd ḥitān (f)	سفينة صيد الحيتان
harpoon	ḥerba (f)	حربة

134. Games. Billiards

billiards	bilyardo (m)	بلياردو
billiard room, hall	qāʿa bilyardo (m)	قاعة بلياردو
ball (snooker, etc.)	kora (f)	كرة
to pocket a ball	dakɣal kora	دخّل كرة
cue	ʿaṣāyet bilyardo (f)	عصاية بلياردو
pocket	geyb bilyardo (m)	جيب بلياردو

135. Games. Playing cards

diamonds	el dinary (m)	الديناري
spades	el bastūny (m)	البستوني
hearts	el koba (f)	الكوبة
clubs	el sebāty (m)	السباتي
ace	ʾāss (m)	آس
king	malek (m)	ملك
queen	maleka (f)	ملكة
jack, knave	walad (m)	ولد
playing card	waraʾa (f)	ورقة
cards	waraʾ (m)	ورق
trump	waraʾa rābeḥa (f)	ورقة رابحة
pack of cards	desta waraʾ ʿenab (f)	دستة ورق اللعب
point	nuʾṭa (f)	نقطة
to deal (vi, vt)	farraʾ	فرّق
to shuffle (cards)	χalaṭ	خلط
lead, turn (n)	dore (m)	دور
cardsharp	moḥtāl fel ʾomār (m)	محتال في القمار

136. Rest. Games. Miscellaneous

to stroll (vi, vt)	tamasʃa	تمشّى
stroll (leisurely walk)	tamʃeya (f)	تمشيّة
car ride	gawla bel sayāra (f)	جولة بالسيّارة
adventure	moɣamra (f)	مغامرة
picnic	nozha (f)	نزهة
game (chess, etc.)	leʿba (f)	لعبة
player	lāʿeb (m)	لاعب
game (one ~ of chess)	dore (m)	دور
collector (e.g. philatelist)	gāmeʿ (m)	جامع
to collect (stamps, etc.)	gammaʿ	جمّع
collection	magmūʿa (f)	مجموعة
crossword puzzle	kalemāt motaqaṭʿa (pl)	كلمات متقاطعة
racecourse (hippodrome)	ḥalabet el sebāʾ (f)	حلبة السباق

disco (discotheque)	disko (m)	ديسكو
sauna	sauna (f)	ساونا
lottery	yanaṣīb (m)	يانصيب
camping trip	reḥlet taχyīm (f)	رحلة تخييم
camp	moχayam (m)	مخيّم
tent (for camping)	χeyma (f)	خيمة
compass	boṣla (f)	بوصلة
camper	moχayam (m)	مخيّم
to watch (film, etc.)	ʃāhed	شاهد
viewer	moʃāhed (m)	مشاهد
TV show (TV program)	barnāmeg televiziony (m)	برنامج تليفزيوني

137. Photography

camera (photo)	kamera (f)	كاميرا
photo, picture	ṣūra (f)	صورة
photographer	moṣawwer (m)	مصوّر
photo studio	estudio taṣwīr (m)	إستوديو تصوير
photo album	albūm el ṣewar (m)	ألبوم الصور
camera lens	ʿadaset kamera (f)	عدسة الكاميرا
telephoto lens	ʿadasa teleskopiya (f)	عدسة تلسكوبيّة
filter	filter (m)	فلتر
lens	ʿadasa (f)	عدسة
optics (high-quality ~)	baṣrīāt (pl)	بصريات
diaphragm (aperture)	saddāda (f)	سدّادة
exposure time (shutter speed)	moddet el taʿarroḍ (f)	مدّة التعرض
viewfinder	el ʿeyn el faḥeṣa (f)	العين الفاحصة
digital camera	kamera diʒital (f)	كاميرا ديجيتال
tripod	tribod (m)	ترايبود
flash	flāʃ (m)	فلاش
to photograph (vt)	ṣawwar	صوّر
to take pictures	ṣawwar	صوّر
to have one's picture taken	etṣawwar	إتصوّر
focus	tarkīz (m)	تركيز
to focus	rakkez	ركّز
sharp, in focus (adj)	ḥādda	حادّة
sharpness	ḥedda (m)	حدّة
contrast	tabāyon (m)	تباين
contrast (as adj)	motabāyen	متباين
picture (photo)	ṣūra (f)	صورة
negative (n)	el nosχa el salba (f)	النسخة السالبة
film (a roll of ~)	film (m)	فيلم
frame (still)	eṭār (m)	إطار
to print (photos)	ṭabaʿ	طبع

138. Beach. Swimming

beach	ʃāṭe' (m)	شاطئ
sand	raml (m)	رمل
deserted (beach)	mahgūr	مهجور
suntan	esmerār el baʃra (m)	إسمرار البشرة
to get a tan	etʃammes	إتشمّس
tanned (adj)	asmar	أسمر
sunscreen	krīm wāqy men el ʃams (m)	كريم واقي من الشمس
bikini	bikini (m)	بكيني
swimsuit, bikini	mayo (m)	مايّوه
swim trunks	mayo regāly (m)	مايّوه رجالي
swimming pool	ḥammām sebāḥa (m)	حمّام سباحة
to swim (vi)	ʿām, sabaḥ	عام, سبح
shower	doʃ (m)	دوش
to change (one's clothes)	ɣayar lebso	غيّر لبسه
towel	fūṭa (f)	فوطة
boat	markeb (m)	مركب
motorboat	lunʃ (m)	لنش
water ski	tazallog ʿalal mā' (m)	تزلّج على الماء
pedalo	el baddāl (m)	البدّال
surfing	surfing (m)	سيرفينج
surfer	rākeb el amwāg (m)	راكب الأمواج
scuba set	gehāz el tanaffos (m)	جهاز التنفّس
flippers (swim fins)	zaʿānef el sebāḥa (pl)	زعانف السباحة
mask (diving ~)	kamāma (f)	كمامة
diver	ɣawwāṣ (m)	غوّاص
to dive (vi)	ɣāṣ	غاص
underwater (adv)	taḥt el maya	تحت المايّة
beach umbrella	ʃamsiya (f)	شمسيّة
beach chair (sun lounger)	korsy blāʒ (m)	كرسي بلاج
sunglasses	naḍḍāret ʃams (f)	نضّارة شمس
air mattress	martaba hawa'iya (f)	مرتبة هوائية
to play (amuse oneself)	leʿeb	لعب
to go for a swim	sebeḥ	سبح
beach ball	koret ʃaṭṭ (f)	كرة شطّ
to inflate (vt)	nafaχ	نفخ
inflatable, air (adj)	qābel lel nafχ	قابل للنفخ
wave	mouga (f)	موجة
buoy (line of ~s)	ʃamandūra (f)	شمندورة
to drown (ab. person)	ɣere'	غرق
to save, to rescue	anqaz	أنقذ
life jacket	sotret nagah (f)	سترة نجاة
to observe, to watch	rāqab	راقب
lifeguard	ḥāres ʃāṭe' (m)	حارس شاطئ

TECHNICAL EQUIPMENT. TRANSPORT

Technical equipment

139. Computer

computer	kombuter (m)	كمبيوتر
notebook, laptop	lab tob (m)	لابتوب
to turn on	fataḥ, ʃagɣal	فتح, شغّل
to turn off	ṭaffa	طفّى
keyboard	lawḥet el mafatīḥ (f)	لوحة المفاتيح
key	meftāḥ (m)	مفتاح
mouse	maws (m)	ماوس
mouse mat	maws bād (m)	ماوس باد
button	zerr (m)	زرّ
cursor	moʾasʃer (m)	مؤشّر
monitor	ʃāʃa (f)	شاشة
screen	ʃāʃa (f)	شاشة
hard disk	hard disk (m)	هارد ديسك
hard disk capacity	seʿet el hard disk (f)	سعة الهارد ديسك
memory	zākera (f)	ذاكرة
random access memory	zākerat el woṣūl el ʿaʃwāʾy (f)	ذاكرة الوصول العشوائي
file	malaff (m)	ملفّ
folder	ḥāfeza (m)	حافظة
to open (vt)	fataḥ	فتح
to close (vt)	ʾafal	قفل
to save (vt)	ḥafaẓ	حفظ
to delete (vt)	masaḥ	مسح
to copy (vt)	nasaχ	نسخ
to sort (vt)	ṣannaf	صنّف
to transfer (copy)	naʾal	نقل
programme	barnāmeg (m)	برنامج
software	barmagīāt (pl)	برمجيّات
programmer	mobarmeg (m)	مبرمج
to program (vt)	barmag	برمج
hacker	haker (m)	هاكر
password	kelmet el serr (f)	كلمة السرّ
virus	virūs (m)	فيروس
to find, to detect	laʾa	لقى
byte	byte (m)	بايت

megabyte	megabayt (m)	ميجا بايت
data	bayanāt (pl)	بيانات
database	qa'edet bayanāt (f)	قاعدة بيانات
cable (USB, etc.)	kabl (m)	كابل
to disconnect (vt)	faṣal	فصل
to connect (sth to sth)	waṣṣal	وصّل

140. Internet. E-mail

Internet	internet (m)	إنترنت
browser	motaṣaffeḥ (m)	متصفّح
search engine	moḥarrek baḥs (m)	محرك بحث
provider	ʃerket el internet (f)	شركة الإنترنت
webmaster	modīr el mawqe' (m)	مدير الموقع
website	mawqe' elektrony (m)	موقع الكتروني
web page	ṣafḥet web (f)	صفحة ويب
address (e-mail ~)	'enwān (m)	عنوان
address book	daftar el 'anawīn (m)	دفتر العناوين
postbox	ṣandū' el barīd (m)	صندوق البريد
post	barīd (m)	بريد
full (adj)	mumtali'	ممتلىء
message	resāla (f)	رسالة
incoming messages	rasa'el wārda (pl)	رسائل واردة
outgoing messages	rasa'el ṣādra (pl)	رسائل صادرة
sender	morsel (m)	مرسل
to send (vt)	arsal	أرسل
sending (of mail)	ersāl (m)	إرسال
receiver	morsel elayh (m)	مرسل إليه
to receive (vt)	estalam	إستلم
correspondence	morasla (f)	مراسلة
to correspond (vi)	tarāsal	تراسل
file	malaff (m)	ملفّ
to download (vt)	ḥammel	حمّل
to create (vt)	'amal	عمل
to delete (vt)	masaḥ	مسح
deleted (adj)	mamsūḥ	ممسوح
connection (ADSL, etc.)	etteṣāl (m)	إتّصال
speed	sor'a (f)	سرعة
modem	modem (m)	مودم
access	woṣūl (m)	وصول
port (e.g. input ~)	maχrag (m)	مخرج
connection (make a ~)	etteṣāl (m)	إتّصال
to connect to ... (vi)	yuwṣel	يوصل
to select (vt)	eχtār	إختار
to search (for ...)	baḥs	بحث

Transport

141. Aeroplane

aeroplane	ṭayāra (f)	طيّارة
air ticket	tazkara ṭayarān (f)	تذكرة طيران
airline	ʃerket ṭayarān (f)	شركة طيران
airport	maṭār (m)	مطار
supersonic (adj)	χāreq lel ṣote	خارق للصوت
captain	kabten (m)	كابتن
crew	ṭa'm (m)	طقم
pilot	ṭayār (m)	طيّار
stewardess	moḍīfet ṭayarān (f)	مضيفة طيران
navigator	mallāḥ (m)	ملاّح
wings	agneḥa (pl)	أجنحة
tail	deyl (m)	ذيل
cockpit	kabīna (f)	كابينة
engine	motore (m)	موتور
undercarriage (landing gear)	ʿagalāt el hobūṭ (pl)	عجلات الهبوط
turbine	torbīna (f)	توربينة
propeller	marwaḥa (f)	مروّحة
black box	mosaggel el ṭayarān (m)	مسجّل الطيران
yoke (control column)	moqawwed el ṭayāra (m)	مقوّد الطيّارة
fuel	woqūd (m)	وقود
safety card	beṭā'et el salāma (f)	بطاقة السلامة
oxygen mask	mask el oksyʒīn (m)	ماسك الاوكسيجين
uniform	zayī muwaḥḥad (m)	زيّ موحّد
lifejacket	sotret nagah (f)	سترة نجاة
parachute	baraʃot (m)	باراشوت
takeoff	eqlāʿ (m)	إقلاع
to take off (vi)	aqlaʿet	أقلعت
runway	modarrag el ṭa'erāṭ (m)	مدرّج الطائرات
visibility	ro'ya (f)	رؤية
flight (act of flying)	ṭayarān (m)	طيران
altitude	ertefāʿ (m)	إرتفاع
air pocket	geyb hawā'y (m)	جيب هوائي
seat	meqʿad (m)	مقعد
headphones	sammaʿāt ra'siya (pl)	سمّاعات رأسية
folding tray (tray table)	ṣeniya qabela lel ṭayī (f)	صينية قابلة للطيّ
airplane window	ʃebbāk el ṭayāra (m)	شبّاك الطيّارة
aisle	mamarr (m)	ممرّ

142. Train

train	qeṭār, 'aṭṭr (m)	قطار
commuter train	qeṭār rokkāb (m)	قطار ركّاب
express train	qeṭār saree' (m)	قطار سريع
diesel locomotive	qāṭeret dīzel (f)	قاطرة ديزل
steam locomotive	qāṭera boχariya (f)	قاطرة بخاريّة
coach, carriage	'araba (f)	عربة
buffet car	'arabet el ṭa'ām (f)	عربة الطعام
rails	qoḍbān (pl)	قضبان
railway	sekka ḥadīdiya (f)	سكّة حديديّة
sleeper (track support)	'āreḍa sekket ḥadīd (f)	عارضة سكّة الحديد
platform (railway ~)	raṣīf (m)	رصيف
platform (~ 1, 2, etc.)	χaṭṭ (m)	خطّ
semaphore	semafore (m)	سيمافور
station	maḥaṭṭa (f)	محطّة
train driver	sawwā' (m)	سوّاق
porter (of luggage)	ʃayāl (m)	شيّال
carriage attendant	mas'ūl 'arabet el qeṭār (m)	مسؤول عربة القطار
passenger	rākeb (m)	راكب
ticket inspector	kamsary (m)	كمسري
corridor (in train)	mamarr (m)	ممرّ
emergency brake	farāmel el ṭawāre' (pl)	فرامل الطوارئ
compartment	ɣorfa (f)	غرفة
berth	serīr (m)	سرير
upper berth	serīr 'olwy (m)	سرير علوّي
lower berth	serīr sofly (m)	سرير سفلي
bed linen, bedding	aɣṭeyet el serīr (pl)	أغطيّة السرير
ticket	tazkara (f)	تذكرة
timetable	gadwal (m)	جدوّل
information display	lawḥet ma'lomāt (f)	لوحة معلومات
to leave, to depart	ɣādar	غادر
departure (of a train)	moɣadra (f)	مغادرة
to arrive (ab. train)	weṣel	وصل
arrival	woṣūl (m)	وصول
to arrive by train	weṣel bel qeṭār	وصل بالقطار
to get on the train	rekeb el qeṭār	ركب القطار
to get off the train	nezel men el qeṭār	نزل من القطار
train crash	ḥeṭām qeṭār (m)	حطام قطار
to derail (vi)	χarag 'an χaṭṭ sīru	خرج عن خطّ سيره
steam locomotive	qāṭera boχariya (f)	قاطرة بخاريّة
stoker, fireman	'atʃagy (m)	عطشجي
firebox	forn el moḥarrek (m)	فرن المحرّك
coal	faḥm (m)	فحم

143. Ship

ship	safīna (f)	سفينة
vessel	safīna (f)	سفينة
steamship	baχera (f)	باخرة
riverboat	baχera nahriya (f)	باخرة نهرية
cruise ship	safīna seyaḥiya (f)	سفينة سياحيّة
cruiser	ṭarrād safīna baḥariya (m)	طرّاد سفينة بحريّة
yacht	yaχt (m)	يخت
tugboat	qāṭera baḥariya (f)	قاطرة بحريّة
barge	ṣandal (m)	صندل
ferry	ʿabbāra (f)	عبّارة
sailing ship	safīna ʃeraʿiya (m)	سفينة شراعيّة
brigantine	markeb ʃerāʿy (m)	مركب شراعي
ice breaker	moḥaṭṭemet galīd (f)	محطّمة جليد
submarine	ɣawwāṣa (f)	غوّاصة
boat (flat-bottomed ~)	markeb (m)	مركب
dinghy (lifeboat)	zawraʾ (m)	زورق
lifeboat	qāreb nagah (m)	قارب نجاة
motorboat	lunʃ (m)	لنش
captain	ʾobṭān (m)	قبطان
seaman	baḥḥār (m)	بحّار
sailor	baḥḥār (m)	بحّار
crew	ṭāqem (m)	طاقم
boatswain	rabbān (m)	ربّان
ship's boy	ṣaby el safīna (m)	صبي السفينة
cook	ṭabbāχ (m)	طبّاخ
ship's doctor	ṭabīb el safīna (m)	طبيب السفينة
deck	saṭ-ḥ el safīna (m)	سطح السفينة
mast	sāreya (f)	سارية
sail	ʃerāʿ (m)	شراع
hold	ʿanbar (m)	عنبر
bow (prow)	moʾaddema (m)	مقدّمة
stern	moʾaχeret el safīna (f)	مؤخّرة السفينة
oar	megdāf (m)	مجداف
screw propeller	marwaḥa (f)	مروّحة
cabin	kabīna (f)	كابينة
wardroom	ɣorfet el ṭaʿām wel rāḥa (f)	غرفة الطعام والراحة
engine room	qesm el ʾālāt (m)	قسم الآلات
bridge	borg el qeyāda (m)	برج القيادة
radio room	ɣorfet el lāselky (f)	غرفة اللاسلكي
wave (radio)	mouga (f)	موجة
logbook	segel el safīna (m)	سجل السفينة
spyglass	monzār (m)	منظار
bell	garas (m)	جرس

flag	ʿalam (m)	علم
hawser (mooring ~)	ḥabl (m)	حبل
knot (bowline, etc.)	ʿoʾda (f)	عقدة
deckrails	drabzīn saṭ-ḥ el safīna (m)	درابزين سطح السفينة
gangway	sellem (m)	سلّم
anchor	marsāh (f)	مرساة
to weigh anchor	rafaʿ morsah	رفع مرساة
to drop anchor	rasa	رسا
anchor chain	selselet morsah (f)	سلسلة مرساة
port (harbour)	mināʾ (m)	ميناء
quay, wharf	marsa (m)	مرسى
to berth (moor)	rasa	رسا
to cast off	aqlaʿ	أقلع
trip, voyage	reḥla (f)	رحلة
cruise (sea trip)	reḥla baḥariya (f)	رحلة بحريّة
course (route)	masār (m)	مسار
route (itinerary)	ṭarīʾ (m)	طريق
fairway (safe water channel)	magra melāḥy (m)	مجرى ملاحيّ
shallows	meyāh ḍaḥla (f)	مياه ضحلة
to run aground	ganaḥ	جنح
storm	ʿāṣefa (f)	عاصفة
signal	eʃara (f)	إشارة
to sink (vi)	ɣereʾ	غرق
Man overboard!	saʾaṭ rāgil min el sefīna!	سقط راجل من السفينة!
SOS (distress signal)	nedāʾ eɣāsa (m)	نداء إغاثة
ring buoy	ṭoʾe nagah (m)	طوق نجاة

144. Airport

airport	maṭār (m)	مطار
aeroplane	ṭayāra (f)	طيّارة
airline	ʃerket ṭayarān (f)	شركة طيران
air traffic controller	marākeb el ḥaraka el gawiya (m)	مراكب الحركة الجويّة
departure	moɣadra (f)	مغادرة
arrival	woṣūl (m)	وصول
to arrive (by plane)	weṣel	وصل
departure time	waʾt el moɣadra (m)	وقت المغادرة
arrival time	waʾt el woṣūl (m)	وقت الوصول
to be delayed	taʾakχar	تأخّر
flight delay	taʾaχor el reḥla (m)	تأخّر الرحلة
information board	lawḥet el maʿlomāt (f)	لوحة المعلومات
information	esteʿlamāt (pl)	إستعلامات
to announce (vt)	aʿlan	أعلن

flight (e.g. next ~)	reḥlet ṭayarān (f)	رحلة طيران
customs	gamārek (pl)	جمارك
customs officer	mowazzaf el gamārek (m)	موظّف الجمارك
customs declaration	taṣrīḥ gomroky (m)	تصريح جمركي
to fill in (vt)	mala	ملا
to fill in the declaration	mala el taṣrīḥ	ملأ التصريح
passport control	taftīʃ el gawazāt (m)	تفتيش الجوازات
luggage	el ʃonaṭ (pl)	الشنط
hand luggage	ʃonaṭ el yad (pl)	شنط اليد
luggage trolley	ʿarabet ʃonaṭ (f)	عربة شنط
landing	hobūṭ (m)	هبوط
landing strip	mamarr el hobūṭ (m)	ممرّ الهبوط
to land (vi)	habaṭ	هبط
airstair (passenger stair)	sellem el ṭayāra (m)	سلّم الطيّارة
check-in	tasgīl (m)	تسجيل
check-in counter	makān tasgīl (m)	مكان تسجيل
to check-in (vi)	saggel	سجّل
boarding card	beṭāqet el rokūb (f)	بطاقة الركوب
departure gate	bawwābet el moɣadra (f)	بوّابة المغادرة
transit	tranzīt (m)	ترانزيت
to wait (vt)	estanna	إستنّى
departure lounge	ṣālet el moɣadra (f)	صالة المغادرة
to see off	waddaʿ	ودّع
to say goodbye	waddaʿ	ودّع

145. Bicycle. Motorcycle

bicycle	beskeletta (f)	بيسكلتّة
scooter	fezba (f)	فزبة
motorbike	moṭosekl (m)	موتوسيكل
to go by bicycle	rāḥ bel beskeletta	راح بالبسكلتّة
handlebars	moqawwed (m)	مقوّد
pedal	dawwāsa (f)	دوّاسة
brakes	farāmel (pl)	فرامل
bicycle seat (saddle)	korsy (m)	كرسي
pump	ṭolommba (f)	طلمّبة
pannier rack	raff el amteʿa (m)	رفّ الأمتعة
front lamp	el meṣbāḥ el amāmy (m)	المصباح الأمامي
helmet	χawza (f)	خوذة
wheel	ʿagala (f)	عجلة
mudguard	refrāf (m)	رفراف
rim	eṭār (m)	إطار
spoke	mekbaḥ el ʿagala (m)	مكبح العجلة

Cars

146. Types of cars

car	sayāra (f)	سيّارة
sports car	sayāra reyāḍiya (f)	سيّارة رياضيّة
limousine	limozīn (m)	ليموزين
off-road vehicle	sayāret ṭoro' wa'ra (f)	سيّارة طرق وعرة
drophead coupé (convertible)	kabryoleyh (m)	كابريوليه
minibus	mikrobāṣ (m)	ميكروباص
ambulance	es'āf (m)	إسعاف
snowplough	garrāfet talg (f)	جرّافة ثلج
lorry	ʃāḥena (f)	شاحنة
road tanker	nāqelet betrūl (f)	ناقلة بترول
van (small truck)	'arabiyet na'l (f)	عربيّة نقل
tractor unit	garrār (m)	جرّار
trailer	ma'ṭūra (f)	مقطورة
comfortable (adj)	morīḥ	مريح
used (adj)	mosta'mal	مستعمل

147. Cars. Bodywork

bonnet	kabbūt (m)	كبوّت
wing	refrāf (m)	رفراف
roof	sa'f (m)	سقف
windscreen	ezāz amāmy (f)	إزاز أمامي
rear-view mirror	merāya daχeliya (f)	مراية داخلية
windscreen washer	monazzef el ezāz el amāmy (m)	منظّف الإزاز الأمامي
windscreen wipers	massāḥāt (pl)	مسّاحات
side window	ʃebbāk gāneby (m)	شبّاك جانبي
electric window	ezāz kahrabā'y (m)	إزاز كهربائي
aerial	hawā'y (m)	هوائي
sunroof	fat-ḥet el sa'f (f)	فتحة السقف
bumper	ekṣedām (m)	اكصدام
boot	ʃanṭet el 'arabiya (f)	شنطة العربيّة
roof luggage rack	raff sa'f el 'arabiya (m)	رفّ سقف العربيّة
door	bāb (m)	باب
door handle	okret el bāb (f)	اوكرة الباب
door lock	'efl el bāb (m)	قفل الباب
number plate	lawḥet raqam el sayāra (f)	لوحة رقم السيارة

silencer	kātem lel ṣote (m)	كاتم للصوت
petrol tank	χazzān el banzīn (m)	خزّان البنزين
exhaust pipe	anbūb el ʿādem (m)	أنبوب العادم
accelerator	ɣāz (m)	غاز
pedal	dawwāsa (f)	دوّاسة
accelerator pedal	dawwāset el banzīn (f)	دوّاسة البنزين
brake	farāmel (pl)	فرامل
brake pedal	dawwāset el farāmel (m)	دوّاسة الفرامل
to brake (use the brake)	farmel	فرمل
handbrake	farāmel el enteẓār (pl)	فرامل الإنتظار
clutch	klatʃ (m)	كلتش
clutch pedal	dawwāset el klatʃ (f)	دوّاسة الكلتش
clutch disc	ʾorṣ el klatʃ (m)	قرص الكلتش
shock absorber	momtaṣṣ lel ṣadamāt (m)	ممتصّ للصدمات
wheel	ʿagala (f)	عجلة
spare tyre	ʿagala eḥteyāṭy (f)	عجلة إحتياطية
tyre	eṭār (m)	إطار
wheel cover (hubcap)	ṭīs (m)	طيس
driving wheels	ʿagalāt el qeyāda (pl)	عجلات القيادة
front-wheel drive (as adj)	dafʿ amāmy (m)	دفع أمامي
rear-wheel drive (as adj)	dafʿ χalfy (m)	دفع خلفي
all-wheel drive (as adj)	dafʿ kāmel (m)	دفع كامل
gearbox	gearboks (m)	جير بوكس
automatic (adj)	otomatīky	أوتوماتيكي
mechanical (adj)	mikanīky	ميكانيكي
gear lever	meqbaḍ nāqel lel ḥaraka (m)	مقبض ناقل الحركة
headlamp	el meṣbāḥ el amāmy (m)	المصباح الأمامي
headlights	el maṣabīḥ el amamiya (pl)	المصابيح الأمامية
dipped headlights	nūr moʾaʃer monχafeḍ (pl)	نور مؤشر منخفض
full headlights	nūr moʾasʃer ʿāly (m)	نور مؤشر عالي
brake light	nūr el farāmel (m)	نور الفرامل
sidelights	lambet el enteẓār (f)	لمبة الإنتظار
hazard lights	eʃārāt el taḥzīr (pl)	إشارات التحذير
fog lights	kasʃāf el ḍabāb (m)	كشّاف الضباب
turn indicator	eʃāret el enʿeṭāf (f)	إشارة الإنعطاف
reversing light	ḍūʾ el rogūʿ lel χalf (m)	ضوء الرجوع للخلف

148. Cars. Passenger compartment

car interior	ṣalone el sayāra (m)	صالون السيارة
leather (as adj)	men el geld	من الجلد
velour (as adj)	men el moχmal	من المخمل
upholstery	tangīd (m)	تنجيد
instrument (gage)	gehāz (m)	جهاز
dashboard	lawḥet ag-heza (f)	لوحة أجهزة

speedometer	me'yās sor'a (m)	مقياس سرعة
needle (pointer)	mo'asʃer (m)	مؤشّر
mileometer	'addād el mesafāt (m)	عدّاد المسافات
indicator (sensor)	'addād (m)	عدّاد
level	mostawa (m)	مستوى
warning light	lammbet enzār (f)	لمّبة إنذار
steering wheel	moqawwed (m)	مقوّد
horn	kalaks (m)	كلاكس
button	zerr (m)	زرّ
switch	nāqel, meftāḥ (m)	ناقل, مفتاح
seat	korsy (m)	كرسي
backrest	masnad el ḍahr (m)	مسند الظهر
headrest	masnad el ra's (m)	مسند الرأس
seat belt	ḥezām el amān (m)	حزام الأمان
to fasten the belt	rabaṭ el ḥezām	ربط الحزام
adjustment (of seats)	ḍabṭ (m)	ضبط
airbag	wesāda hawa'iya (f)	وسادة هوائية
air-conditioner	takyīf (m)	تكييف
radio	radio (m)	راديو
CD player	moʃagɣel sidi (m)	مشغّل سي دي
to turn on	fataḥ, ʃagɣal	فتح, شغّل
aerial	hawā'y (m)	هوائي
glove box	dorg (m)	درج
ashtray	ṭa'ṭū'a (f)	طقطوقة

149. Cars. Engine

engine	moḥarrek (m)	محرّك
motor	motore (m)	موتور
diesel (as adj)	'alal diesel	على الديزل
petrol (as adj)	'alal banzīn	على البنزين
engine volume	ḥagm el moḥarrek (m)	حجم المحرّك
power	'owwa (f)	قوّة
horsepower	ḥoṣān (m)	حصان
piston	mekbas (m)	مكبس
cylinder	esṭewāna (f)	أسطوانة
valve	ṣamām (m)	صمام
injector	baχāχa (f)	بخّاخة
generator (alternator)	mowalled (m)	مولّد
carburettor	karburetor (m)	كاربراتير
motor oil	zeyt el moḥarrek (m)	زيت المحرّك
radiator	radiator (m)	رادياتير
coolant	mobarred (m)	مبرّد
cooling fan	marwaḥa (f)	مروحة
battery (accumulator)	baṭṭariya (f)	بطّاريّة
starter	meftāḥ el taʃɣīl (m)	مفتاح التشغيل

ignition	nezām taʃɣīl (m)	نظام تشغيل
sparking plug	ʃam'et el eḥterāq (f)	شمعة الإحتراق
terminal (battery ~)	ṭaraf tawṣīl (m)	طرف توصيل
positive terminal	ṭaraf muwgeb (m)	طرف موجب
negative terminal	ṭaraf sāleb (m)	طرف سالب
fuse	fetīl (m)	فتيل
air filter	ṣaffāyet el hawā' (f)	صفّاية الهواء
oil filter	ṣaffāyet el zeyt (f)	صفّاية الزيت
fuel filter	ṣaffāyet el banzīn (f)	صفّاية البنزين

150. Cars. Crash. Repair

car crash	ḥadset sayāra (f)	حادثة سيارة
traffic accident	ḥādes morūry (m)	حادث مروري
to crash (into the wall, etc.)	χabaṭ	خبط
to get smashed up	daʃdaʃ	دشدش
damage	χesāra (f)	خسارة
intact (unscathed)	salīm	سليم
to break down (vi)	ta'aṭṭal	تعطّل
towrope	ḥabl el saḥb	حبل السحب
puncture	soqb (m)	ثقب
to have a puncture	fasʃ	فشّ
to pump up	nafaχ	نفخ
pressure	ḍaɣṭ (m)	ضغط
to check (to examine)	eχtabar	إختبر
repair	taṣlīḥ (m)	تصليح
garage (auto service shop)	warʃet taṣlīḥ 'arabīāt (f)	ورشة تصليح عربيات
spare part	'eṭ'et ɣeyār (f)	قطعة غيار
part	'eṭ'a (f)	قطعة
bolt (with nut)	mesmār 'alawoze (m)	مسمار قلاووظ
screw (fastener)	mesmār (m)	مسمار
nut	ṣamūla (f)	صامولة
washer	warda (f)	وردة
bearing (e.g. ball ~)	maḥmal (m)	محمل
tube	anbūba (f)	أنبوبة
gasket (head ~)	'az'a (f)	عزقة
cable, wire	selk (m)	سلك
jack	'afrīṭa (f)	عفريطة
spanner	meftāḥ rabṭ (m)	مفتاح ربط
hammer	ʃakūʃ (m)	شاكوش
pump	ṭolommba (f)	طلمّبة
screwdriver	mefakk (m)	مفكّ
fire extinguisher	ṭaffayet ḥarī' (f)	طفّاية حريق
warning triangle	eʃāret taḥzīr (f)	إشارة تحذير
to stall (vi)	et'aṭṭal	إتعطّل

stall (n)	tawaqqof (m)	توقّف
to be broken	kān maksūr	كان مكسور
to overheat (vi)	soχn aktar men el lāzem	سخن أكثر من اللازم
to be clogged up	kān masdūd	كان مسدود
to freeze up (pipes, etc.)	etgammed	إتجمّد
to burst (vi, ab. tube)	enqaṭaʿ - ett'aṭṭaʿ	إنقطع
pressure	ḍaɣṭ (m)	ضغط
level	mostawa (m)	مستوى
slack (~ belt)	ḍaʿīf	ضعيف
dent	ṭaʿga (f)	طعجة
knocking noise (engine)	da'' (m)	دقّ
crack	ʃa'' (m)	شقّ
scratch	χadʃ (m)	خدش

151. Cars. Road

road	ṭarī' (m)	طريق
motorway	ṭarī' sareeʿ (m)	طريق سريع
highway	otostrad (m)	اوتوستراد
direction (way)	ettegāh (m)	إتّجاه
distance	masāfa (f)	مسافة
bridge	kobry (m)	كبري
car park	maw'ef el ʿarabeyāt (m)	موقف العربيات
square	medān (m)	ميدان
road junction	taqāṭoʿ ṭoro' (m)	تقاطع طرق
tunnel	nafa' (m)	نفق
petrol station	maḥaṭṭet banzīn (f)	محطّة بنزين
car park	maw'ef el ʿarabeyāt (m)	موقف العربيات
petrol pump	maḍaχet banzīn (f)	مضخّة بنزين
auto repair shop	warʃet taṣlīḥ ʿarabīāt (f)	ورشة تصليح عربيات
to fill up	mala banzīn	ملى بنزين
fuel	woqūd (m)	وقود
jerrycan	ʒerken (m)	جركن
asphalt, tarmac	asfalt (m)	اسفلت
road markings	ʿalamāt el ṭarī' (pl)	علامات الطريق
kerb	bardora (f)	بردورة
crash barrier	sūr (m)	سور
ditch	terʿa (f)	ترعة
roadside (shoulder)	ḥaffet el ṭarī' (f)	حافّة الطريق
lamppost	ʿamūd nūr (m)	عمود نور
to drive (a car)	sā'	ساق
to turn (e.g., ~ left)	ḥād	حاد
to make a U-turn	laff fe u-turn	لفّ في يو تيرن
reverse (~ gear)	ḥaraka ela al warā' (f)	حركة إلى الوراء
to honk (vi)	zammar	زمّر
honk (sound)	kalaks (m)	كلاكس

to get stuck (in the mud, etc.)	ɣaraz	غرّز
to spin the wheels	dawwar	دوّر
to cut, to turn off (vt)	awqaf	أوقف
speed	sorʿa (f)	سرعة
to exceed the speed limit	ʿadda el sorʿa	عدّى السرعة
to give a ticket	farad ɣarāma	فرض غرامة
traffic lights	eʃārāt el morūr (pl)	إشارات المرور
driving licence	roxset el qeyāda (f)	رخصة قيادة
level crossing	maʿbar (m)	معبر
crossroads	taqāṭoʿ (m)	تقاطع
zebra crossing	maʿbar (m)	معبر
bend, curve	monʿaṭaf (m)	منعطف
pedestrian precinct	manteʾa lel moʃāh (f)	منطقة للمشاة

PEOPLE. LIFE EVENTS

152. Holidays. Event

celebration, holiday	ʿīd (m)	عيد
national day	ʿīd waṭany (m)	عيد وطني
public holiday	agāza rasmiya (f)	أجازة رسميّة
to commemorate (vt)	eḥtafal be zekra	إحتفل بذكرى
event (happening)	ḥadass (m)	حدث
event (organized activity)	monasba (f)	مناسبة
banquet (party)	walīma (f)	وليمة
reception (formal party)	ḥaflet esteʾbāl (f)	حفلة إستقبال
feast	walīma (f)	وليمة
anniversary	zekra sanawiya (f)	ذكرى سنوية
jubilee	yobeyl (m)	يوبيل
to celebrate (vt)	eḥtafal	إحتفل
New Year	raʾs el sanna (m)	رأس السنة
Happy New Year!	koll sana wenta ṭayeb!	كلّ سنة وأنت طيّب!
Father Christmas	baba neweyl (m)	بابا نويل
Christmas	ʿīd el melād (m)	عيد الميلاد
Merry Christmas!	ʿīd melād saʿīd!	عيد ميلاد سعيد!
Christmas tree	ʃagaret el kresmas (f)	شجرة الكريسمس
fireworks (fireworks show)	alʿāb nāriya (pl)	ألعاب ناريّة
wedding	faraḥ (m)	فرح
groom	ʿarīs (m)	عريس
bride	ʿarūsa (f)	عروسة
to invite (vt)	ʿazam	عزم
invitation card	beṭāʾet daʿwa (f)	بطاقة دعوة
guest	ḍeyf (m)	ضيف
to visit (~ your parents, etc.)	zār	زار
to meet the guests	estaʾbal ḍoyūf	إستقبل ضيوف
gift, present	hediya (f)	هديّة
to give (sth as present)	edda	إدّى
to receive gifts	estalam hadāya	إستلم هدايا
bouquet (of flowers)	bokeyh (f)	بوكيه
congratulations	tahneʾa (f)	تهنئة
to congratulate (vt)	hanna	هنّأ
greetings card	beṭāʾet tahneʾa (f)	بطاقة تهنئة
to send a postcard	baʿat beṭāʾet tahneʾa	بعت بطاقة تهنئة
to get a postcard	estalam beṭāʾa tahneʾa	استلم بطاقة تهنئة

toast	naχab (m)	نخب
to offer (a drink, etc.)	ḍayaf	ضيّف
champagne	ʃambania (f)	شمبانيا
to enjoy oneself	estamtaʿ	إستمتع
merriment (gaiety)	bahga (f)	بهجة
joy (emotion)	saʿāda (f)	سعادة
dance	raʾṣa (f)	رقصة
to dance (vi, vt)	raʾaṣ	رقص
waltz	valles (m)	فالس
tango	tango (m)	تانجو

153. Funerals. Burial

cemetery	maqbara (f)	مقبرة
grave, tomb	ʾabr (m)	قبر
cross	ṣalīb (m)	صليب
gravestone	ḥagar el maʾʾbara (m)	حجر المقبرة
fence	sūr (m)	سور
chapel	kenīsa saɣīra (f)	كنيسة صغيرة
death	mote (m)	موت
to die (vi)	māt	مات
the deceased	el motawaffy (m)	المتوّفي
mourning	ḥedād (m)	حداد
to bury (vt)	dafan	دفن
undertakers	maktab motaʿahhed el dafn (m)	مكتب متعهّد الدفن
funeral	ganāza (f)	جنازة
wreath	eklīl (m)	إكليل
coffin	tabūt (m)	تابوت
hearse	naʿʃ (m)	نعش
shroud	kafan (m)	كفن
funeral procession	ganāza (f)	جنازة
funerary urn	garra ganaʾeziya (f)	جرّة جنائزية
crematorium	maḥraʾet gosas el mawta (f)	محرقة جثث الموتى
obituary	segel el wafīāt (m)	سجل الوفيات
to cry (weep)	baka	بكى
to sob (vi)	nawwaḥ	نوّح

154. War. Soldiers

platoon	faṣīla (f)	فصيلة
company	serriya (f)	سريّة
regiment	foge (m)	فوج
army	geyʃ (m)	جيش

division	fer'a (f)	فرقة
section, squad	weḥda (f)	وحدة
host (army)	geyʃ (m)	جيش
soldier	gondy (m)	جنّدي
officer	ḍābeṭ (m)	ضابط
private	gondy (m)	جنّدي
sergeant	raqīb tāny (m)	رقيب تاني
lieutenant	molāzem tāny (m)	ملازم تاني
captain	naqīb (m)	نقيب
major	rā'ed (m)	رائد
colonel	'aqīd (m)	عقيد
general	ʒenerāl (m)	جنرال
sailor	baḥḥār (m)	بحّار
captain	'obṭān (m)	قبطان
boatswain	rabbān (m)	ربّان
artilleryman	gondy fe selāḥ el madfa'iya (m)	جنّدي في سلاح المدفعيّة
paratrooper	selāḥ el maẓallāt (m)	سلاح المظلّلات
pilot	ṭayār (m)	طيّار
navigator	mallāḥ (m)	ملاّح
mechanic	mikanīky (m)	ميكانيكي
pioneer (sapper)	mohandes 'askary (m)	مهندس عسكري
parachutist	gondy el baraʃot (m)	جنّدي الباراشوت
reconnaissance scout	kaʃāfet el esteṭlā' (f)	كشّافة الإستطلاع
sniper	qannāṣ (m)	قنّاص
patrol (group)	dawriya (f)	دوّريّة
to patrol (vt)	'ām be dawriya	قام بدوريّة
sentry, guard	ḥāres (m)	حارس
warrior	muḥāreb (m)	محارب
patriot	waṭany (m)	وطني
hero	baṭal (m)	بطل
heroine	baṭala (f)	بطلة
traitor	χāyen (m)	خاين
to betray (vt)	χān	خان
deserter	hāreb men el gondiya (m)	هارب من الجنديّة
to desert (vi)	farr men el geyʃ	فرّ من الجيش
mercenary	ma'gūr (m)	مأجور
recruit	gondy gedīd (m)	جنّدي جديد
volunteer	motaṭawwe' (m)	متطوّع
dead (n)	'atīl (m)	قتيل
wounded (n)	garīḥ (m)	جريح
prisoner of war	asīr ḥarb (m)	أسير حرب

155. War. Military actions. Part 1

war	ḥarb (f)	حرب
to be at war	ḥārab	حارب
civil war	ḥarb ahliya (f)	حرب أهليّة
treacherously (adv)	ɣadran	غدراً
declaration of war	eʿlān ḥarb (m)	إعلان حرب
to declare (~ war)	aʿlan	أعلن
aggression	ʿedwān (m)	عدوان
to attack (invade)	hagam	هجم
to invade (vt)	eḥtall	إحتلّ
invader	moḥtell (m)	محتلّ
conqueror	fāteḥ (m)	فاتح
defence	defāʿ (m)	دفاع
to defend (a country, etc.)	dāfaʿ	دافع
to defend (against ...)	dāfaʿ ʿan ...	... دافع عن
enemy	ʿadeww (m)	عدوّ
foe, adversary	χeṣm (m)	خصم
enemy (as adj)	ʿadeww	عدوّ
strategy	estrateʒiya (f)	إستراتيجيّة
tactics	taktīk (m)	تكتيك
order	amr (m)	أمر
command (order)	amr (m)	أمر
to order (vt)	amar	أمر
mission	mohemma (f)	مهمّة
secret (adj)	serry	سرّي
battle	maʿraka (f)	معركة
combat	ʾetāl (m)	قتال
attack	hogūm (m)	هجوم
charge (assault)	enqeḍāḍ (m)	إنقضاض
to storm (vt)	enqaḍḍ	إنقضّ
siege (to be under ~)	ḥeṣār (m)	حصار
offensive (n)	hogūm (m)	هجوم
to go on the offensive	hagam	هجم
retreat	enseḥāb (m)	إنسحاب
to retreat (vi)	ensaḥab	إنسحب
encirclement	eḥāṭa (f)	إحاطة
to encircle (vt)	aḥāṭ	أحاط
bombing (by aircraft)	ʾaṣf (m)	قصف
to drop a bomb	asqaṭ qonbola	أسقط قنبلة
to bomb (vt)	ʾaṣaf	قصف
explosion	enfegār (m)	إنفجار
shot	ṭalʾa (f)	طلقة

to fire (~ a shot)	aṭlaq el nār	أطلق النار
firing (burst of ~)	eṭlāq nār (m)	إطلاق نار
to aim (to point a weapon)	ṣawwab ʿala …	صوّب على ...
to point (a gun)	ṣawwab	صوّب
to hit (the target)	aṣāb el hadaf	أصاب الهدف
to sink (~ a ship)	aɣraʾ	أغرق
hole (in a ship)	soqb (m)	ثقب
to founder, to sink (vi)	ɣereʾ	غرق
front (war ~)	gabha (f)	جبهة
evacuation	eχlāʾ (m)	إخلاء
to evacuate (vt)	aχla	أخلى
trench	χondoq (m)	خندق
barbed wire	aslāk ʃāʾeka (pl)	أسلاك شائكة
barrier (anti tank ~)	ḥāgez (m)	حاجز
watchtower	borg moraʾba (m)	برج مراقبة
military hospital	mostaʃfa ʿaskary (m)	مستشفى عسكري
to wound (vt)	garaḥ	جرح
wound	garḥ (m)	جرح
wounded (n)	garīḥ (m)	جريح
to be wounded	oṣīb bel garḥ	أصيب بالجرح
serious (wound)	χaṭīr	خطير

156. Weapons

weapons	asleḥa (pl)	أسلحة
firearms	asleḥa nāriya (pl)	أسلحة ناريّة
cold weapons (knives, etc.)	asleḥa bayḍāʾ (pl)	أسلحة بيضاء
chemical weapons	asleḥa kemawiya (pl)	أسلحة كيماويّة
nuclear (adj)	nawawy	نووي
nuclear weapons	asleḥa nawawiya (pl)	أسلحة نوويّة
bomb	qonbela (f)	قنبلة
atomic bomb	qonbela nawawiya (f)	قنبلة نوويّة
pistol (gun)	mosaddas (m)	مسدّس
rifle	bondoqiya (f)	بندقيّة
submachine gun	mosaddas rasʃāʃ (m)	مسدّس رشّاش
machine gun	rasʃāʃ (m)	رشّاش
muzzle	fawha (f)	فوهة
barrel	anbūba (f)	أنبوبة
calibre	ʿeyār (m)	عيار
trigger	zanād (m)	زناد
sight (aiming device)	moṣawweb (m)	مصوّب
magazine	maχzan (m)	مخزن
butt (shoulder stock)	ʿaqab el bondoʾiya (m)	عقب البندقيّة
hand grenade	qonbela yadawiya (f)	قنبلة يدويّة

explosive	mawād motafaggera (pl)	مواد متفجّرة
bullet	roṣāṣa (f)	رصاصة
cartridge	χarṭūʃa (f)	خرطوشة
charge	ḥaʃwa (f)	حشوة
ammunition	zaχīra (f)	ذخيرة
bomber (aircraft)	qazefet qanābel (f)	قاذفة قنابل
fighter	ṭayāra muqātela (f)	طيّارة مقاتلة
helicopter	heliokobter (m)	هليكوبتر
anti-aircraft gun	madfaʿ moḍād lel ṭaʾerāṭ (m)	مدفع مضاد للطائرات
tank	dabbāba (f)	دبّابة
tank gun	madfaʿ el dabbāba (m)	مدفع الدبّابة
artillery	madfaʿiya (f)	مدفعيّة
gun (cannon, howitzer)	madfaʿ (m)	مدفع
to lay (a gun)	ṣawwab	صوّب
shell (projectile)	qazīfa (f)	قذيفة
mortar bomb	qonbela hawn (f)	قنبلة هاون
mortar	hawn (m)	هاون
splinter (shell fragment)	ʃazya (f)	شظية
submarine	ɣawwāṣa (f)	غوّاصة
torpedo	ṭorbīd (m)	طوربيد
missile	ṣarūχ (m)	صاروخ
to load (gun)	ʿammar	عمّر
to shoot (vi)	ḍarab bel nār	ضرب بالنار
to point at (the cannon)	ṣawwab ʿala …	صوّب على ...
bayonet	ḥerba (f)	حربة
rapier	seyf zu ḥaddeyn (m)	سيف ذو حدّين
sabre (e.g. cavalry ~)	seyf monḥany (m)	سيف منحني
spear (weapon)	remḥ (m)	رمح
bow	qose (m)	قوس
arrow	sahm (m)	سهم
musket	musket (m)	مسكيت
crossbow	qose mostaʿraḍ (m)	قوس مستعرض

157. Ancient people

primitive (prehistoric)	bedāʾy	بدائي
prehistoric (adj)	ma qabl el tarīχ	ما قبل التاريخ
ancient (~ civilization)	ʾadīm	قديم
Stone Age	el ʿaṣr el ḥagary (m)	العصر الحجري
Bronze Age	el ʿaṣr el bronzy (m)	العصر البرونزي
Ice Age	el ʿaṣr el galīdy (m)	العصر الجليدي
tribe	qabīla (f)	قبيلة
cannibal	ʾākel loḥūm el baʃar (m)	آكل لحوم البشر
hunter	ṣayād (m)	صيّاد
to hunt (vi, vt)	eṣṭād	إصطاد

mammoth	mamūθ (m)	ماموث
cave	kahf (m)	كهف
fire	nār (f)	نار
campfire	nār moχayem (m)	نار مخيّم
cave painting	rasm fel kahf (m)	رسم في الكهف
tool (e.g. stone axe)	adah (f)	أداة
spear	remḥ (m)	رمح
stone axe	fa'ʼs ḥagary (m)	فأس حجري
to be at war	ḥārab	حارب
to domesticate (vt)	estaʼnas	استئنس
idol	ṣanam (m)	صنم
to worship (vt)	ʻabad	عبد
superstition	χorāfa (f)	خرافة
rite	mansak (m)	منسك
evolution	taṭṭawwor (m)	تطوّر
development	nomoww (m)	نموّ
disappearance (extinction)	enqerāḍ (m)	إنقراض
to adapt oneself	takayaf (maʻ)	(تكيّف (مع
archaeology	ʻelm el ʼāsār (m)	علم الآثار
archaeologist	ʻālem āsār (m)	عالم آثار
archaeological (adj)	asary	أثري
excavation site	mawqeʻ ḥafr (m)	موّقع حفر
excavations	tanqīb (m)	تنقيب
find (object)	ekteʃāf (m)	إكتشاف
fragment	ʼeṭʻa (f)	قطعة

158. Middle Ages

people (ethnic group)	ʃaʻb (m)	شعب
peoples	ʃoʻūb (pl)	شعوب
tribe	qabīla (f)	قبيلة
tribes	qabāʼel (pl)	قبائل
barbarians	el barabra (pl)	البرابرة
Gauls	el ɣaliyūn (pl)	الغاليّون
Goths	el qūṭiyūn (pl)	القوطيون
Slavs	el selāf (pl)	السلاف
Vikings	el viking (pl)	الفايكينج
Romans	el romān (pl)	الرومان
Roman (adj)	romāny	روماني
Byzantines	bizanṭiyūn (pl)	بيزنطيون
Byzantium	bīzanṭa (f)	بيزنطة
Byzantine (adj)	bīzanṭy	بيزنطي
emperor	embraṭore (m)	إمبراطور
leader, chief (tribal ~)	zaʻīm (m)	زعيم
powerful (~ king)	gabbār	جبّار

king	malek (m)	ملك
ruler (sovereign)	ḥākem (m)	حاكم
knight	fāres (m)	فارس
feudal lord	eqṭāʿy (m)	إقطاعي
feudal (adj)	eqṭāʿy	إقطاعي
vassal	ḥākem tābeʿ (m)	حاكم تابع
duke	dūʾ (m)	دوق
earl	earl (m)	ايرل
baron	barūn (m)	بارون
bishop	asqof (m)	أسقف
armour	derʿ (m)	درع
shield	derʿ (m)	درع
sword	seyf (m)	سيف
visor	ḥaffa amamiya lel χoza (f)	حافة أماميّة للخوذة
chainmail	derʿ el zard (m)	درع الزرد
Crusade	ḥamla ṣalībiya (f)	حملة صليبيّة
crusader	ṣalīby (m)	صليبي
territory	arḍ (f)	أرض
to attack (invade)	hagam	هجم
to conquer (vt)	fataḥ	فتح
to occupy (invade)	eḥtall	إحتلّ
siege (to be under ~)	ḥeṣār (m)	حصار
besieged (adj)	moḥāṣar	محاصر
to besiege (vt)	ḥāṣar	حاصر
inquisition	maḥākem el taftīʃ (pl)	محاكم التفتيش
inquisitor	mofatteʃ (m)	مفتّش
torture	taʿzīb (m)	تعذيب
cruel (adj)	waḥʃy	وحشي
heretic	moharṭeq (m)	مهرطق
heresy	harṭaʾa (f)	هرطقة
seafaring	el safar bel baḥr (m)	السفر بالبحر
pirate	ʾorṣān (m)	قرصان
piracy	ʾarṣana (f)	قرصنة
boarding (attack)	mohagmet safīna (f)	مهاجمة سفينة
loot, booty	ɣanīma (f)	غنيمة
treasure	konūz (pl)	كنوز
discovery	ekteʃāf (m)	إكتشاف
to discover (new land, etc.)	ektaʃaf	إكتشف
expedition	beʿsa (f)	بعثة
musketeer	fāres (m)	فارس
cardinal	kardinal (m)	كاردينال
heraldry	ʃeʿārāt el nabāla (pl)	شعارات النبالة
heraldic (adj)	χāṣṣ be ʃeʿarāt el nebāla	خاصّ بشعارات النبالة

159. Leader. Chief. Authorities

king	malek (m)	ملك
queen	maleka (f)	ملكة
royal (adj)	malaky	ملكي
kingdom	mamlaka (f)	مملكة
prince	amīr (m)	أمير
princess	amīra (f)	أميرة
president	ra'īs (m)	رئيس
vice-president	nā'eb el ra'īs (m)	نائب الرئيس
senator	'oḍw magles el ʃoyūχ (m)	عضو مجلس الشيوخ
monarch	'āhel (m)	عاهل
ruler (sovereign)	ḥākem (m)	حاكم
dictator	dektatore (m)	ديكتاتور
tyrant	ṭāɣeya (f)	طاغية
magnate	ra'smāly kebīr (m)	رأسمالي كبير
director	modīr (m)	مدير
chief	ra'īs (m)	رئيس
manager (director)	modīr (m)	مدير
boss	ra'īs (m)	رئيس
owner	ṣāḥeb (m)	صاحب
leader	za'īm (m)	زعيم
head (~ of delegation)	ra'īs (m)	رئيس
authorities	solṭāt (pl)	سلطات
superiors	ro'asā' (pl)	رؤساء
governor	muḥāfeẓ (m)	محافظ
consul	qonṣol (m)	قنصل
diplomat	deblomāsy (m)	دبلوماسي
mayor	ra'īs el baladiya (m)	رئيس البلديّة
sheriff	ʃerīf (m)	شريف
emperor	embraṭore (m)	إمبراطور
tsar, czar	qayṣar (m)	قيصر
pharaoh	fer'one (m)	فرعون
khan	χān (m)	خان

160. Breaking the law. Criminals. Part 1

bandit	qāṭe' ṭarī' (m)	قاطع طريق
crime	garīma (f)	جريمة
criminal (person)	mogrem (m)	مجرم
thief	sāre' (m)	سارق
to steal (vi, vt)	sara'	سرق
stealing, theft	ser'a (f)	سرقة
to kidnap (vt)	χaṭaf	خطف
kidnapping	χaṭf (m)	خطف

kidnapper	χāṭef (m)	خاطف
ransom	fedya (f)	فدية
to demand ransom	ṭalab fedya	طلب فدية
to rob (vt)	nahab	نهب
robbery	nahb (m)	نهب
robber	nahhāb (m)	نهّاب
to extort (vt)	balṭag	بلطج
extortionist	balṭagy (m)	بلطجي
extortion	balṭaga (f)	بلطجة
to murder, to kill	ʾatal	قتل
murder	ʾatl (m)	قتل
murderer	qātel (m)	قاتل
gunshot	ṭalʾet nār (f)	طلقة نار
to fire (~ a shot)	aṭlaq el nār	أطلق النار
to shoot to death	ʾatal bel roṣāṣ	قتل بالرصاص
to shoot (vi)	ḍarab bel nār	ضرب بالنار
shooting	ḍarb nār (m)	ضرب نار
incident (fight, etc.)	ḥādes (m)	حادث
fight, brawl	χenāʾa (f)	خناقة
Help!	sāʿidni	ساعدني!
victim	ḍaḥiya (f)	ضحيّة
to damage (vt)	χarrab	خرّب
damage	χesāra (f)	خسارة
dead body, corpse	gossa (f)	جثّة
grave (~ crime)	χaṭīra	خطيرة
to attack (vt)	hagam	هجم
to beat (to hit)	ḍarab	ضرب
to beat up	ḍarab	ضرب
to take (rob of sth)	salab	سلب
to stab to death	ṭaʿan ḥatta el mote	طعن حتّى الموت
to maim (vt)	ʃawwah	شوّه
to wound (vt)	garaḥ	جرح
blackmail	ebtezāz (m)	إبتزاز
to blackmail (vt)	ebtazz	إبتزّ
blackmailer	mobtazz (m)	مبتزّ
protection racket	balṭaga (f)	بلطجة
racketeer	mobtazz (m)	مبتزّ
gangster	ragol ʿeṣāba (m)	رجل عصابة
mafia	mafia (f)	مافيا
pickpocket	nasʃāl (m)	نشّال
burglar	leṣṣ beyūt (m)	لص بيوت
smuggling	tahrīb (m)	تهريب
smuggler	moharreb (m)	مهرّب
forgery	tazwīr (m)	تزوير
to forge (counterfeit)	zawwar	زوّر
fake (forged)	mozawwara	مزوّرة

161. Breaking the law. Criminals. Part 2

rape	eɣteṣāb (m)	إغتصاب
to rape (vt)	eɣtaṣab	إغتصب
rapist	moɣtaṣeb (m)	مغتصب
maniac	mahwūs (m)	مهووس
prostitute (fem.)	mommos (f)	مومّس
prostitution	da'āra (f)	دعارة
pimp	qawwād (m)	قوّاد
drug addict	modmen moχaddarāt (m)	مدمن مخدّرات
drug dealer	tāger moχaddarāt (m)	تاجر مخدّرات
to blow up (bomb)	faggar	فجّر
explosion	enfegār (m)	إنفجار
to set fire	aʃ'al el nār	أشعل النار
arsonist	moʃ'el ḥarīq 'an 'amd (m)	مشعل حريق عن عمد
terrorism	erhāb (m)	إرهاب
terrorist	erhāby (m)	إرهابي
hostage	rahīna (m)	رهينة
to swindle (deceive)	eḥtāl	إحتال
swindle, deception	eḥteyāl (m)	إحتيال
swindler	moḥtāl (m)	محتال
to bribe (vt)	raʃa	رشا
bribery	erteʃā' (m)	إرتشاء
bribe	raʃwa (f)	رشوة
poison	semm (m)	سمّ
to poison (vt)	sammem	سمّم
to poison oneself	sammem nafsoh	سمّم نفسه
suicide (act)	enteḥār (m)	إنتحار
suicide (person)	montaḥer (m)	منتحر
to threaten (vt)	hadded	هدّد
threat	tahdīd (m)	تهديد
to make an attempt	ḥāwel eɣteyāl	حاول إغتيال
attempt (attack)	moḥawlet eɣteyāl (f)	محاولة إغتيال
to steal (a car)	sara'	سرق
to hijack (a plane)	eχtaṭaf	إختطف
revenge	enteqām (m)	إنتقام
to avenge (get revenge)	entaqam	إنتقم
to torture (vt)	'azzeb	عذّب
torture	ta'zīb (m)	تعذيب
to torment (vt)	'azzeb	عذّب
pirate	'orṣān (m)	قرصان
hooligan	wabaʃ (m)	وبش

armed (adj)	mosallaḥ	مسلّح
violence	ʿonf (m)	عنف
illegal (unlawful)	meʃ qanūniy	مش قانونيّ
spying (espionage)	tagassas (m)	تجسّس
to spy (vi)	tagassas	تجسّس

162. Police. Law. Part 1

justice	qaḍāʾ (m)	قضاء
court (see you in ~)	maḥkama (f)	محكمة
judge	qāḍy (m)	قاضي
jurors	moḥallafīn (pl)	محلّفين
jury trial	qaḍāʾ el muḥallafīn (m)	قضاء المحلّفين
to judge, to try (vt)	ḥakam	حكم
lawyer, barrister	muḥāmy (m)	محامي
defendant	moddaʿy ʿaleyh (m)	مدّعي عليه
dock	ʾafaṣ el ettehām (m)	قفص الإتّهام
charge	ettehām (m)	إتّهام
accused	mottaham (m)	متّهم
sentence	ḥokm (m)	حكم
to sentence (vt)	ḥakam	حكم
guilty (culprit)	gāny (m)	جاني
to punish (vt)	ʿāqab	عاقب
punishment	ʿeqāb (m)	عقاب
fine (penalty)	ɣarāma (f)	غرامة
life imprisonment	segn mada el ḥayah (m)	سجن مدى الحياة
death penalty	ʿoqūbet ʾeʿdām (f)	عقوبة إعدام
electric chair	el korsy el kaharabāʾy (m)	الكرسي الكهربائي
gallows	maʃnaʾa (f)	مشنقة
to execute (vt)	aʿdam	أعدم
execution	eʿdām (m)	إعدام
prison	segn (m)	سجن
cell	zenzāna (f)	زنزانة
escort (convoy)	ḥerāsa (f)	حراسة
prison officer	ḥāres segn (m)	حارس سجن
prisoner	sagīn (m)	سجين
handcuffs	kalabʃāt (pl)	كلابشات
to handcuff (vt)	kalbeʃ	كلبش
prison break	horūb men el segn (m)	هروب من السجن
to break out (vi)	hereb	هرب
to disappear (vi)	eχtafa	إختفى
to release (from prison)	aχla sabīl	أخلى سبيل

amnesty	ʿafw ʿām (m)	عفو عام
police	ʃorṭa (f)	شرطة
police officer	ʃorṭy (m)	شرطي
police station	qesm ʃorṭa (m)	قسم شرطة
truncheon	ʿaṣāya maṭṭāṭiya (f)	عصاية مطّاطية
megaphone (loudhailer)	būʾ (m)	بوق
patrol car	ʿarabiyet dawrīāt (f)	عربيّة دوريات
siren	sarīna (f)	سرينة
to turn on the siren	wallaʿ el sarīna	ولّع السرينة
siren call	ṣote sarīna (m)	صوت سرينة
crime scene	masraḥ el garīma (m)	مسرح الجريمة
witness	ʃāhed (m)	شاهد
freedom	ḥorriya (f)	حرّيّة
accomplice	ʃerīk fel garīma (m)	شريك في الجريمة
to flee (vi)	hereb	هرب
trace (to leave a ~)	asar (m)	أثر

163. Police. Law. Part 2

search (investigation)	baḥs (m)	بحث
to look for ...	dawwar ʿala	دوّر على
suspicion	ʃobha (f)	شبهة
suspicious (e.g., ~ vehicle)	maʃbūh	مشبوه
to stop (cause to halt)	awqaf	أوقّف
to detain (keep in custody)	eʿtaqal	إعتقل
case (lawsuit)	ʾaḍiya (f)	قضيّة
investigation	taḥʾīʾ (m)	تحقيق
detective	moḥaqqeq (m)	محقّق
investigator	mofatteʃ (m)	مفتّش
hypothesis	rewāya (f)	رواية
motive	dāfeʿ (m)	دافع
interrogation	estegwāb (m)	إستجواب
to interrogate (vt)	estagweb	إستجوب
to question (~ neighbors, etc.)	estanṭaʾ	إستنطق
check (identity ~)	faḥṣ (m)	فحص
round-up (raid)	gamʿ (m)	جمع
search (~ warrant)	taftīʃ (m)	تفتيش
chase (pursuit)	moṭarda (f)	مطاردة
to pursue, to chase	ṭārad	طارد
to track (a criminal)	tatabbaʿ	تتبّع
arrest	eʿteqāl (m)	إعتقال
to arrest (sb)	eʿtaqal	اعتقل
to catch (thief, etc.)	ʾabaḍ ʿala	قبض على
capture	ʾabḍ (m)	قبض
document	wasīqa (f)	وثيقة
proof (evidence)	dalīl (m)	دليل

to prove (vt)	asbat	أثبت
footprint	baṣma (f)	بصمة
fingerprints	baṣamāt el aṣābe' (pl)	بصمات الأصابع
piece of evidence	'eṭ'a men el adella (f)	قطعة من الأدلّة
alibi	ḥegget ɣeyāb (f)	حجّة غياب
innocent (not guilty)	barī'	بريء
injustice	ẓolm (m)	ظلم
unjust, unfair (adj)	meʃ 'ādel	مش عادل
criminal (adj)	mogrem	مجرم
to confiscate (vt)	ṣādar	صادر
drug (illegal substance)	moχaddarāt (pl)	مخدّرات
weapon, gun	selāḥ (m)	سلاح
to disarm (vt)	garrad men el selāḥ	جرّد من السلاح
to order (command)	amar	أمر
to disappear (vi)	eχtafa	إختفى
law	qanūn (m)	قانون
legal, lawful (adj)	qanūny	قانوني
illegal, illicit (adj)	meʃ qanūny	مش قانوني
responsibility (blame)	mas'oliya (f)	مسؤوليّة
responsible (adj)	mas'ūl (m)	مسؤول

NATURE

The Earth. Part 1

164. Outer space

space	faḍā' (m)	فضاء
space (as adj)	faḍā'y	فضائي
outer space	el faḍā' el χāregy (m)	الفضاء الخارجي
world	'ālam (m)	عالم
universe	el kōn (m)	الكون
galaxy	el magarra (f)	المجرّة
star	negm (m)	نجم
constellation	borg (m)	برج
planet	kawwkab (m)	كوكب
satellite	'amar ṣenā'y (m)	قمر صناعي
meteorite	nayzek (m)	نيزك
comet	mozannab (m)	مذنّب
asteroid	kowaykeb (m)	كويكب
orbit	madār (m)	مدار
to revolve (~ around the Earth)	dār	دار
atmosphere	el ɣelāf el gawwy (m)	الغلاف الجوّي
the Sun	el ʃams (f)	الشمس
solar system	el magmū'a el ʃamsiya (f)	المجموعة الشمسيّة
solar eclipse	kosūf el ʃams (m)	كسوف الشمس
the Earth	el arḍ (f)	الأرض
the Moon	el 'amar (m)	القمر
Mars	el marrīχ (m)	المرّيخ
Venus	el zahra (f)	الزهرة
Jupiter	el moʃtary (m)	المشتري
Saturn	zoḥḥol (m)	زحل
Mercury	'aṭāred (m)	عطارد
Uranus	uranus (m)	اورانوس
Neptune	nibtūn (m)	نبتون
Pluto	bluto (m)	بلوتو
Milky Way	darb el tebbāna (m)	درب التبّانة
Great Bear (Ursa Major)	el dobb el akbar (m)	الدب الأكبر
North Star	negm el 'oṭb (m)	نجم القطب
Martian	sāken el marrīχ (m)	ساكن المرّيخ
extraterrestrial (n)	faḍā'y (m)	فضائي

alien	kā'en faḍā'y (m)	كائن فضائي
flying saucer	ṭaba' ṭā'er (m)	طبق طائر
spaceship	markaba faḍa'iya (f)	مركبة فضائية
space station	maḥaṭṭet faḍā' (f)	محطّة فضاء
blast-off	enṭelāq (m)	إنطلاق
engine	motore (m)	موتور
nozzle	manfaθ (m)	منفث
fuel	woqūd (m)	وقود
cockpit, flight deck	kabīna (f)	كابينة
aerial	hawā'y (m)	هوائي
porthole	kowwa mostadīra (f)	كوّة مستديرة
solar panel	lawḥa ʃamsiya (f)	لوحة شمسيّة
spacesuit	badlet el faḍā' (f)	بدّلة الفضاء
weightlessness	enʿedām wazn (m)	إنعدام الوزن
oxygen	oksiʒīn (m)	أوكسجين
docking (in space)	rasw (m)	رسو
to dock (vi, vt)	rasa	رسى
observatory	marṣad (m)	مرصد
telescope	teleskop (m)	تلسكوب
to observe (vt)	rāqab	راقب
to explore (vt)	estakʃef	إستكشف

165. The Earth

the Earth	el arḍ (f)	الأرض
the globe (the Earth)	el kora el arḍiya (f)	الكرة الأرضيّة
planet	kawwkab (m)	كوّكب
atmosphere	el ɣelāf el gawwy (m)	الغلاف الجوّي
geography	goɣrafia (f)	جغرافيا
nature	ṭabeeʿa (f)	طبيعة
globe (table ~)	namūzag lel kora el arḍiya (m)	نموذج للكرة الأرضيّة
map	χarīṭa (f)	خريطة
atlas	aṭlas (m)	أطلس
Europe	orobba (f)	أوروبّا
Asia	asya (f)	آسيا
Africa	afreqia (f)	أفريقيا
Australia	ostorālya (f)	أستراليا
America	amrīka (f)	أمريكا
North America	amrīka el ʃamaliya (f)	أمريكا الشماليّة
South America	amrīka el ganūbiya (f)	أمريكا الجنوبيّة
Antarctica	el qoṭb el ganūby (m)	القطب الجنوبي
the Arctic	el qoṭb el ʃamāly (m)	القطب الشمالي

166. Cardinal directions

north	ʃemāl (m)	شمال
to the north	lel ʃamāl	للشمال
in the north	fel ʃamāl	في الشمال
northern (adj)	ʃamāly	شمالي
south	ganūb (m)	جنوب
to the south	lel ganūb	للجنوب
in the south	fel ganūb	في الجنوب
southern (adj)	ganūby	جنوبي
west	ɣarb (m)	غرب
to the west	lel ɣarb	للغرب
in the west	fel ɣarb	في الغرب
western (adj)	ɣarby	غربي
east	ʃarʾ (m)	شرق
to the east	lel ʃarʾ	للشرق
in the east	fel ʃarʾ	في الشرق
eastern (adj)	ʃarʾy	شرقي

167. Sea. Ocean

sea	baḥr (m)	بحر
ocean	moḥīṭ (m)	محيط
gulf (bay)	χalīg (m)	خليج
straits	maḍīq (m)	مضيق
land (solid ground)	barr (m)	برّ
continent (mainland)	qārra (f)	قارّة
island	gezīra (f)	جزيرة
peninsula	ʃebh gezeyra (f)	شبه جزيرة
archipelago	magmūʿet gozor (f)	مجموعة جزر
bay, cove	χalīg (m)	خليج
harbour	mināʾ (m)	ميناء
lagoon	lagūn (m)	لاجون
cape	raʾs (m)	رأس
atoll	gezīra morganiya estwaʾiya (f)	جزيرة مرجانية إستوائيّة
reef	ʃoʿāb (pl)	شعاب
coral	morgān (m)	مرجان
coral reef	ʃoʿāb morganiya (pl)	شعاب مرجانية
deep (adj)	ʿamīq	عميق
depth (deep water)	ʿomq (m)	عمق
abyss	el ʿomq el saḥīq (m)	العمق السحيق
trench (e.g. Mariana ~)	χondoq (m)	خندق
current (Ocean ~)	tayār (m)	تيّار
to surround (bathe)	ḥāṭ	حاط
shore	sāḥel (m)	ساحل

coast	sāḥel (m)	ساحل
flow (flood tide)	tayār (m)	تيّار
ebb (ebb tide)	gozor (m)	جزر
shoal	meyāh ḍaḥla (f)	مياه ضحلة
bottom (~ of the sea)	qāʿ (m)	قاع
wave	mouga (f)	موجة
crest (~ of a wave)	qemma (f)	قمّة
spume (sea foam)	zabad el baḥr (m)	زبد البحر
storm (sea storm)	ʿāṣefa (f)	عاصفة
hurricane	eʿṣār (m)	إعصار
tsunami	tsunāmy (m)	تسونامي
calm (dead ~)	hodūʾ (m)	هدوء
quiet, calm (adj)	hady	هادئ
pole	ʾoṭb (m)	قطب
polar (adj)	ʾoṭby	قطبي
latitude	ʿarḍ (m)	عرض
longitude	χaṭṭ ṭūl (m)	خطّ طول
parallel	motawāz (m)	متواز
equator	χaṭṭ el estewāʾ (m)	خطّ الإستواء
sky	samāʾ (f)	سماء
horizon	ofoq (m)	أفق
air	hawāʾ (m)	هواء
lighthouse	manāra (f)	منارة
to dive (vi)	ɣāṣ	غاص
to sink (ab. boat)	ɣereʾ	غرق
treasure	konūz (pl)	كنوز

168. Mountains

mountain	gabal (m)	جبل
mountain range	selselet gebāl (f)	سلسلة جبال
mountain ridge	notūʾ el gabal (m)	نتوء الجبل
summit, top	qemma (f)	قمّة
peak	qemma (f)	قمّة
foot (~ of the mountain)	asfal (m)	أسفل
slope (mountainside)	monḥadar (m)	منحدر
volcano	borkān (m)	بركان
active volcano	borkān naʃeṭ (m)	بركان نشط
dormant volcano	borkān χāmed (m)	بركان خامد
eruption	sawarān (m)	ثوّران
crater	fawhet el borkān (f)	فوهة البركان
magma	magma (f)	ماجما
lava	ḥomam borkāniya (pl)	حمم بركانية
molten (~ lava)	monṣahera	منصهرة
canyon	wādy ḍayeʾ (m)	وادي ضيّق

gorge	mamarr ḍaye' (m)	ممرّ ضيّق
crevice	ʃa'' (m)	شقّ
abyss (chasm)	hāwya (f)	هاوية
pass, col	mamarr gabaly (m)	ممرّ جبلي
plateau	haḍaba (f)	هضبة
cliff	garf (m)	جرف
hill	tall (m)	تلّ
glacier	nahr galīdy (m)	نهر جليدي
waterfall	ʃallāl (m)	شلّال
geyser	nabʿ maya ḥāra (m)	نبع ميّة حارة
lake	boḥeyra (f)	بحيرة
plain	sahl (m)	سهل
landscape	manzar ṭabeeʿy (m)	منظر طبيعي
echo	ṣada (m)	صدى
alpinist	motasalleq el gebāl (m)	متسلّق الجبال
rock climber	motasalleq ṣoχūr (m)	متسلّق صخور
to conquer (in climbing)	taɣallab ʿala	تغلّب على
climb (an easy ~)	tasalloq (m)	تسلّق

169. Rivers

river	nahr (m)	نهر
spring (natural source)	ʿeyn (m)	عين
riverbed (river channel)	magra el nahr (m)	مجرى النهر
basin (river valley)	ḥoḍe (m)	حوض
to flow into …	ṣabb fe …	صبّ في…
tributary	rāfed (m)	رافد
bank (river ~)	ḍaffa (f)	ضفّة
current (stream)	tayār (m)	تيّار
downstream (adv)	maʿ ettigāh magra el nahr	مع إتّجاه مجرى النهر
upstream (adv)	ḍed el tayār	ضد التيار
inundation	ɣamr (m)	غمر
flooding	fayaḍān (m)	فيضان
to overflow (vi)	fāḍ	فاض
to flood (vt)	ɣamar	غمر
shallow (shoal)	meyāh ḍaḥla (f)	مياه ضحلة
rapids	monḥadar el nahr (m)	منحدر النهر
dam	sadd (m)	سدّ
canal	qanah (f)	قناة
reservoir (artificial lake)	χazzān mā'y (m)	خزّان مائي
sluice, lock	bawwāba qanṭara (f)	بوّابة قنطرة
water body (pond, etc.)	berka (f)	بركة
swamp (marshland)	mostanqaʿ (m)	مستنقع
bog, marsh	mostanqaʿ (m)	مستنقع

whirlpool	dawwāma (f)	دوّامة
stream (brook)	gadwal (m)	جدوّل
drinking (ab. water)	el ʃorb	الشرب
fresh (~ water)	ʿazb	عذب
ice	galīd (m)	جليد
to freeze over (ab. river, etc.)	etgammed	إتجمّد

170. Forest

forest, wood	ɣāba (f)	غابة
forest (as adj)	ɣāba	غابة
thick forest	ɣāba kasīfa (f)	غابة كثيفة
grove	bostān (m)	بستان
forest clearing	ezālet el ɣābāt (f)	إزالة الغابات
thicket	agama (f)	أجمة
scrubland	arāḍy el ʃogayrāt (pl)	أراضي الشجيرات
footpath (troddenpath)	mamarr (m)	ممرّ
gully	wādy ḍayeʾ (m)	وادي ضيّق
tree	ʃagara (f)	شجرة
leaf	waraʾa (f)	ورقة
leaves (foliage)	waraʾ (m)	ورق
fall of leaves	tasāʾoṭ el awrāʾ (m)	تساقط الأوراق
to fall (ab. leaves)	saqaṭ	سقط
top (of the tree)	raʾs (m)	رأس
branch	ɣoṣn (m)	غصن
bough	ɣoṣn raʾīsy (m)	غصن رئيسي
bud (on shrub, tree)	borʿom (m)	برعم
needle (of the pine tree)	ʃawka (f)	شوكة
fir cone	kūz el ṣnowbar (m)	كوز الصنوبر
tree hollow	gofe (m)	جوف
nest	ʿeʃ (m)	عشّ
burrow (animal hole)	goḥr (m)	جحر
trunk	gezʿ (m)	جذع
root	gezr (m)	جذر
bark	leḥāʾ (m)	لحاء
moss	ṭaḥlab (m)	طحلب
to uproot (remove trees or tree stumps)	eqtalaʿ	إقتلع
to chop down	ʾaṭṭaʿ	قطّع
to deforest (vt)	azāl el ɣabāt	أزال الغابات
tree stump	gezʿ el ʃagara (m)	جذع الشجرة
campfire	nār moxayem (m)	نار مخيّم
forest fire	ḥarīʾ ɣāba (m)	حريق غابة

to extinguish (vt)	ṭaffa	طفّى
forest ranger	ḥāres el ɣāba (m)	حارس الغابة
protection	ḥemāya (f)	حماية
to protect (~ nature)	ḥama	حمى
poacher	sāreʾ el ṣeyd (m)	سارق الصيد
steel trap	maṣyada (f)	مصيّدة
to gather, to pick (vt)	gammaʿ	جمّع
to lose one's way	tāh	تاه

171. Natural resources

natural resources	sarawāt ṭabiʿiya (pl)	ثروات طبيعيّة
minerals	maʿāden (pl)	معادن
deposits	rawāseb (pl)	رواسب
field (e.g. oilfield)	ḥaql (m)	حقل
to mine (extract)	estaχrag	إستخرج
mining (extraction)	esteχrāg (m)	إستخراج
ore	χām (m)	خام
mine (e.g. for coal)	mangam (m)	منجم
shaft (mine ~)	mangam (m)	منجم
miner	ʿāmel mangam (m)	عامل منجم
gas (natural ~)	ɣāz (m)	غاز
gas pipeline	χaṭṭ anabīb ɣāz (m)	خطّ أنابيب غاز
oil (petroleum)	nafṭ (m)	نفط
oil pipeline	anabīb el nafṭ (pl)	أنابيب النفط
oil well	bīr el nafṭ (m)	بير النفط
derrick (tower)	ḥaffāra (f)	حفّارة
tanker	nāqelet betrūl (f)	ناقلة بترول
sand	raml (m)	رمل
limestone	ḥagar el kals (m)	حجر الكلس
gravel	ḥaṣa (m)	حصى
peat	χaθ faḥm nabāty (m)	خث فحم نباتي
clay	ṭīn (m)	طين
coal	faḥm (m)	فحم
iron (ore)	ḥadīd (m)	حديد
gold	dahab (m)	ذهب
silver	faḍḍa (f)	فضّة
nickel	nikel (m)	نيكل
copper	neḥās (m)	نحاس
zinc	zink (m)	زنك
manganese	manganīz (m)	منجنيز
mercury	zeʾbaq (m)	زئبق
lead	roṣāṣ (m)	رصاص
mineral	maʿdan (m)	معدن
crystal	kristāl (m)	كريستال
marble	roχām (m)	رخام
uranium	yuranuim (m)	يورانيوم

The Earth. Part 2

172. Weather

weather	ṭa'ʾs (m)	طقس
weather forecast	naʃra gawiya (f)	نشرة جويّة
temperature	ḥarāra (f)	حرارة
thermometer	termometr (m)	ترمومتر
barometer	barometr (m)	بارومتر
humid (adj)	roṭob	رطب
humidity	roṭūba (f)	رطوبة
heat (extreme ~)	ḥarāra (f)	حرارة
hot (torrid)	ḥarr	حارّ
it's hot	el gaww ḥarr	الجّو حرّ
it's warm	el gaww dafa	الجوّ دفا
warm (moderately hot)	dāfeʾ	دافئ
it's cold	el gaww bāred	الجوّ بارد
cold (adj)	bāred	بارد
sun	ʃams (f)	شمس
to shine (vi)	nawwar	نوّر
sunny (day)	moʃmes	مشمس
to come up (vi)	ʃaraʾ	شرق
to set (vi)	ɣarab	غرب
cloud	saḥāba (f)	سحابة
cloudy (adj)	meɣayem	مغيّم
rain cloud	saḥābet maṭar (f)	سحابة مطر
somber (gloomy)	meɣayem	مغيّم
rain	maṭar (m)	مطر
it's raining	el donia betmaṭṭar	الدنيا بتمطّر
rainy (~ day, weather)	momṭer	ممطر
to drizzle (vi)	maṭṭaret razāz	مطّرت رذاذ
pouring rain	maṭar monhamer (f)	مطر منهمر
downpour	maṭar ɣazīr (m)	مطر غزير
heavy (e.g. ~ rain)	ʃedīd	شديد
puddle	berka (f)	بركة
to get wet (in rain)	ettbal	إتّبل
fog (mist)	ʃabbūra (f)	شبّورة
foggy	fih ʃabbūra	فيه شبّورة
snow	talg (m)	ثلج
it's snowing	fih talg	فيه ثلج

173. Severe weather. Natural disasters

thunderstorm	ʿāṣefa raʿdiya (f)	عاصفة رعدية
lightning (~ strike)	barʾ (m)	برق
to flash (vi)	baraq	برق
thunder	raʿd (m)	رعد
to thunder (vi)	dawa	دوّى
it's thundering	el samāʾ dawat raʿd (f)	السماء دوّت رعد
hail	maṭar bard (m)	مطر برد
it's hailing	maṭṭaret bard	مطّرت برد
to flood (vt)	ɣamar	غمر
flood, inundation	fayaḍān (m)	فيضان
earthquake	zelzāl (m)	زلزال
tremor, shoke	hazza arḍiya (f)	هزّة أرضية
epicentre	markaz el zelzāl (m)	مركز الزلزال
eruption	sawarān (m)	ثوران
lava	ḥomam borkāniya (pl)	حمم بركانية
twister, tornado	eʿṣār (m)	إعصار
typhoon	tyfūn (m)	طوفان
hurricane	eʿṣār (m)	إعصار
storm	ʿāṣefa (f)	عاصفة
tsunami	tsunāmy (m)	تسونامي
cyclone	eʿṣār (m)	إعصار
bad weather	ṭaʾs sayeʾ (m)	طقس سئ
fire (accident)	ḥarīʾ (m)	حريق
disaster	karsa (f)	كارثة
meteorite	nayzek (m)	نيّزك
avalanche	enheyār talgy (m)	إنهيار ثلجي
snowslide	enheyār talgy (m)	إنهيار ثلجي
blizzard	ʿāṣefa talgiya (f)	عاصفة ثلجيّة
snowstorm	ʿāṣefa talgiya (f)	عاصفة ثلجيّة

Fauna

174. Mammals. Predators

predator	moftares (m)	مفترس
tiger	nemr (m)	نمر
lion	asad (m)	أسد
wolf	ze'b (m)	ذئب
fox	ta'lab (m)	ثعلب
jaguar	nemr amrīky (m)	نمر أمريكي
leopard	fahd (m)	فهد
cheetah	fahd ṣayād (m)	فهد صيّاد
black panther	nemr aswad (m)	نمر أسوّد
puma	asad el gebāl (m)	أسد الجبال
snow leopard	nemr el tolūg (m)	نمر الثلوج
lynx	waʃaq (m)	وشق
coyote	qayūṭ (m)	قيوط
jackal	ebn 'āwy (m)	ابن آوى
hyena	ḍeb' (m)	ضبع

175. Wild animals

animal	ḥayawān (m)	حيوان
beast (animal)	waḥʃ (m)	وحش
squirrel	sengāb (m)	سنجاب
hedgehog	qonfoz (m)	قنفذ
hare	arnab barry (m)	أرنب برّي
rabbit	arnab (m)	أرنب
badger	ɣarīr (m)	غرير
raccoon	rakūn (m)	راكون
hamster	hamster (m)	هامستر
marmot	marmoṭ (m)	مرموط
mole	χold (m)	خلد
mouse	fār (m)	فأر
rat	gerz (m)	جرذ
bat	χoffāʃ (m)	خفّاش
ermine	qāqem (m)	قاقم
sable	sammūr (m)	سمّور
marten	fara'īāt (m)	فرائيات
weasel	ebn 'ers (m)	ابن عرس
mink	mink (m)	منك

beaver	qondos (m)	قندس
otter	taʿlab maya (m)	ثعلب الميّة
horse	ḥoṣān (m)	حصان
moose	eyl el mūz (m)	أيّل الموظ
deer	ayl (m)	أيل
camel	gamal (m)	جمل
bison	bison (m)	بيسون
wisent	byson orobby (m)	بيسون أوروبي
buffalo	gamūs (m)	جاموس
zebra	ḥomār waḥʃy (m)	حمار وحشي
antelope	ẓaby (m)	ظبي
roe deer	yaḥmūr orobby (m)	يحمورأوروبيّ
fallow deer	eyl asmar orobby (m)	أيّل أسمر أوروبي
chamois	ʃamwah (f)	شامواه
wild boar	χenzīr barry (m)	خنزير برّي
whale	ḥūt (m)	حوت
seal	foqma (f)	فقمة
walrus	el kabʿ (m)	الكبع
fur seal	foqmet el farāʾ (f)	فقمة الفراء
dolphin	dolfīn (m)	دولفين
bear	dobb (m)	دبّ
polar bear	dobb ʾoṭṭby (m)	دبّ قطبي
panda	banda (m)	باندا
monkey	ʾerd (m)	قرد
chimpanzee	ʃimbanzy (m)	شيمبانزي
orangutan	orangutan (m)	أورنغوتان
gorilla	ɣorella (f)	غوريلا
macaque	ʾerd el makāk (m)	قرد المكاك
gibbon	gibbon (m)	جيبون
elephant	fīl (m)	فيل
rhinoceros	χartīt (m)	خرتيت
giraffe	zarāfa (f)	زرافة
hippopotamus	faras el nahr (m)	فرس النهر
kangaroo	kangarū (m)	كانجّارو
koala (bear)	el koala (m)	الكوالا
mongoose	nems (m)	نمس
chinchilla	ʃenʃīla (f)	شنشيلة
skunk	ẓerbān (m)	ظربان
porcupine	nīṣ (m)	نيص

176. Domestic animals

cat	ʾoṭṭa (f)	قطّة
tomcat	ʾoṭṭ (m)	قطّ
dog	kalb (m)	كلب

horse	ḥoṣān (m)	حصان
stallion (male horse)	χeyl faḥl (m)	خيل فحل
mare	faras (f)	فرس
cow	ba'ara (f)	بقرة
bull	sore (m)	ثور
ox	sore (m)	ثور
sheep (ewe)	χarūf (f)	خروف
ram	kebʃ (m)	كبش
goat	me'za (f)	معزة
billy goat, he-goat	mā'ez zakar (m)	ماعز ذكر
donkey	ḥomār (m)	حمار
mule	baɣl (m)	بغل
pig	χenzīr (m)	خنزير
piglet	χannūṣ (m)	خنّوص
rabbit	arnab (m)	أرنب
hen (chicken)	farχa (f)	فرخة
cock	dīk (m)	ديك
duck	baṭṭa (f)	بطّة
drake	dakar el baṭṭ (m)	ذكر البط
goose	wezza (f)	وزّة
tom turkey, gobbler	dīk rūmy (m)	ديك رومي
turkey (hen)	dīk rūmy (m)	ديك رومي
domestic animals	ḥayawānāt dawāgen (pl)	حيوانات دواجن
tame (e.g. ~ hamster)	alīf	أليف
to tame (vt)	rawweḍ	روّض
to breed (vt)	rabba	ربّى
farm	mazra'a (f)	مزرعة
poultry	dawāgen (pl)	دواجن
cattle	māʃeya (f)	ماشية
herd (cattle)	qaṭee' (m)	قطيع
stable	esṭabl χeyl (m)	إسطبل خيل
pigsty	ḥazīret χanazīr (f)	حظيرة الخنازير
cowshed	zerībet el ba'ar (f)	زريبة البقر
rabbit hutch	qan el arāneb (m)	قن الأرانب
hen house	qan el ferāχ (m)	قن الفراخ

177. Dogs. Dog breeds

dog	kalb (m)	كلب
sheepdog	kalb rā'y (m)	كلب رعي
German shepherd	kalb rā'y almāny (m)	كلب راعي ألمانيّ
poodle	būdle (m)	بودل
dachshund	daʃhund (m)	داشهند
bulldog	bulldog (m)	بولدوج

boxer	bokser (m)	بوكسر
mastiff	mastiff (m)	ماستيف
Rottweiler	rottfeyler (m)	روت فايلر
Doberman	doberman (m)	دوبرمان
basset	basset (m)	باسيت
bobtail	bobtayl (m)	بوبتيل
Dalmatian	delmāṭy (m)	دلماطي
cocker spaniel	kokker spaniel (m)	كوكر سبانييل
Newfoundland	nyu faundland (m)	نيوفاوندلاند
Saint Bernard	sant bernard (m)	سانت بيرنارد
husky	hasky (m)	هاسكي
Chow Chow	tʃaw tʃaw (m)	تشاوتشاو
spitz	esbitz (m)	إسبتز
pug	bug (m)	بج

178. Sounds made by animals

barking (n)	nebāḥ (m)	نباح
to bark (vi)	nabaḥ	نبح
to miaow (vi)	mawmaw	موّمو
to purr (vi)	χarχar	خرخر
to moo (vi)	χār	خار
to bellow (bull)	χār	خار
to growl (vi)	damdam	دمدم
howl (n)	ʿawāʾ (m)	عواء
to howl (vi)	ʿawa	عوى
to whine (vi)	ann	أنّ
to bleat (sheep)	maʾmaʾ	مأمأ
to oink, to grunt (pig)	qabaʿ	قبع
to squeal (vi)	qabaʿ	قبع
to croak (vi)	naʾʾ	نقّ
to buzz (insect)	ṭann	طنّ
to chirp (crickets, grasshopper)	ʿarʿar	عرعر

179. Birds

bird	ṭāʾer (m)	طائر
pigeon	ḥamāma (f)	حمامة
sparrow	ʿaṣfūr dawri (m)	عصفور دوري
tit (great tit)	qarqaf (m)	قرقف
magpie	ʿaʾʿaʾ (m)	عقعق
raven	ɣorāb aswad (m)	غراب أسود
crow	ɣorāb (m)	غراب

jackdaw	zāɣ zarʿy (m)	زاغ زرعي
rook	ɣorāb el qeyẓ (m)	غراب القيظ
duck	baṭṭa (f)	بطّة
goose	wezza (f)	وزّة
pheasant	tadarrog (m)	تدرج
eagle	ʿeqāb (m)	عقاب
hawk	el bāz (m)	الباز
falcon	ṣaʾr (m)	صقر
vulture	nesr (m)	نسر
condor (Andean ~)	kondor (m)	كندور
swan	el temm (m)	التمّ
crane	karkiya (m)	كركية
stork	loqloq (m)	لقلق
parrot	babaɣāʾ (m)	ببغاء
hummingbird	ṭannān (m)	طنّان
peacock	ṭawūs (m)	طاووس
ostrich	naʿāma (f)	نعامة
heron	belʃone (m)	بلشون
flamingo	flamingo (m)	فلامينجو
pelican	bagʿa (f)	بجعة
nightingale	ʿandalīb (m)	عندليب
swallow	el sonūnū (m)	السنونو
thrush	somnet el ḥoqūl (m)	سمنة الحقول
song thrush	somna moɣarreda (m)	سمنة مغرّدة
blackbird	ʃaḥrūr aswad (m)	شحرور أسود
swift	semmāma (m)	سمّامة
lark	qabra (f)	قبرة
quail	semmān (m)	سمّان
woodpecker	naʾār el χaʃab (m)	نقار الخشب
cuckoo	weqwāq (m)	وقواق
owl	būma (f)	بومة
eagle owl	būm orāsy (m)	بوم أوراسي
wood grouse	dīk el χalang (m)	ديك الخلنج
black grouse	ṭyhūg aswad (m)	طيهوج أسوّد
partridge	el ḥagal (m)	الحجل
starling	zerzūr (m)	زرزور
canary	kanāry (m)	كناري
hazel grouse	ṭyhūg el bondoʾ (m)	طيهوج البندق
chaffinch	ʃarʃūr (m)	شرشور
bullfinch	deɣnāʃ (m)	دغناش
seagull	nawras (m)	نورس
albatross	el qoṭros (m)	القطرس
penguin	beṭrīq (m)	بطريق

180. Birds. Singing and sounds

to sing (vi)	ɣanna	غنّى
to call (animal, bird)	nāda	نادى
to crow (cock)	ṣāḥ	صاح
cock-a-doodle-doo	kokokūko	كوكوكوكو
to cluck (hen)	kāky	كاكي
to caw (crow call)	naʿaq	نعق
to quack (duck call)	baṭbaṭ	بطبط
to cheep (vi)	ṣawṣaw	صوّصو
to chirp, to twitter	zaʾzaʾ	زقزق

181. Fish. Marine animals

bream	abramīs (m)	أبراميس
carp	ʃabbūṭ (m)	شبّوط
perch	farχ (m)	فرخ
catfish	ʾarmūṭ (m)	قرموط
pike	karāky (m)	كراكي
salmon	salamon (m)	سلمون
sturgeon	ḥafʃ (m)	حفش
herring	renga (f)	رنجة
Atlantic salmon	salamon aṭlasy (m)	سلمون أطلسي
mackerel	makerel (m)	ماكريل
flatfish	samak mefalṭah (f)	سمك مفلطح
zander, pike perch	samak sandar (m)	سمك سندر
cod	el qadd (m)	القد
tuna	tuna (f)	تونة
trout	salamon meraʾʾaṭ (m)	سلمون مرقّط
eel	ḥankalīs (m)	حنكليس
electric ray	raʿād (m)	رعاد
moray eel	moraya (f)	موراية
piranha	bīrana (f)	بيرانا
shark	ʾerʃ (m)	قرش
dolphin	dolfīn (m)	دولفين
whale	ḥūt (m)	حوت
crab	kaboria (m)	كابوريا
jellyfish	ʾandīl el baḥr (m)	قنديل البحر
octopus	aχṭabūṭ (m)	أخطبوط
starfish	negmet el baḥr (f)	نجمة البحر
sea urchin	qonfoz el baḥr (m)	قنفذ البحر
seahorse	ḥoṣān el baḥr (m)	حصان البحر
oyster	maḥār (m)	محار
prawn	gammbary (m)	جمّبري

lobster	estakoza (f)	استكوزا
spiny lobster	estakoza (m)	استاكوزا

182. Amphibians. Reptiles

snake	teʿbān (m)	ثعبان
venomous (snake)	sām	سام
viper	afʿa (f)	أفعى
cobra	kobra (m)	كوبرا
python	teʿbān byton (m)	ثعبان بايثون
boa	bawāʾ el ʿaṣera (f)	بواء العاصرة
grass snake	teʿbān el ʿoʃb (m)	ثعبان العشب
rattle snake	afʿa megalgela (f)	أفعى مجلجلة
anaconda	anakonda (f)	أناكوندا
lizard	seḥliya (f)	سحليّة
iguana	eɣwana (f)	إغوانة
monitor lizard	warl (m)	ورل
salamander	salamander (m)	سلمندر
chameleon	ḥerbāya (f)	حرباية
scorpion	ʿaʾrab (m)	عقرب
turtle	solḥefah (f)	سلحفاة
frog	ḍeffḍaʿ (m)	ضفدع
toad	ḍeffḍaʿ el ṭeyn (m)	ضفدع الطين
crocodile	temsāḥ (m)	تمساح

183. Insects

insect	ḥaʃara (f)	حشرة
butterfly	farāʃa (f)	فراشة
ant	namla (f)	نملة
fly	debbāna (f)	دبّانة
mosquito	namūsa (f)	ناموسة
beetle	χonfesa (f)	خنفسة
wasp	dabbūr (m)	دبّور
bee	naḥla (f)	نحلة
bumblebee	naḥla ṭannāna (f)	نحلة طنّانة
gadfly (botfly)	naʿra (f)	نعرة
spider	ʿankabūt (m)	عنكبوت
spider's web	nasīg ʿankabūt (m)	نسيج عنكبوت
dragonfly	yaʿsūb (m)	يعسوب
grasshopper	garād (m)	جراد
moth (night butterfly)	ʿetta (f)	عثّة
cockroach	ṣarṣūr (m)	صرصور
tick	qarāda (f)	قرادة

flea	barɣūt (m)	برغوث
midge	baʿūḍa (f)	بعوضة
locust	garād (m)	جراد
snail	ḥalazōn (m)	حلزون
cricket	ṣarṣūr el ḥaql (m)	صرصور الحقل
firefly	yarāʿa (f)	يراعة
ladybird	χonfesa menaʾṭṭa (f)	خنفسة منقّطة
cockchafer	χonfesa motlefa lel nabāt (f)	خنفسة متّلفة للنبات
leech	ʿalaqa (f)	علقة
caterpillar	yasrūʿ (m)	يسروع
earthworm	dūda (f)	دودة
larva	yaraqa (f)	يرقة

184. Animals. Body parts

beak	monqār (m)	منقار
wings	agneḥa (pl)	أجنحة
foot (of the bird)	regl (f)	رجل
feathers (plumage)	rīʃ (m)	ريش
feather	rīʃa (f)	ريشة
crest	ʿorf el dīk (m)	عرف الديك
gills	χāyaʃīm (pl)	خياشيم
spawn	beyḍ el samak (pl)	بيض السمك
larva	yaraqa (f)	يرقة
fin	zaʿnafa (f)	زعنفة
scales (of fish, reptile)	ḥarāfeʃ (pl)	حرافش
fang (canine)	nāb (m)	ناب
paw (e.g. cat's ~)	yad (f)	يد
muzzle (snout)	χaṭm (m)	خطم
mouth (cat's ~)	boʾ (m)	بوء
tail	deyl (m)	ذيل
whiskers	ʃawāreb (pl)	شوارب
hoof	ḥāfer (m)	حافر
horn	ʾarn (m)	قرن
carapace	derʿ (m)	درع
shell (mollusk ~)	maḥāra (f)	محارة
eggshell	ʾeʃret beyḍa (f)	قشرة بيضة
animal's hair (pelage)	ʃaʿr (m)	شعر
pelt (hide)	geld (m)	جلد

185. Animals. Habitats

habitat	mawṭen (m)	موّطن
migration	hegra (f)	هجرة
mountain	gabal (m)	جبل

reef	ʃoʿāb (pl)	شعاب
cliff	garf (m)	جرف
forest	ɣāba (f)	غابة
jungle	adɣāl (pl)	أدغال
savanna	savanna (f)	سافانّا
tundra	tundra (f)	تندرا
steppe	barāry (pl)	براري
desert	ṣaḥraʾ (f)	صحراء
oasis	wāḥa (f)	واحة
sea	baḥr (m)	بحر
lake	boḥeyra (f)	بحيرة
ocean	moḥīṭ (m)	محيط
swamp (marshland)	mostanqaʿ (m)	مستنقع
freshwater (adj)	maya ʿazba	ميّة عذبة
pond	berka (f)	بركة
river	nahr (m)	نهر
den (bear's ~)	wekr (m)	وكر
nest	ʿeʃ (m)	عشّ
tree hollow	gofe (m)	جوف
burrow (animal hole)	goḥr (m)	جحر
anthill	ʿeʃ naml (m)	عش نمل

Flora

186. Trees

tree	ʃagara (f)	شجرة
deciduous (adj)	nafḍiya	نفضيّة
coniferous (adj)	ṣonoberiya	صنوبرية
evergreen (adj)	dā'emet el χoḍra	دائمة الخضرة
apple tree	ʃagaret toffāḥ (f)	شجرة تفّاح
pear tree	ʃagaret komettra (f)	شجرة كمثّرى
cherry tree	ʃagaret karaz (f)	شجرة كرز
plum tree	ʃagaret bar'ū' (f)	شجرة برقوق
birch	batola (f)	بتولا
oak	ballūṭ (f)	بلّوط
linden tree	zayzafūn (f)	زيزفون
aspen	ḥūr rāgef	حور راجف
maple	qayqab (f)	قيقب
spruce	rateng (f)	راتينج
pine	ṣonober (f)	صنوبر
larch	arziya (f)	أرزية
fir tree	tanūb (f)	تنوب
cedar	el orz (f)	الأرز
poplar	ḥūr (f)	حور
rowan	ɣobayrā' (f)	غبيراء
willow	ṣefsāf (f)	صفصاف
alder	gār el mā' (m)	جار الماء
beech	el zān (f)	الزان
elm	derdar (f)	دردار
ash (tree)	marān (f)	مران
chestnut	kastanā' (f)	كستناء
magnolia	maɣnolia (f)	ماغنوليا
palm tree	naχla (f)	نخلة
cypress	el soro (f)	السرو
mangrove	mangrūf (f)	مانجروف
baobab	baobab (f)	باوباب
eucalyptus	eukalyptus (f)	أوكالبتوس
sequoia	sequoia (f)	سيكويا

187. Shrubs

bush	ʃogeyra (f)	شجيرة
shrub	ʃogayrāt (pl)	شجيرات

grapevine	karma (f)	كرمة
vineyard	karam (m)	كرم
raspberry bush	zarʿet tūt el ʿalīʾ el aḥmar (f)	زرعة توت العليق الأحمر
redcurrant bush	keʃmeʃ aḥmar (m)	كشمش أحمر
gooseberry bush	ʿenab el saʿlab (m)	عنب الثعلب
acacia	aqaqia (f)	أقاقيا
barberry	berbarīs (m)	برباريس
jasmine	yasmīn (m)	ياسمين
juniper	ʿarʿar (m)	عرعر
rosebush	ʃogeyret ward (f)	شجيرة ورد
dog rose	ward el seyāg (pl)	ورد السياج

188. Mushrooms

mushroom	feṭr (f)	فطر
edible mushroom	feṭr ṣāleḥ lel akl (m)	فطر صالح للأكل
poisonous mushroom	feṭr sām (m)	فطر سام
cap	ṭarbūʃ el feṭr (m)	طربوش الفطر
stipe	sāq el feṭr (m)	ساق الفطر
cep, penny bun	feṭr boleṭe maʾkūl (m)	فطر بوليط مأكول
orange-cap boletus	feṭr aḥmar (m)	فطر أحمر
birch bolete	feṭr boleṭe (m)	فطر بوليط
chanterelle	feṭr el ʃanterel (m)	فطر الشانتريل
russula	feṭr russula (m)	فطر روسولا
morel	feṭr el ɣoʃna (m)	فطر الغوشنة
fly agaric	feṭr amanīt el ṭāʾer (m)	فطر أمانيت الطائر
death cap	feṭr amanīt falusyāny el sām (m)	فطر أمانيت فالوسياني السام

189. Fruits. Berries

fruit	tamra (f)	تمرة
fruits	tamr (m)	تمر
apple	toffāḥa (f)	تفّاحة
pear	komettra (f)	كمّثرى
plum	barʾūʾ (m)	برقوق
strawberry (garden ~)	farawla (f)	فراولة
cherry	karaz (m)	كرز
grape	ʿenab (m)	عنب
raspberry	tūt el ʿalīʾ el aḥmar (m)	توت العليق الأحمر
blackcurrant	keʃmeʃ aswad (m)	كشمش أسود
redcurrant	keʃmeʃ aḥmar (m)	كشمش أحمر
gooseberry	ʿenab el saʿlab (m)	عنب الثعلب
cranberry	ʿenabiya ḥāda el χebāʾ (m)	عنبية حادة الخباء
orange	bortoqāl (m)	برتقال

tangerine	yosfy (m)	يوسفي
pineapple	ananās (m)	أناناس
banana	moze (m)	موز
date	tamr (m)	تمر
lemon	lymūn (m)	ليمون
apricot	meʃmeʃ (f)	مشمش
peach	χawχa (f)	خوخة
kiwi	kiwi (m)	كيوي
grapefruit	grabe frūt (m)	جريب فروت
berry	tūt (m)	توت
berries	tūt (pl)	توت
cowberry	ʿenab el sore (m)	عنب الثور
wild strawberry	farawla barriya (f)	فراولة برّيّة
bilberry	ʿenab al aḥrāg (m)	عنب الأحراج

190. Flowers. Plants

flower	zahra (f)	زهرة
bouquet (of flowers)	bokeyh (f)	بوكيه
rose (flower)	warda (f)	وردة
tulip	tolīb (f)	توليب
carnation	ʾoronfol (m)	قرنفل
gladiolus	el dalbūs (f)	الدّلَبُوثُ
cornflower	qanṭeryūn ʿanbary (m)	قنطريون عنبري
harebell	garīs mostadīr el awrāʾ (m)	جريس مستدير الأوراق
dandelion	handabāʾ (f)	هندباء
camomile	kamomile (f)	كاموميل
aloe	el alowa (m)	الألوّة
cactus	ṣabbār (m)	صبّار
rubber plant, ficus	faykas (m)	فيكس
lily	zanbaq (f)	زنبق
geranium	ɣarnūqy (f)	غرنوقي
hyacinth	el lavender (f)	اللافندر
mimosa	mimoza (f)	ميموزا
narcissus	nerges (f)	نرجس
nasturtium	abo χangar (f)	أبو خنجر
orchid	orkid (f)	أوركيد
peony	fawnia (f)	فاوانيا
violet	el banafseg (f)	البنفسج
pansy	bansy (f)	بانسي
forget-me-not	ʾāzān el faʾr (pl)	آذان الفأر
daisy	aqwaḥān (f)	أقحوان
poppy	el χoʃχāʃ (f)	الخشخاش
hemp	qanb (m)	قنب

mint	neʿnāʿ (m)	نعناع
lily of the valley	zanbaq el wādy (f)	زنبق الوادي
snowdrop	zahrat el laban (f)	زهرة اللبن
nettle	ʾarrāṣ (m)	قرّاص
sorrel	ḥammāḍ bostāny (m)	حمّاض بستاني
water lily	niloferiya (f)	نيلوفرية
fern	sarχas (m)	سرخس
lichen	aʃna (f)	أشنة
conservatory (greenhouse)	ṣoba (f)	صوبة
lawn	ʿoʃb aχḍar (m)	عشب أخضر
flowerbed	geneynet zohūr (f)	جنينة زهور
plant	nabāt (m)	نبات
grass	ʿoʃb (m)	عشب
blade of grass	ʿoʃba (f)	عشبة
leaf	waraʾa (f)	ورقة
petal	waraʾet el zahra (f)	ورقة الزهرة
stem	sāq (f)	ساق
tuber	darna (f)	درنة
young plant (shoot)	nabta saɣīra (f)	نبتة صغيرة
thorn	ʃawka (f)	شوكة
to blossom (vi)	fattaḥet	فتّحت
to fade, to wither	debel	ذبل
smell (odour)	rīḥa (f)	ريحة
to cut (flowers)	ʾaṭaʿ	قطع
to pick (a flower)	ʾaṭaf	قطف

191. Cereals, grains

grain	ḥobūb (pl)	حبوب
cereal crops	maḥaṣīl el ḥubūb (pl)	محاصيل الحبوب
ear (of barley, etc.)	sonbola (f)	سنبلة
wheat	ʾamḥ (m)	قمح
rye	ʃelm mazrūʿ (m)	شيلم مزروع
oats	ʃofān (m)	شوفان
millet	el deχn (m)	الدُخن
barley	ʃeʿīr (m)	شعير
maize	dora (f)	ذرة
rice	rozz (m)	رزّ
buckwheat	ḥanṭa sodaʾ (f)	حنطة سوداء
pea plant	besella (f)	بسلّة
kidney bean	faṣolya (f)	فاصوليا
soya	fūl el ṣoya (m)	فول الصويا
lentil	ʿads (m)	عدس
beans (pulse crops)	fūl (m)	فول

REGIONAL GEOGRAPHY

192. Politics. Government. Part 1

politics	seyāsa (f)	سياسة
political (adj)	seyāsy	سياسي
politician	seyāsy (m)	سياسي
state (country)	dawla (f)	دولة
citizen	mowāṭen (m)	مواطن
citizenship	mewaṭna (f)	مواطنة
national emblem	ʃeʿār waṭany (m)	شعار وطني
national anthem	naʃīd waṭany (m)	نشيد وطني
government	ḥokūma (f)	حكومة
head of state	ra'ʾs el dawla (m)	رأس الدولة
parliament	barlamān (m)	برلمان
party	ḥezb (m)	حزب
capitalism	raʾsmaliya (f)	رأسماليّة
capitalist (adj)	raʾsmāly	رأسمالي
socialism	eʃterakiya (f)	إشتراكيّة
socialist (adj)	eʃterāky	إشتراكي
communism	ʃeyūʿiya (f)	شيوعيّة
communist (adj)	ʃeyūʿy	شيوعي
communist (n)	ʃeyūʿy (m)	شيوعي
democracy	dīmoqraṭiya (f)	ديموقراطيّة
democrat	demoqrāṭy (m)	ديموقراطي
democratic (adj)	demoqrāṭy	ديموقراطي
Democratic party	el ḥezb el demokrāṭy (m)	الحزب الديموقراطي
liberal (n)	librāly (m)	ليبيرالي
Liberal (adj)	librāly	ليبيرالي
conservative (n)	moḥāfeẓ (m)	محافظ
conservative (adj)	moḥāfeẓ	محافظ
republic (n)	gomhoriya (f)	جمهورية
republican (n)	gomhūry (m)	جمهوري
Republican party	el ḥezb el gomhūry (m)	الحزب الجمهوري
elections	entaχabāt (pl)	إنتخابات
to elect (vt)	entaχab	إنتخب
elector, voter	nāχeb (m)	ناخب
election campaign	ḥamla enteχabiya (f)	حملة إنتخابيّة
voting (n)	taṣwīt (m)	تصويت
to vote (vi)	ṣawwat	صوّت

suffrage, right to vote	ḥa' el enteχāb (m)	حق الإنتخاب
candidate	morasʃaḥ (m)	مرشّح
to run for (~ President)	rasʃaḥ nafsoh	رشّح نفسه
campaign	ḥamla (f)	حملة
opposition (as adj)	mo'āreḍ	معارض
opposition (n)	mo'arḍa (f)	معارضة
visit	zeyāra (f)	زيارة
official visit	zeyāra rasmiya (f)	زيارة رسميّة
international (adj)	dawly	دوّلي
negotiations	mofawḍāt (pl)	مفاوضات
to negotiate (vi)	tafāwaḍ	تفاوض

193. Politics. Government. Part 2

society	mogtama' (m)	مجتمع
constitution	dostūr (m)	دستور
power (political control)	solṭa (f)	سلطة
corruption	fasād (m)	فساد
law (justice)	qanūn (m)	قانون
legal (legitimate)	qanūny	قانوني
justice (fairness)	'adāla (f)	عدالة
just (fair)	'ādel	عادل
committee	lagna (f)	لجنة
bill (draft law)	maʃrū' qanūn (m)	مشروع قانون
budget	mowazna (f)	موازنة
policy	seyāsa (f)	سياسة
reform	eṣlāḥ (m)	إصلاح
radical (adj)	oṣūly	أصولي
power (strength, force)	'owwa (f)	قوّة
powerful (adj)	'awy	قوّي
supporter	mo'ayed (m)	مؤيد
influence	ta'sīr (m)	تأثير
regime (e.g. military ~)	nezām ḥokm (m)	نظام حكم
conflict	χelāf (m)	خلاف
conspiracy (plot)	mo'amra (f)	مؤامرة
provocation	estefzāz (m)	إستفزاز
to overthrow (regime, etc.)	asqaṭ	أسقط
overthrow (of a government)	esqāṭ (m)	إسقاط
revolution	sawra (f)	ثوّرة
coup d'état	enqelāb (m)	إنقلاب
military coup	enqelāb 'askary (m)	إنقلاب عسكري
crisis	azma (f)	أزمة
economic recession	rokūd eqteṣādy (m)	ركود إقتصادي

demonstrator (protester)	motaẓāher (m)	متظاهر
demonstration	mozahra (f)	مظاهرة
martial law	ḥokm ʿorfy (m)	حكم عرفي
military base	qaʿeda ʿaskariya (f)	قاعدة عسكريّة
stability	esteqrār (m)	إستقرار
stable (adj)	mostaqerr	مستقرّ
exploitation	esteɣlāl (m)	إستغلال
to exploit (workers)	estaɣall	إستغلّ
racism	ʿonṣoriya (f)	عنصريّة
racist	ʿonṣory (m)	عنصري
fascism	faʃiya (f)	فاشيّة
fascist	fāʃy (m)	فاشي

194. Countries. Miscellaneous

foreigner	agnaby (m)	أجنبي
foreign (adj)	agnaby	أجنبي
abroad (in a foreign country)	fel χāreg	في الخارج
emigrant	mohāger (m)	مهاجر
emigration	hegra (f)	هجرة
to emigrate (vi)	hāgar	هاجر
the West	el ɣarb (m)	الغرب
the East	el ʃarʾ (m)	الشرق
the Far East	el ʃarʾ el aqṣa (m)	الشرق الأقصى
civilization	ḥaḍāra (f)	حضارة
humanity (mankind)	el baʃariya (f)	البشريّة
the world (earth)	el ʿālam (m)	العالم
peace	salām (m)	سلام
worldwide (adj)	ʿālamy	عالمي
homeland	waṭan (m)	وطن
people (population)	ʃaʿb (m)	شعب
population	sokkān (pl)	سكّان
people (a lot of ~)	nās (pl)	ناس
nation (people)	omma (f)	أمّة
generation	gīl (m)	جيل
territory (area)	arḍ (f)	أرض
region	manteʾa (f)	منطقة
state (part of a country)	welāya (f)	ولاية
tradition	taʾlīd (m)	تقليد
custom (tradition)	ʿāda (f)	عادة
ecology	ʿelm el bīʾa (m)	علم البيئة
Indian (Native American)	hendy aḥmar (m)	هندي أحمر
Gypsy (masc.)	ɣagary (m)	غجري
Gypsy (fem.)	ɣagariya (f)	غجريّة

Gypsy (adj)	ɣagary	غجري
empire	embraṭoriya (f)	إمبراطورية
colony	mostaʿmara (f)	مستعمرة
slavery	ʿobūdiya (f)	عبودية
invasion	ɣazw (m)	غزو
famine	magāʿa (f)	مجاعة

195. Major religious groups. Confessions

religion	dīn (m)	دين
religious (adj)	dīny	ديني
faith, belief	emān (m)	إيمان
to believe (in God)	aman	أمن
believer	moʾmen (m)	مؤمن
atheism	el elḥād (m)	الإلحاد
atheist	molḥed (m)	ملحد
Christianity	el masīḥiya (f)	المسيحيّة
Christian (n)	mesīḥy (m)	مسيحي
Christian (adj)	mesīḥy	مسيحي
Catholicism	el kasolekiya (f)	الكاثوليكيّة
Catholic (n)	kasolīky (m)	كاثوليكي
Catholic (adj)	kasolīky	كاثوليكي
Protestantism	brotestantiya (f)	بروتستانتية
Protestant Church	el kenīsa el brotestantiya (f)	الكنيسة البروتستانتية
Protestant (n)	brotestanty (m)	بروتستانتي
Orthodoxy	orsozeksiya (f)	الأرثوذكسيّة
Orthodox Church	el kenīsa el orsozeksiya (f)	الكنيسة الأرثوذكسيّة
Orthodox (n)	arsazoksy (m)	أرثوذكسي
Presbyterianism	maʃīχiya (f)	مشيخية
Presbyterian Church	el kenīsa el maʃīχiya (f)	الكنيسة المشيخية
Presbyterian (n)	maʃīχiya (f)	مشيخية
Lutheranism	el luseriya (f)	اللوثرية
Lutheran (n)	luterriya (m)	لوثرية
Baptist Church	el kenīsa el meʿmedaniya (f)	الكنيسة المعمدانية
Baptist (n)	meʿmedāny (m)	معمداني
Anglican Church	el kenīsa el anʒlekaniya (f)	الكنيسة الإنجليكانية
Anglican (n)	enʒelikāny (m)	أنجليكاني
Mormonism	el moromoniya (f)	المورمونية
Mormon (n)	mesīḥy mormōn (m)	مسيحي مرمون
Judaism	el yahūdiya (f)	اليهودية
Jew (n)	yahūdy (m)	يهودي
Buddhism	el būziya (f)	البوذية
Buddhist (n)	būzy (m)	بوذي

Hinduism	el hindūsiya (f)	الهندوسية
Hindu (n)	hendūsy (m)	هندوسي
Islam	el islām (m)	الإسلام
Muslim (n)	muslim (m)	مسلم
Muslim (adj)	islāmy	إسلامي
Shiah Islam	el mazhab el ʃeeʿy (m)	المذهب الشيعي
Shiite (n)	ʃeeʿy (m)	شيعي
Sunni Islam	el mazhab el sunny (m)	المذهب السنّي
Sunnite (n)	sunni (m)	سنّي

196. Religions. Priests

priest	kāhen (m)	كاهن
the Pope	el bāba (m)	البابا
monk, friar	rāheb (m)	راهب
nun	rāheba (f)	راهبة
pastor	ʾessīs (m)	قسّيس
abbot	raʾīs el deyr (m)	رئيس الدير
vicar (parish priest)	viqār (m)	فيقار
bishop	asqof (m)	أسقف
cardinal	kardinal (m)	كاردينال
preacher	mobasʃer (m)	مبشّر
preaching	tabʃīr (f)	تبشير
parishioners	raʿyet el abraʃiya (f)	رعية الأبرشية
believer	moʾmen (m)	مؤمن
atheist	molḥed (m)	ملحد

197. Faith. Christianity. Islam

Adam	ʾādam (m)	آدم
Eve	ḥawwāʾ (f)	حوّاء
God	allah (m)	الله
the Lord	el rabb (m)	الربّ
the Almighty	el qadīr (m)	القدير
sin	zanb (m)	ذنب
to sin (vi)	aznab	أذنب
sinner (masc.)	mozneb (m)	مذنب
sinner (fem.)	mozneba (f)	مذنبة
hell	el gaḥīm (f)	الجحيم
paradise	el ganna (f)	الجنّة
Jesus	yasūʿ (m)	يسوع
Jesus Christ	yasūʿ el masīḥ (m)	يسوع المسيح

the Holy Spirit	el rūḥ el qods (m)	الروح القدس
the Saviour	el masīḥ (m)	المسيح
the Virgin Mary	maryem el ʿazrāʾ (f)	مريم العذراء
the Devil	el ʃayṭān (m)	الشيطان
devil's (adj)	ʃeyṭāny	شيطاني
Satan	el ʃayṭān (m)	الشيطان
satanic (adj)	ʃeyṭāny	شيطاني
angel	malāk (m)	ملاك
guardian angel	malāk ḥāres (m)	ملاك حارس
angelic (adj)	malāʾeky	ملائكي
apostle	rasūl (m)	رسول
archangel	el malāk el raʾīsy (m)	الملاك الرئيسي
the Antichrist	el masīḥ el daggāl (m)	المسيح الدجّال
Church	el kenīsa (f)	الكنيسة
Bible	el ketāb el moqaddas (m)	الكتاب المقدّس
biblical (adj)	tawrāty	توراتي
Old Testament	el ʿahd el ʾadīm (m)	العهد القديم
New Testament	el ʿahd el gedīd (m)	العهد الجديد
Gospel	engīl (m)	إنجيل
Holy Scripture	el ketāb el moqaddas (m)	الكتاب المقدّس
Heaven	el ganna (f)	الجنّة
Commandment	waṣiya (f)	وصيّة
prophet	naby (m)	نبي
prophecy	nobūʾa (f)	نبوءة
Allah	allah (m)	الله
Mohammed	moḥammed (m)	محمّد
the Koran	el qorʾān (m)	القرآن
mosque	masged (m)	مسجد
mullah	mullah (m)	ملا
prayer	ṣalāh (f)	صلاة
to pray (vi, vt)	ṣalla	صلّى
pilgrimage	ḥagg (m)	حج
pilgrim	ḥagg (m)	حاج
Mecca	makka el mokarrama (f)	مكة المكرّمة
church	kenīsa (f)	كنيسة
temple	maʿbad (m)	معبد
cathedral	katedraʾiya (f)	كاتدرائية
Gothic (adj)	qūṭy	قوطي
synagogue	kenīs (m)	كنيس
mosque	masged (m)	مسجد
chapel	kenīsa saɣīra (f)	كنيسة صغيرة
abbey	deyr (m)	دير
convent	deyr (m)	دير
monastery	deyr (m)	دير
bell (church ~s)	garas (m)	جرس

bell tower	borg el garas (m)	برج الجرس
to ring (ab. bells)	da''	دقّ
cross	ṣalīb (m)	صليب
cupola (roof)	'obba (f)	قبّة
icon	ramz (m)	رمز
soul	nafs (f)	نفس
fate (destiny)	maṣīr (m)	مصير
evil (n)	ʃarr (m)	شرّ
good (n)	χeyr (m)	خير
vampire	maṣṣāṣ demā' (m)	مصّاص دماء
witch (evil ~)	sāḥera (f)	ساحرة
demon	ʃeṭān (m)	شيطان
spirit	roḥe (m)	روح
redemption (giving us ~)	takfīr (m)	تكفير
to redeem (vt)	kaffar ʿan	كفّر عن
church service	qedās (m)	قداس
to say mass	'ām be χedma dīniya	قام بخدمة دينية
confession	eʿterāf (m)	إعتراف
to confess (vi)	eʿtaraf	إعترف
saint (n)	qeddīs (m)	قدّيس
sacred (holy)	moqaddas (m)	مقدّس
holy water	maya moqaddesa (f)	ماية مقدّسة
ritual (n)	ʃaʿā'er (pl)	شعائر
ritual (adj)	ʃaʿā'ery	شعائري
sacrifice	zabīḥa (f)	ذبيحة
superstition	χorāfa (f)	خرافة
superstitious (adj)	mo'men bel χorafāt (m)	مؤمن بالخرافات
afterlife	aχra (f)	الآخرة
eternal life	ḥayat el abadiya (f)	حياة الأبدية

MISCELLANEOUS

198. Various useful words

background (green ~)	χalefiya (f)	خلفية
balance (of the situation)	tawāzon (m)	توازن
barrier (obstacle)	ḥāgez (m)	حاجز
base (basis)	asās (m)	أساس
beginning	bedāya (f)	بداية
category	fe'a (f)	فئة
cause (reason)	sabab (m)	سبب
choice	eχteyār (m)	إختيار
coincidence	ṣodfa (f)	صدّفة
comfortable (~ chair)	morīḥ	مريح
comparison	moqarna (f)	مقارنة
compensation	ta'wīḍ (m)	تعويض
degree (extent, amount)	daraga (f)	درجة
development	tanmeya (f)	تنمية
difference	far' (m)	فرق
effect (e.g. of drugs)	ta'sīr (m)	تأثير
effort (exertion)	mag-hūd (m)	مجهود
element	'onṣor (m)	عنصر
end (finish)	nehāya (f)	نهاية
example (illustration)	mesāl (m)	مثال
fact	ḥa'ī'a (f)	حقيقة
frequent (adj)	motakarrer (m)	متكرّر
growth (development)	nomoww (m)	نموّ
help	mosa'da (f)	مساعدة
ideal	mesāl (m)	مثال
kind (sort, type)	nū' (m)	نوع
labyrinth	matāha (f)	متاهة
mistake, error	χaṭa' (m)	خطأ
moment	laḥza (f)	لحظة
object (thing)	mawḍū' (m)	موضوع
obstacle	'aqaba (f)	عقبة
original (original copy)	aṣl (m)	أصل
part (~ of sth)	goz' (m)	جزء
particle, small part	goz' (m)	جزء
pause (break)	estrāḥa (f)	إستراحة
position	mawqef (m)	موّقف
principle	mabda' (m)	مبدأ
problem	moʃkela (f)	مشكلة
process	'amaliya (f)	عمليّة

progress	ta'addom (m)	تقدّم
property (quality)	χaṣṣa (f)	خاصّة
reaction	radd fe'l (m)	ردّ فعل
risk	moχaṭra (f)	مخاطرة
secret	serr (m)	سرّ
series	selsela (f)	سلسلة
shape (outer form)	ʃakl (m)	شكل
situation	ḥāla (f), waḍ' (m)	حالة, وضع
solution	ḥall (m)	حلّ
standard (adj)	'ādy -qeyāsy	عادي, قياسي
standard (level of quality)	'eyās (m)	قياس
stop (pause)	estrāḥa (f)	إستراحة
style	oslūb (m)	أسلوب
system	nezām (m)	نظام
table (chart)	gadwal (m)	جدوّل
tempo, rate	eqā' (m)	إيقاع
term (word, expression)	moṣṭalaḥ (m)	مصطلح
thing (object, item)	ḥāga (f)	حاجة
truth (e.g. moment of ~)	ḥaʔʔa (f)	حقيقة
turn (please wait your ~)	dore (m)	دور
type (sort, kind)	nū' (m)	نوع
urgent (adj)	mesta'gel	مستعجل
urgently	be ʃakl 'āgel	بشكل عاجل
utility (usefulness)	manf'a (f)	منفعة
variant (alternative)	ʃakl moχtalef (m)	شكل مختلف
way (means, method)	ṭarīʔa (f)	طريقة
zone	mante'a (f)	منطقة

www.ingramcontent.com/pod-product-compliance
Lightning Source LLC
LaVergne TN
LVHW051340080426
835509LV00020BA/3223